QUITTING TIME

by James McDonald

Introduction

Quitting Time is the story about how God took this former jockey, trainer, and thoroughbred horse owner, to the top of his profession. Then, at the peak of his career, He brought him back down to the bottom.

When it was quitting time, God arranged for his sudden decline. The very same One, who had made life a dream, arranged for this man's worst nightmare. His career came to a crashing halt. Then his physical freedom was taken away. At that point he did not have anywhere to look but up.

He discovered God, in his sovereignty, had even arranged for the horse, Quitting Time, to come into his possession in order to fulfill His purpose. Although James thought Quitting Time was jump-starting his career, his Creator was actually getting ready to pull the rug out from under him. In His time and in accordance with His plan, He knocked him off of his high horse.

Afterwards, God graciously brought him through a prison experience of about 15 years. His purpose in all of this was to bring this strong-willed man of the world into submission. In order to give him a truly productive life, He had to first bring him to his quitting time.

Although he thought he had life all figured out, God showed James how far off base he really was. In his own eyes he was totally on point, but in reality he had missed the mark by a mile. He thought he was in total control. By the world's standards, he had everything. But, his life was totally out of control.

By God's grace, he learned possessions, fame, and having the connections to more or less write his own ticket were not the answer to his deepest needs-Jesus is. Although it was God who had opened the necessary doors for him to obtain any position of privilege he had enjoyed in life, he never for an instant suspected it was His Creator who was the master of his fate. But, James had to learn the hard way He had actually arranged for the success he enjoyed just so He could show him worldly achievement isn't all it's cracked up to be, .

Suddenly, he was on the bottom bunk in a jail cell looking up. At that point, he didn't know it but that was the best place he could possibly be. What seemed like the end of the road for him was actually a new beginning. At this point in his life, God began teaching him what life is really all about.

Even though he had lived a life of ungodliness, God was there with open arms just waiting for him to come to his senses. When he needed the help which no man could give him, he cried out and His merciful Father answered that desperate plea for help. James learned firsthand what amazing grace is.

Then, for reasons beyond our human comprehension, God chose to reveal Himself to this lost soul in the most awesome ways. In the process, He proved Jesus is indeed alive and very much in control of all of our circumstances. This book is a living testimony God's Word is alive. Through the events described by James, He proved again and again His Word does exactly what He has told us it would do thousands of years ago. He is still "the Lord who changes not."

God orchestrated the events contained in this book to let you know He changes people. If you want to change and cannot change yourself, do not give up. You are not alone. There is One who can do the impossible. He did it for the author of this incredible story and He will do it for you. He cares for you and He is willing to change the ones who are ready to come to their quitting time. You did not find this book on your own. You were led to it by the Author of your salvation.

There are several reasons why QUITTING TIME was written. The first one being God wants all people to know He is indeed the God of Abraham, Isaac, and Jacob-the great I AM and that He is the same yesterday, today, and forever."

The same God who parted the Red Sea is the very One who changed James from the inside out.

Furthermore, He wishes to reveal Himself to those who will seek Him with all their heart. Most importantly, He wants to assure you there is still hope. No matter where you are God will meet you right there. Both James and God hope this knowledge will challenge others- Christian and non-Christian alike- to come to their quitting time.

God gave James the inspiration to write this book while he was in prison. As he witnessed the aftermath of broken lives, He assured His newly-born again child that he could do something to help his fellow prisoners. Although he was in physical bondage for almost 15 years, he was free. During that period, God gave him the keys to set others free. Many of the men he met in prison are still chasing after rainbows, but God wants them and everyone else who comes into possession of this book to know fame and fortune are not the answer- Jesus is.

Speaking from experience, James can testify to the fact material goods and notoriety will not fill anyone's void. He thought those things would make his life complete. Instead, he became bound by the god of this world. Still, God gave him the experiences he shares in this book just so he could be a witness of His grace and thereby help keep others from being deceived by the riches of this world and the Prince of darkness.

It is his prayer our awesome heavenly Father will use the words in this book to help others. May the story he tells be the catalyst which leads others right into the Master's arms. Then, they too will gladly quit living for themselves. After all, the fact of the matter is when one surrenders their life to God they lose nothing. In reality, they gain far more than they could imagine through an awesome relationship with the Creator. This in turn will prepare them for an eternal future.

Hopefully, this book will inspire many people to seize the opportunity God is offering. James prays that all who read this book will see it is the time to start a real life in Christ. After all, only things you do for Jesus will really matter in the end.

No one is beyond the reach of God's grace. No matter how corrupt they have become, He will welcome them into His kingdom with open arms. Jesus is truly the "way the truth, and the life." He is willing and able to give life to those who simply ask for it. He is truly the hope for the hopeless. Only He has the power to completely change us - from the inside out.

The awesome power of God's spoken Word is revealed in this book and is available to everyone searching for a better way. Our heavenly Father really wants people to experience the transforming power and truth of it all. "You shall know the truth, and the truth shall set you free." He is still doing everything in His power to help all people to know that Jesus is the answer to every problem they will ever face in this life.

James wishes to encourage his fellow believers our blessed Redeemer will indeed take you to victory in every area of your life when you fully commit your life to Him. Once you become a doer of the Word and not a hearer only, miracles in your everyday life will become as common as the air you breathe.

God has clearly revealed Himself to us in the Bible. Indeed He has made it simple enough for anyone to understand His will. However, far too many of His children have never even read the entire Bible. In it, He tells us, you do this and I'll do that. There is no simpler way to victory in this life or the next. Although you may think your plan for your life is best, God has a better future planned for you. "Eye has not seen, nor ear heard, neither has it entered into the heart of man the things God has planned for those who love Him." (1 Corinthians 2:9)

May the God of all creation use this book to inspire others to dig into their Bibles and find out how they too can live victoriously in Christ- "from faith to faith" After all, Jesus paid for this victory with His very own blood! "And they overcame him, by the blood of the Lamb, and by the word of their testimony."

Acknowledgments

First and foremost, I would like to give thanks to my Creator for this book and for the awesome life He has given me. Although there are many other testimonies and books God has used to reveal His goodness to the world, I don't intend for this to be just another account of how the lost got found. I pray this book will be used as an awesome testimony of the power of His word and His faithfulness to the written word He has so painstakingly preserved for His children. This book was created for His glory and His people. He alone deserves all the glory and He alone can give you the victory in this life and the one to come. I pray He has enabled me to present this to you in the best way possible. I also pray He will use it to bless you even more than He has blessed me.

I would also like to take the liberty to give thanks and accolades to those whom our heavenly Father sent across my path during the preparation of this book. He used all of these dear saints of His to inspire, assist, encourage, and enable me to complete the work. I could not have done it without Him or them.

Me dear brother-in-Christ, the late G. Booth Lusteg, spent countless hours reviewing and editing the first draft of Quitting Time with me. His having already authored a very enlightening book concerning the AFL and the NFL paid off for me. His book, entitled: Kick Rejection…and Win!! Is an attention getting revelation of his experiences as a league leading kicker for the Green Bay Packers, New York Jets, Buffalo Bills, and the Miami Dolphins. He really inspired me and urged me on to bring out the passion in me to write this book to the very best of any ability our Father has placed in me to do so. In his lifetime, G. Booth freely gave countless hours of service to the furtherance of the Gospel and he freely donated much time and effort to assist me in getting the message God has given me to share with His people. For this I am eternally grateful and I look forward to my reunion with G. Booth in glory so I can shake his hand one more time and thank him.

A short time after G. Booth went to be with Jesus, Carol Lusteg Herdock, his former wife, volunteered to help me to edit this book for the second time. She selflessly took the time out of her busy schedule as a realtor to assist me in correcting the errors we overlooked during our first try at editing the work. I am so grateful for her contribution and her encouragement throughout the process.

Another dear brother-in-Christ of mine, John Michael Domino, was instrumental in getting this book published. He not only inspired me by writing about me in his own book: 'Can't Wait to Get Back to Prison,' he connected me to the publisher which enabled me to finish the process of getting this book into print. In John's first book, he expounds on the joys of participating in a prison ministry. He received the inspiration for this book by a dear friend of ours, Lester Lemke. Les was also in the prison ministry before he went to be with Jesus. Les was also a great inspiration to me. At any rate, John's experience as the author of a multitude of publications paid off for me. He cheerfully assisted me whenever I asked for his help and encouraged me in more ways than you can imagine.

Another dear sister-in-Christ I would like to thank is Linette Escobar. Strangely enough, she is also an author. I say 'strangely' because God chose to send a multitude of Christian authors across my path to assist me as I was preparing this book. This would be considered a coincidence to some, but we know better. He is amazing. At any rate, Linette wrote a book: Journey Behind Prison Walls. I read it and I absolutely had no problems relating to her ordeal. In the book, she explains how she went through the federal prison system and how God used her 'down' time to reveal Himself to her in many miraculous ways. The difference between her and I is that she was falsely imprisoned. It turns out she was innocent of the charges she was convicted of and sentenced for. However, God used it all for His glory. Her account of how He did this is a must read for anyone seeking a serious relationship with our Father. The similarities in how God introduced Himself to her and I are striking and a real encouragement. He is truly no respecter of persons. I thank Him for leading her to share her walk with Him with others. I also appreciate her willingness to help me in whatever ways she was able to. She is a tribute to how a committed child of God's can overcome any circumstances they are faced with.

Speaking of serious believers, Ron and Amy Marriage are two people who were very greatly used by our Father to get this book into the hands of the publisher. If it weren't for Amy putting together the covers for the front and back of the book, it probably would still be sitting in my computer unpublished. She has been a great help to me as I have been blessed by her faithfulness to Him over the years I have had the pleasure to have known her. Her husband, Ron, is also an answer to my prayers-in more ways than one. Whenever I needed his assistance for anything I asked him about, he undertook the task with great zeal. His sacrificial attitude is and was so refreshing to me. Together, this dynamic duo for Christ helped me to arrange the pictures, newspaper articles, and captions for the book using whatever spare time they could muster up-this in spite of their busy schedules. Both are self-employed and I so appreciate them sacrificing their valuable time to assist me. Besides being prayer warriors and unprecedented helps, they brought me a taste of heavenly fellowship each time we all came together to work on this testimony of our Father's faithfulness you are about to read. I have yet to meet two Christians as dedicated to living out the great commandment Jesus gave us to love one another as He loved us. I sincerely thank God for them and their generosity to me and to so many others our Father has brought across their paths

After I had received one of the early Proofs, I

presented it to my dear sister-in-Christ, Julianna Castranova. At that time, I thought I was finished with my labor of love. However, our Father soon used Julie to show me there was still work to be done. This resulted in many more hours of work for me-and her. She faithfully navigated through her busy schedule as a Broward county school psychiatrist and single mother of two and sacrificially put many of the final touches on this publication. Thanks again.

Last but not least, I would like to give mention to Gloria Rosenblatt. Gloria is the mother of my sister, Geri's fiancée, Lindy. After she had read Quitting Time for the second time, she took the liberty of correcting some still unnoticed errors in the manuscript for me. I really appreciate her making this effort. This act of kindness inspired me to make the final copy as is it should be-fit for a king. After all, it is the King's work. I also want to thank Gloria for confirming to me that God has already used this book and will continue to use it to bless others. This reminds to tell others this book is not about me-it is about Him.

Actually, Gloria is not the last one I would like to give thanks to. Now that I think of it, God has used so many of His people to assist me along the way. I don't mean to exclude anyone who deserves credit for helping me in getting the final product to the publisher. If I have left any of you out, God knows who you are and your reward awaits you. Forgive me for my oversight. Believe it or not, I truly appreciate every single effort anyone has made in order to help me to get Quitting Time into the hands of the people God has chosen to present it to. I sincerely pray He will bless you all a hundredfold more than you have blessed me, in Jesus' name.

Contents

ALWAYS A BRIDESMAID

The bell rang. The latch sprung. The gates flew open. The field of horses leaped forward. Then the old familiar phrase: "And they're off!" came spouting out of the sports caster's mouth. The chase was on. The sound of jockeys cracking whips, and their horses thundering hoof beats filled the air. The place: the Blue Bonnet Racetrack in Montreal, Canada.

I was aboard a horse named Sunny Fritz in this particular race. A few jumps after the field came busting out of the gate, my mount and I were right smack in the middle of the pack. Although we were getting sandblasted from the dirt being ejected out of the hooves of the horses we followed, neither my horse nor I were seriously affected.

As I gripped the reins tighter, I felt raw power in my hands. As far as I could tell, on the other end of those leather controls was a locomotive just waiting for me to open it full throttle. In spite of very close quarters, I managed to carefully maneuver my horse into an ever diminishing opening situated between two horses.

The race in which we were competing would be over in less than a minute. I knew there wasn't a fraction of a second to waste. About four strides later, I saw the opportunity to drop my mount down alongside the rail. Without hesitation, I abruptly steered my horse into the 'fast lane'. This move enabled us to gain relief from the sand storm and I knew it would also help us to save some valuable ground.

After we had traveled the first half mile, some of the horses in front and those alongside of us started fading back. This was to be expected. Since most of the competition wasn't quite fit enough to travel the whole distance of the race. I knew it was time for us to take advantage of the open space as the tired thoroughbreds began drifting out. The window was open. It was now or never.

I steered my horse off the rail and we quickly burst through an available opening. As we pursued the leaders of this pack, Sunny Fritz took a nice hold of the bit. This was exactly what I had hoped for. However, before I could relish in the fact I finally had a live horse under me for the run down the stretch, we were beginning to be shut out by one of the tiring leaders who was drifting in at this point in the race.

Thankfully, Sunny Fritz had as much heart as me and didn't hesitate as I urged him on to force his way in between horses. A fraction of a second later, we had already made our way up to fourth place. A few strides after that, we were third.

At this point, the adrenalin rush being experienced by my mount and I simultaneously was immeasurable. As we reached the middle of the stretch, we edged our way into second place. I could taste victory. I was in another dimension. We seemed to be going at warp speed and I sensed my horse still had plenty more run left in him.

However, my ecstasy soon turned to disappointment. As we neared the finish line, I discovered the leader of the race was not tiring at all and we were running out of ground. With less than a sixteenth of a mile to go, I realized victory was going to elude me once again.

To my utter dismay the leader was drawing away from us at this point. It turned out he had quite a bit more ability than my mount did. Consequently, he won the race by 5 lengths. I was disheartened, but I was satisfied we had finished in the top three. In my estimation, Sunny Fritz and I would definitely win our next race over this track as long as we were racing against this same caliber of competition.

No doubt the winning horse was much the better on that occasion. He had an added advantage due to the fact he had already raced over this track once before. He was also carrying less weight than Sunny Fritz. All things considered, I figured my horse would only improve on the performance he had just given. But, this wasn't much consolation to me. I desperately needed a win.

To some of my competitors this may have been just another race. To me, it was a do or die situation. I really needed a victory. Up to that point in time, I hadn't yet ridden a horse capable enough to bring me into the winner's circle. Even though I was just an apprentice jockey and had only ridden in about 30 races during my budding career, I was in desperate straits.

I was fighting a war on two fronts. I was in a major battle against the pound- many a jockey's arch enemy. It seemed the harder I tried the harder it got to keep my weight down low enough to make my horse's assigned weight. At the current time, I had been resorting to a strict diet, lots of exercise, and innumerable trips to the 'hot box' in an effort to keep off unwanted pounds. (Hot box is a term jockeys' use to describe the steam room).

It was torturous to my body. Depriving my self from eating most of the foods I loved to eat was bad enough. To top it off, I could hardly even take a drink of water when I was thirsty; because this would cause me to put back on the pounds I had previously worked so hard to shed off in the hot box.

It was a vicious cycle I had endured for all too long. To add to my misery, I was in the fight of my life to jump start my career and somehow obtain financial stability. At the time, I had a wife and a newborn son. I was striving to make a better life for us all. However, my career was at a standstill.

Being an apprentice jockey is not that rewarding- at least not until your first win. Up until this point in my career, I had spent about six years scraping my pennies while working for the elite in the sport of kings. It seemed as though I was never going to get that pot of gold at the end of this rainbow. Hopefully, winning this race would be the catalyst for my dreams to finally become a reality. Not so.

After the valet unsaddled my horse in front of the grandstand, I made my way back to the jockey's room. As I entered, one of the clerks called out my name. When I replied, he told me I had a phone call. I couldn't imagine who it was. He handed me the phone and it turned out my caller was a gentleman who was a close friend of Sunny Fritz's owner. As I acknowledged I was jockey McDonald, this total stranger congratulated me for giving my mount such a perfect ride.

It turned out he was delighted the horse had just paid a whopping $66.00 for a two dollar second place wager. Evidently, this guy had bet a fair amount of money on my mount. I was delighted too. I was pleased this man had seen the race and was going to tell his friend about my riding skills. After we ended our conversation, I was all smiles.

However, the world always seemed to find a way to steal my joy. A short time after my phone conversation with the owner's friend, I found out I didn't make a dime from this good fortune. It turned out that nobody had placed a bet for me. I expected the trainer of Sunny Fritz to do so, but he didn't.

At the time I couldn't afford to bet any money of my own so I was flat out of luck. This was due to the fact my finances were not under my control. In fact, it seemed to me as though I had absolutely no control over anything in my life.

Worse yet, I soon found out the trainer, Ron, was not as ecstatic as I was about the fact Sunny Fritz had finished second. Even though he wasn't there to see the race in person he was under the impression I should have won the race. Undoubtedly, this was because the assistant trainer passed the buck again.

When I discussed the matter of our second place finish with Ron the following morning, it was clear my situation had worsened. Instead of complimenting my performance the night before, he only gave me criticism. In fact, due to his assistant's report, he blamed me for our loss.

I couldn't deal with it anymore. The way I saw it, I had been striving in vain for too many years. At the tender age of 16, I was first introduced to the world of horse racing. This was in 1965. By the grace of God, I was given what I considered a golden opportunity. Although I was born and raised in a run down area in the city of Newark, New Jersey, He had big plans for my future.

It was only by His grace I have ever amounted to anything in this world. My first childhood memories are of my mom being a nervous wreck. She was gone most of the time. She was out working to support my siblings and me. My dad had left my mom with three young children. He was an alcoholic. I never met him until I was 13 years old. Consequently, my early years were not very pleasant.

The one thing I remember most is the fact we never seemed to have enough of anything. Although most of my friends seemed to have everything they needed, my family was always lacking. While I was growing up, I longed for stability and a loving family environment. However, throughout my childhood I never experienced any of those things.

At the age of 13, my dad came back into my life. At the time, he had been remarried and was actually living in a town across the river from Newark, named Kearny. Since my mom could hardly deal with all of the responsibilities of rearing five kids, she had allowed my older brother, Joe, to move in with my dad.

Joe seemed to be happy and I missed him a lot, so one day I made my way over to my dad's. A few months later, I made the move to live with my dad too. I liked my brother's new environment. However, I soon found out the grass was not greener on the other side. My dad was still an alcoholic and very difficult to live with.

By the time I turned 16 years of age, I was desperate to make some changes in my life. I dropped out of high school. I hadn't had a good high school experience anyway. In fact, I was always getting into some kind of trouble there. I hated school.

As far as I was concerned, dropping out of school was my opportunity to quit living my life on other people's terms. My plan was to earn what I could and save as much as possible in order to move away from my dad. It seemed as though I always had people telling me what to do with my life. In my mind, quitting school was the first step towards gaining control over my life.

Once I had quit school, I took a job as a messenger for a printing company located in Newark. The pay was minimal, and there was little opportunity for advancement. However, this job was the doorway to the stars for me.

I didn't know it at the time, but God had a much better plan. He used one of the printers working in that small company to change my future. His name was Vinny. He was a middle-aged man with a medium build. He was an Italian and he was quite the conversationalist. I met him one day while I was picking up some inks from the printing shop for one of my deliveries.

Vinny quickly took note of my small stature. (I was about 5'2" and weighed a mere 98 pounds). We had barely become acquainted when he asked me if I had ever considered becoming a jockey. I replied by telling him I loved to ride horses and would love to be a jockey someday. Then I told him I didn't even know where a racetrack was located. Since I didn't know anybody connected with horse racing, I didn't see any way I would ever get the opportunity to become a jockey.

Vinny soon explained to me he knew a couple of jockeys from New York. He told me he lived there and the jockeys he knew happened to live in the same building as him. He also informed me the two were brothers and they were twins.

During our conversation, Vinny promised me he would talk to those jockeys and ask them if they would help me get started on a career in horse racing. He explained he would arrange for me to go to New York with him one day after work and he would introduce me to them both. To make a long story short, Vinny made good on his promise and one day the brothers, Ray and Carl Cummings, took me to Belmont Park Racetrack in Elmont, Long Island. When we arrived there the Cummings brothers dropped me off at the stable gate. The twins had informed me I first had to get a temporary pass from security. Otherwise, I would not have been allowed to enter the stable area.

After I applied for and received my temporary badge, I entered the stable area at Belmont Park. As I began my search for employment as a 'hot walker,' (a hot walker is one who walks the racehorses around the barn which helps them to cool out after their morning workouts). I was mesmerized by what I encountered on the backside of the racetrack.

As I walked towards the first set of barns I had set my sights on, I realized how sturdily these structures were built. They were not at all like I imagined they would be. In fact, I remember thinking these massive structures looked more habitable than any of the places I had ever lived in.

Something else quickly caught my attention. Outside of most of these barns I saw Mercedes Benz's, limos, Jaguars, Ferrari's, and just about every other expensive car I could imagine. My first thoughts were: *This is it! I am where I have always dreamed of being. I am going to get mine at this place.*

It was a long haul, but after five years struggling, I rode in my first race at Aqueduct Racetrack in Queens, New York. I had finally received my first break. This turn of events came about unexpectedly. I had just about given up hope of ever riding in a race. Then, one day a friend of mine suggested I hire a jockey agent. Since I hadn't ridden in any races, I didn't think any reputable agent would care to represent me. However, God had a plan.

Shortly after my friends' suggestion, I was

shooting pool in the recreation hall at Belmont Park Racetrack. God chose this time to introduce me to a jockey agent. His name was Dell. He and I hit it off really well and the next thing I knew he offered to take my ‘book‘. (In other words become my agent). To my surprise, Dell had seen me exercising race horses and liked my style.

Shortly after Dell took my book, he hooked me up with Corbellini Stable. A few days later, I was realizing my dream of becoming an apprentice jockey. Since I was gung ho for my first victory, I took chances most of the other riders would never attempt. This made some of the more established riders quite nervous. In fact, one of them really took a disliking to me and used his sway with the New York racing stewards to make my life as an apprentice very difficult. Eventually, this put a halt to my meteoric rise to fame on the New York racing circuit.

Since I was having much trouble with the racing stewards in New York, my agent suggested I try racing in New Jersey. I took his advice and soon hooked up with a trainer there by the name of Ron Gibbs. Shortly after I hooked up with him, he sent me to Canada with a string of horses.

After I had ridden in about 10 races at Blue Bonnet Racetrack Ron started getting itchy because our stable hadn't yet won any races. The assistant trainer who was in charge of this string of horses started blaming me for our lack of victories.

Up until this time, I had received more than my fair share of criticism and broken promises from this assistant. I wasn't pleased with him slandering me as well. However, there wasn’t much I could do to remedy my situation.

It didn’t look to me as though I had any future in my current position. The way I saw it, I had to win a race, get an agent, and then break away from my current handlers. Hopefully, then I could start earning some serious money.

However, we didn't have much noteworthy stock in our stable for me to work with. Therefore, my chances to achieve my goal were minimal at best. From what I had observed, the assistant trainer had a habit of running his horses 'over their heads'. (That is to say a few notches above their abilities). This had caused most of our stable's financial woes. We couldn't win any purses racing in spots where we were outclassed by the competition. I tried to point this out, but he ignored my advice.

However, there was light at the end of the tunnel for me. We had a horse named, Sunny Fritz. Ron had suggested to the assistant what slot on the claiming scale this particular horse should be racing at. When the assistant entered Sunny Fritz accordingly, I was elated. I had been working him out in the mornings and I knew the horse was going to race in the right spot.

Finally, I saw opportunity. I told my handlers they could bet their money on Sunny Fritz. I explained to them he might not get the win his first time out, but I was sure he was fit enough to finish in the top three racing against this caliber of horses. Since the morning line on him was astronomical, I saw an opportunity for all of us to cash in. I was so happy because I figured I finally actually had a chance of winning a race and making some real money.

As usual, things didn't' work out the way I planned. At this point in time, the race was finished and so was I. I was frustrated to say the least. Subsequently, I painfully made the decision it was quitting time. As far as I was concerned, starving my body and subjecting myself to the hardships I had endured was all for naught. I can't even begin to describe the anger which had built up inside of me. All I could think about was the way I had been taken advantage of during the past six years. Life on the racetrack for me definitely was not what I had expected.

All of my hopes of ever having a career as a

jockey were devastated. However, I decided I was not about to give up on my dream of becoming wealthy. I had one more option. From what I had already learned during those years of dealing with thoroughbreds, I knew what it took to win races. I had no doubts that I could still reach my goals by training horses. Then, I wouldn't have to be concerned about my weight problem and I could call the shots. I was determined I would make my come back in horseracing some day as a successful thoroughbred horse trainer.

As far as I was concerned, I had ridden on the merry-go-round of life long enough. The gold ring I had been reaching for had eluded me for far too long. However, I knew in my heart I wasn't totally defeated. Although I was bitter and bewildered, I wasn't through with horseracing.

I was discouraged, but this only made me more determined to make my way to the top. I knew if I could become a successful trainer, I could beat the 'big boys' at their own game. Although I was never given the right opportunity to win races as a jockey, I was convinced there was still hope for me to make my mark in horseracing.

At that point in my life, I could not have been more resolute. I was going to be a winner some day. I was sick and tired of being on the bottom. It seemed I could never catch a break in
life. I felt I knew as much about training horses - probably even more- than most of the trainers I had dealt with. I figured the one thing which stood in between me and the top was the lack of money.

Since I didn't have any connections with any horse owners who would give me a horse of theirs to train, I made up my mind I was going to go out and get my hands on enough money of my own to finance my future as a horse trainer. I didn't care what I had to do to get the funds. I was totally optimistic I would someday buy a horse of my own and jumpstart my new career.

At this point, I was more determined in my heart

than I had ever been about anything in my life. I swore to myself I would beg, borrow, or steal until I had raised enough money to accomplish my goal. I would be a winning trainer someday. Up until then, I hadn't tasted victory. However, I just knew the time would come when I would be a source to reckon with in the world of thoroughbred horseracing. Although I was still a maiden, I was determined to prove I was a winner-whatever the cost.

"To accept his lot and be happy in the work-this is a gift of God" (Ecclesiastes 5:19b)

RISING STAR

After I left the race track, I took on jobs in the automotive field. I was mechanically inclined, so I became a mechanic's helper. I received quite an education in auto repair from the man I worked for. I also made an important ‘connection.’ This came by way of a career criminal I met through my boss. This opened the door for me to earn more money than I had ever laid my hands on before.

While I was working in this garage, I became involved with Tony. Eventually, I teamed up with him and we committed numerous crimes together. For obvious reasons, I dare not use his real name so Tony will suffice.

He was quite an operator. He was born and raised in Brooklyn, New York. His son was in the mob there. He seemed to know every angle and always came up with new ways to make 'fast' money. I am not going to give the Devil glory by going into details concerning my evil escapades with Tony.

Suffice it to say Tony and I pulled off insurance scams, robbed a few drug dealers, sold drugs, stole tons of construction equipment, and multiple thousands of dollars in cash.

Once I figured I had enough cash stashed away, I funneled all of my energies back into horse racing. I felt it was time to bring this dark chapter of my life to a close. I really didn't want to live the life of a criminal.

I just wanted to live life to the fullest and I thought getting rich was the answer to all my problems. Although I was dumb enough to buy into that lie, I was smart enough to know a career in crime would eventually lead to my incarceration.

With the money I had been able to amass up to that point in time, I felt I had enough to invest in my future as a trainer and start making money legally again. I soon discovered the road leading up to my goal was almost as bumpy as the one I had traveled on as an apprentice jockey.

However, my career as a trainer did start out with a bit of a bang. I had begun this new pursuit for fame and fortune by going to Monmouth Park Racetrack in New Jersey. Since I knew it was important for me to be on the backside of the racetrack during the early morning training hours, I landed myself a job as an exercise boy with Budd Lepman Stables. At the time, Budd was one of the leading trainers at Monmouth Park Racetrack.

By being there every morning, I knew I would have access to information which would be helpful to my goal. I planned on learning which horses were available for sale. Eventually, I had hoped to single out the ones I felt were worthy of buying or claiming and take the next step towards my career as a trainer.

Budd and I soon became good friends. He was a wonderful person. He would always help the ones he could. His hired help always knew they could turn to him in time of need. During the years I knew Budd, he did lots of favors for me. He was one of the few true friends I ever had.

Shortly after I started working for him in the summer of 1975, I told him I wanted to buy a horse and become a trainer. He asked me how much I could afford to invest. I told him I had about $10,000 and he told me he would look around and try to find a horse which he felt I could work with.

Several weeks later, Budd made good on his promise. Turns out another trainer had told him about a horse for sale. He was sure I could move this horse up. The horse was a 3-year old filly named Patriotic Petunia. Budd told me she just needed some 'schooling' and he was sure I could fill the bill.

I purchased her later on that same day for $5,000. Budd had promised, if I purchased her, he would get a stall for her at Monmouth Park. This was another Godsend. You see, I didn't even have my trainer's license at the time. Therefore, I had no way of obtaining stalls at the racetrack. Budd delivered.

Once I had her in my possession, I made arrangements with one of Budd's grooms, Marc Shappy, to groom and care for Patriotic Petunia. I had met him years earlier when he and I had been working for Budd. At the time, Marc had told me he wanted to become a trainer. I promised him, if I ever got into the position to help him realize his dream, I would do so. As soon as he learned I had purchased Patriotic Petunia, he told me he could acquire a trainer's license. Then, he asked me if he could train her. I was quite willing to help Marc get his start, so I made good on my word.

Although I was her real trainer, I put Marc down as the official trainer of Patriotic Petunia. I didn't care who was listed as trainer. I was only interested in getting my first thoroughbred into the winner's circle at Monmouth Park. When this happened, I figure we would all be winners.

I agreed to pay Marc 10% of Patriotic Petunia's winnings. I wasn't about to pay the average daily training fees a trainer would have charged. (In those days it was about $50 a day for each horse in training). Since I was doing the training anyway, I felt this was a good arrangement for both of us.

When I felt I had corrected my horse's problem-which was her erratic behavior in the starting gate-I entered her into a race. Budd helped me to line up one of the leading riders at Monmouth Park as her jockey for the event. This was a work of God. Since Patriotic Petunia was well know for causing problems at the start of her previous races, none of the leading riders wanted to risk riding such a horse.

At this point, I felt confident my horse would make a good showing. However, I had no idea she was actually going to win her first race under my silks. To say I was surprised is an understatement. I was shocked.

I expected to succeed as a trainer some day, but I had no clue it would be this day.

However, by God's grace I chalked up a win on the first try. Wow. This was much more to my liking than being a jockey who was under someone else's control. Now, I was sure I had a great future ahead of me as a trainer.

I always knew I could be a winner. By God's grace, I had been given the opportunity to prove it. All my life I felt I had to prove I was good enough. It seemed as though I was always second best. As far as I could tell, this was a major turning pointing in my life. I thought I was going to be the one calling the shots from then on. I had no idea was my Maker who was in control and not me. Nor did I have any idea I would not have succeeded had He not ordained it.

After Patriotic Petunia's winning effort, Budd informed me he knew someone who was willing to buy her from me. The gentleman offered me a few thousand dollars more than the purchase price I had paid for her. Upon my dear friend's recommendation, I didn't hesitate to sell her.

The main reason I did so was because she was a bit whacky and I was fully aware of the danger she posed to my investment. At any given moment, she could have hurt herself and I would have been out of business. Although nothing is a sure thing in horseracing, I had quite a large profit from my first venture as a trainer and I was sure I had made the right choice. At this point, I was confident my future in horseracing was going to be a lucrative career.

Patriotic Petunia was the first horse I owned. Subsequently, she won the first race I entered her into. I couldn't have been more elated. This was also the first win of my career in horseracing. Little did I know, the Father had a long list of surprises in store for me. I didn't deserve it-nor acknowledge it-but it was He who had prepared the way for my rise to fame in my chosen profession. All these undeserved blessings He showered upon me-in spite of me. "How excellent is Your lovingkindness, O God! Therefore the children of men put their trust under the shadow of thy wings." (Pslams 36:7)

After I sold Patriotic Petunia, I experienced a series of ups and downs as a trainer. I should have known it was coming. Nothing ever came easy in my life. But, being the optimist I am, I expected after my first winner I was just going to continue right on up the ladder to stardom.

Lady Technion's victory was another one of the Father's pleasant surprises. However, it got ugly because-unbeknownst to me-my horse was drugged before the race. Although I was standing in the winner's circle, I had no way of knowing beforehand this was about to happen. When I entered this horse in this race, I was merely hoping she would finish the race in good health and get some conditioning under her belt.

Consequently, I felt like a complete idiot after the race; because I had told my partner-prior to the race-not to bet on our horse on this day. Little did I know what went on behind the scenes before post time. A local veterinarian and a trusted friend and horse trainer of mine chose to give my horse some stimulants and make a bet on her. God used this situation to remind me that, when the stakes are high, you can't afford to trust anyone-even those you consider to be true friends. When people aren't saved and living their life for God, and they have their focus on making money, they are then subject to do anything in order to get some. "The love of money is the root of all evil." (1 Timothy 6:10) Notice this verse does not say money is the root of all evil. It is the love of money which leads people into sin and corruption.

I was sadly disappointed. At one point, I became so low on finances I looked up my old 'buddy', Tony. He was still up to his old tricks. In fact, he had moved to Florida and was involved in the illegal drug trade there. When I found this out, I knew I could team back up with him and I could make some 'fast' money. Tony welcomed me with open arms.

After our reunion, he was quick to put me to work as a 'mule'. (A mule is one who transports drugs from one location to another). Although the money for my services as a mule was a most welcome benefit, I knew the risk I was taking by moving kilos of cocaine from Miami to New York far outweighed my profits. In light of this, I came up with an alternate plan. I decided I would only stay involved in the drug trade with Tony long enough to find out where he got his drugs. Once I zeroed in on some unsuspecting dealers, I figured I could figure out how I could rip them off. I completely ignored the fact I would be putting my life in grave danger attempting to rob such dangerous criminals.

One day, Tony introduced me to another drug dealer. It turned out he was seeking to do the same thing as I was. His name was Billy. Since Billy liked to play tennis- and this was my favorite sport- he and I hit it off real well. Once we became more familiar with one another, we both decided our best option for a quick profit would be to team up and rip off some unsuspecting dealer.

None of these drug dealers knew me. Therefore our plan was for Billy to steer me to the drugs and any money they had on hand. I was to keep a low profile. Then, when the opportunity presented itself, the rip off was up to me.

We were 'successful' in our very first venture. I managed to steal over $150,000 in drugs from one of Billy's suppliers. Thankfully, I didn't have to hurt anyone in the process. After we had sold the stolen drugs, we decided to invest our newfound wealth into horse racing.

He also loved the sport and I convinced him we could make a lot of money together legally. Since Tony had told Billy I was a former jockey and a thoroughbred horse owner/trainer, he was quick to seize the opportunity to partner with me in the venture.

I loved the idea I wouldn't have to pay all the bills connected with running a stable; because Billy would be responsible for 50%

of them. He agreed to be a 'silent' partner and this meant I could still be in total control of the operation.

A short time later, Billy and I went to Calder Racecourse in order to get acquainted with South Florida racing. I had no idea God had ordained this. Since I was living in sin, I didn't deserve the opportunity which was presented to me later on that afternoon. Yet, my heavenly Father opened the door for me to reach success in a far greater degree than I had imagined through a horse named Newmarket Lady.

While Billy and I were enjoying the races that fateful afternoon, an old acquaintance of mine, Alan Sherman, approached me. He was never one to mince words and he quickly asked me if I were interested in claiming a horse that day.

I explained to Alan I hadn't yet obtained a trainer's license in Florida. However, I also explained I was in the process of getting my own stable going again. At that point, he told me he had been observing a really hot prospect which had been racing at Calder. According to him, the horse's name was Newmarket Lady and she was scheduled to race in the very next race. She was entered for a $15,000 claiming tag that day.

Alan had barely finished explaining why he thought Newmarket Lady was such a hot prospect when the filly came walking into the paddock area. At the time, Billy, Alan, and I were standing at the entrance to the saddling paddock at Calder.

My partner in crime took an immediate liking to Newmarket Lady. In fact, he quickly urged me to put in a claim for her. However, because of a past experience I had had with Alan's brother, who was also a horse trainer, I didn't feel I could trust his judgment.

I had known the brothers for some years and I knew only too well their lack of expertise. Although they had both worked training horses for years, neither had been able to win any races up to that point in their careers.

A year or so prior to this occasion, Alan's brother, Mark, had instructed me to claim a horse. Just like Alan, he had approached me at the Monmouth Park Racetrack one afternoon. This also took place shortly before the horse he was trying to get me to claim was scheduled to race.

On that occasion, Mark swore to me he had spoken to the guy who normally exercised this particular horse in the mornings. According to him, the horse had great potential and the trainer was trying to ‘steal’ a race by running him against a cheaper caliber of horses. (Mark had 'tipped' me off figuring I would give him a financial reward after I had claimed this horse)

At the time, I was under the impression Mark knew what he was talking about, so I placed a claim in for this horse based solely on the information he had passed on to me. I learned a valuable lesson that day and thank God it didn't cost me a dime.

During the running of the race, the horse actually broke down and became lame. After the race, I was in shock. However, luckily (at least at the time I thought it was ‘luck’ causing me to dodge the bullet. It turned out someone else besides me had placed a claim in for that particular horse and they took ownership of him after the race and not me. (Consequently, when more than one person places a claim in on a horse, the racing secretary assigns a number to each potential claimant and places the numbers in a bottle. Then, the secretary shakes the bottle and pours out a number. Whoever has the selected number assigned to them gets ownership of the horse which is being claimed).

Had my number come out of the bottle that day, I would have lost a substantial amount of money. The reason being the lame horse would have been my property after the race that day. (The rules of claiming make it clear one who places a claim in for a horse in a race is granted ownership from the finish of that particular race. Whatever the outcome of the race is, the horse has been paid for by the claimant and is now under their ownership).

Based on that experience, I had reservations about forking out $15,000 for a horse I really knew nothing about. However, my partner was gung-ho to invest some money into horse racing. This alone wasn't enough to sway my vote. However, when Alan suggested we could run the horse under his license until I obtained mine, I had second thoughts about his offer.

Alan also made it clear I would actually train the horse. Furthermore, he volunteered to help us out by grooming and caring for Newmarket Lady. Since Billy was so willing to invest at his time, I figured he was serious about horseracing. I was sure, once he had taken the plunge he would also be a good prospect for investing more money into my stable's future.

As I weighed the options, it seemed as though claiming Newmarket Lady was a good proposition for everyone involved. Since Alan didn't have any horses to train and he didn't have any prospects, being the trainer on record could give him some much needed publicity.

At that point, something seemed to be urging me on to take the plunge. Billy and I put up the necessary capital and got our stable going in Florida. At that time,

I had no idea I was about to be blessed beyond my wildest dreams.

Why me? Considering the way I was living? Although I had no clue, God was going to use my success to prepare me for the ministry. He had a special plan for me and He was going to use my love of horses and my lust for money to bring me to the exact place where He wanted me to be.

However, first we had to get Newmarket Lady claimed. Unbeknownst to me, there were several others attempting to claim her that day. However, I now know beyond any shadow of a doubt it was God's plan for me to get her into my stable. The Father of lights was in effect fulfilling His Word which states: "he takes the base things of the world and uses them to bring to nought things that are." He was arranging for me to become a force to be reckoned with in the field of horseracing. He does indeed work in mysterious ways.

After I placed our claim in, He saw to it my number came up and this enabled me to gain control of Newmarket Lady's future. She won the race she competed in that day. This was a good sign. At that point, I at least knew she was physically and mentally prepared for competition.

At that point, I had no doubt she was well worth what we had paid for her. Once we had her in our barn, we began to fatten her up and give her the TLC she needed. I personally exercised her on a daily basis. This proved to be quite a task. Consequently, the treatment we were giving her affected her performance on the racetrack immensely. Since I galloped her two miles each morning, I had to use all of my riding ability and strength to keep her from 'running off'. (This is a term used to describe when a horse overpowers their rider and runs out of control at full throttle).

Less than a month after Newmarket Lady was brought under our shed row she won her first race under our stable silks. At that very moment, I knew I had a champion in my grasp. After all the years I had toiled as a pauper in the sport of Kings, my day had come. I didn't understand it at the time, but this was not happening to me as a result of good 'luck'. Also, I know now it was not because of any special skills on my part. God was directing this show.

After the astronomical performance Newmarket Lady put forth in her debut, while representing HBF Stable, (the stable name I chose which is an abbreviation for Horse Brokers of Florida; a corporation my partner and I owned) I had no doubt in my mind that she was a true champion in the making. However, at that time I had no idea that God was in the process of creating quite the 'Cinderella' story. I never could have even imagined He was going to take us both as far as He eventually did. Come to think of it: "Eye has not seen, nor ear heard; neither has it entered into the heart of man, the things which God has prepared for them that love Him." (I Corinthians 2:9)

At any rate, Newmarket Lady responded to my

special care and long distance training far better than I had imagined. As a result, she won race after race for our stable. In fact, following her first victory, she went on to win three allowance races back to back. (Allowance races are a step above claiming races and a short step below stakes races. Stakes races are the highest caliber of races. Also, no one is allowed to claim a horse placed into an allowance race or a stakes race, so we didn't have to fear losing her).

Eventually, Newmarket Lady moved up the ladder even further when she proved herself a worthy opponent in stakes race competition. She brought my abilities as a trainer into the forefront of thoroughbred horse racing. Although, not everyone was aware I was actually training Newmarket Lady at the first.

Alan got the publicity and was even put on television in an interview in the beginning months of Newmarket Lady's career with our stable. This resulted in his receiving some wealthy new clients. Afterwards, my partner got the impression Alan was the brains of the outfit.

Since Alan and Billy both hit it off pretty well, Billy tended to lean towards Alan's perspective as to how we should train Newmarket Lady. This presented a problem for me. Eventually, Alan ran her in a race in which I had insisted he scratch her from. This particular day the track was in a very sloppy condition. For this reason I feared she would sustain an injury running over the slick surface. Contrary to my instruction, he failed to withdraw her from the race.

Consequently, she raced over the slippery surface and sustained a major injury to one of her front ankles in the process. I was infuriated. I fired Alan because of this blunder. Billy didn't like this move. He began to criticize my handling of the whole situation.

Then, Alan began to feed Billy more propaganda on the whole matter of caring for Newmarket Lady. Afterwards, he was left with the impression I did not have the ability to get her back to the races without

Alan's help. To make matters worse, he started complaining about how much money I had spent getting our stable up and running.

Since I wanted to do everything first class, I didn't pinch pennies when I purchased our equipment. Billy saw this as being too extravagant. I saw it as a major investment. He saw it as a major unnecessary expense.

At any rate, after Newmarket Lady was sidelined for about 6 months, Billy began to get more and more impatient. He complained about having to keep pouring money into our stable. When he told me he didn't believe he would ever see Newmarket Lady in the winners circle again, I had had enough. This was the final straw. As far as I was concerned, Billy was out.

I knew I had to find another partner as soon as possible. However, I didn't really have any immediate prospects at the time. At this point, my main objective was to get a win under my belt and bring some money into our stable's account.

Therefore, I focused on obtaining my trainer's license. A short time later, I took the test and was issued my license at Calder Racecourse. However, I struggled to get stalls for my horses. At the time, they were doing some construction on the racetrack and were moving everybody out of the stable area. As a result, it was next to impossible to obtain stalls in the South Florida area.

Thankfully, this didn't take God by surprise. He used my good friend Budd Lepman to get me over that hurdle. Since I couldn't get any stalls, he suggested I go to Florida Downs for a few months. When I agreed, he arranged for me to have three stalls at that track. I figured racing at Florida Downs was good experience for me and Newmarket Lady could recuperate there.

At the time we only had two horses in our stable and they were both incapacitated. Therefore, I didn't want to go to Florida Downs with no racing prospects. I wanted to at least have a chance to win a race while I was there in order to pay for our expenses.

Once again, my unkown Benafactor had this part all figured out as well. It just so happened, a gentleman, who was stabled right next to me, had a horse he was trying to sell. This particular horse was a three year old filly. She had only won one race in her lifetime. She had a lot of speed, but she was running at the bottom of the claiming ladder at Calder.

The filly's name was Girl Queen. Her trainer knew she wasn't quite good enough to race at the track he was about to move his stable to, so he had to unload her. As far as I was concerned, she was a perfect investment for Billy and me.

I assured my 'partner' she would win at least one race at Florida Downs and this would pay for all of our expenses. He quickly accepted my plan and we purchased the filly. Eventually, it all worked out -but not the way I had planned. Girl Queen did win a race at Florida Downs, but, this was only because of Divine assistance. You see, she really didn't like the deep surface of the track there.

I raced Girl Queen three times at Florida Downs. During those three outings, she never even finished in the money. She just didn't seem to want to run over that track. At that point, I was at my wits end. To top it off, Billy was really giving me a hard time about not winning any races.

I had no idea what I was going to do next. At the time, I was down to my last couple of dollars. Although I didn't know it then, God came to my rescue via an elderly trainer who was stabled a few stalls away from me at Florida Downs.

At that time, I was quite hungry for my first official win as a trainer. But, Girl Queen was not cooperating. Therefore, neither of us were making much of an impression on anyone. I knew she was fit and in sound racing condition. What I didn't know was the reason she hadn't been performing up to her ability.

I had no idea what my next move was. This in itself should have told me something; because I always seemed to find the right angles. At any rate, the Lord led this trainer to offer me the help I so desperately needed. He hadn't spoken two words to me in the few months we had been stabled next to one another. Suddenly, he approached me and explained to me he had been watching Girl Queen and he had an idea as to how I could get her to put in a winning performance.

Thankfully, I wasn't too proud and I listened to this old timer's advice. I did what this trainer suggested I do with her. To make a long story short, she won the next race I placed her in. "The way of a fool is right in his own eyes; but he that hearkens unto counsel is wise". (Proverbs 12:15)

To add icing to the cake, someone claimed Girl Queen from us on that same day she won. This could not have come at a more perfect time. We were scheduled to leave Florida Downs the following week and I didn't want to take Girl Queen back to South Florida anyway. Since I knew she didn't have enough ability to win races at the tracks there, I was grateful someone had claimed her.

Between the money we earned from betting on Girl Queen, the purse we won that day, and the money we received from the person who claimed her we had a major influx of cash. We managed to pay off all of our bills and had a few bucks left over.

H.B.F. STABLE, owner
Swindon - second
Busy March - third
Six furlongs - 1:13

"Girl Queen"

JOCKEY CARL BURNS up
Florida Downs, Fla.
March 20th, 1980
J.E. McDONALD, trainer

"The GLEN ELLEN MOBILE HOME PARK of CLEARWATER"

Needless to say, Billy was happy. I was too. I had finally chalked up my first victory as the trainer on record. Again, I feel all the glory for this win belongs to God. I know I couldn't have done it without someone's help. At just the right time, He sent that someone to get me the help I needed.

A few days after Girl Queen's victory, I moved our stable's two remaining horses, back to South Florida. It turned out a former friend of mine, Lou Rafferty, had just become the racing secretary of the Hialeah Park Racetrack. He had offered to give me five stalls there. At the time I couldn't have imagined it, but this too was a blessing from God.

At any rate, everything seemed to be going along according to plan for me and for Newmarket Lady. She had been training quite well and I was looking forward to her return to the races. However, I must confess I couldn't be sure whether or not her previously injured ankle would hold up in the heat of competition I was about to enter her into.

Meanwhile, Billy was becoming way too anxious for my liking. I really just wanted to dissolve our partnership. However, I still didn't have any prospects to replace him. Although patience had never been one of my strong points, I had no choice but to wait.

I didn't know it at the time, but the Lord was going to use a catastrophic incident to bring my old partner in crime back into my life. Once we rejoined forces, I was able me to move Billy out of my life for good. I arranged for Tony to purchase Billy's half of the stable and welcomed my new 'silent' partner into the business. I couldn't have been more pleased. Tony's wife loved horses and he had plenty of money to invest. His drug business was booming.

"O Lord, I know that the way of man is not in himself; it is not in man that walks to direct his steps." (Jeremiah 10:23)

BITTERSWEET VICTORY

A few months after I fired Alan, I had rented a plane with the intention of flying my two sons, James and Allen, my niece, Tammy, and my girlfriend, to Orlando. We had planned on going to Disney World for the day.

Flying had been my ultimate high. After I had moved from New Jersey to Florida, I flew planes almost as much as I had driven my car. As long as there was an airstrip near my destination-even short, grassy ones- I preferred flying over driving.

I had no idea where I got the thought that I should not fly on this particular day. Even though I absolutely loved to fly, the moment that idea had entered my mind, I felt troubled and looked for a reason not to go to the airport and pick up the 185 Cessna aircraft I had reserved for the trip we had planned for on that fateful day.

I even called the weather bureau in hopes there were going to be storms in our flight path that day. However, the weather checked out fine and, for some 'strange' reason, I felt disappointed that it did.

Since my two sons had their heart set on a trip to Disney World that afternoon, I didn't want to disappoint them. Therefore, against my better judgment, I went to the airport to pick up the plane as scheduled.

We drove to Tamiami Airport and I picked up the plane I had made a reservation for on that day.

I checked the aircraft out very carefully and everything seemed to be normal. At the approach to the runway I was using, I did a complete run up on the plane. Again, everything seemed to be normal. The kids were looking forward to the trip, so I didn't see any reason to delay the flight any longer.

I put the aircraft on the runway and we headed

for our destination. I thank God our destination was not eternity; because at the time none of us knew Jesus as our personal Savior. "And as it is appointed unto man once to die, but after this the judgment." (Hebrews 9:27)

I taxied down the runway and took off. It was a smooth takeoff. A very short time later while I was attempting to gain altitude, the plane's engine began to shriek as though it were starving for oil. Immediately, I knew I should have listened to the still small voice which was trying to warn me earlier that day. As I think back on it now, I realize the troubling thought which had come into my mind must have been a warning directly from the spirit of God.

At any rate, it was too late to correct my near fatal mistake. As I quickly glanced over at my oil pressure gage, I discovered what I feared most. We did indeed have a major problem. According to the oil pressure reading, my aircraft's engine had zero oil pressure.

I glanced over at the altimeter-which measures how high the plane is flying-and to my dismay the aircraft had only climbed up to 1500 feet. We were in serious trouble. There wasn't any room for error. Immediately, I leveled the aircraft and started looking for somewhere to land. While I was attempting to do a 360, my sons, and my niece began crying out: "We're going to die!"

I tried to calm everybody down. However, the plane began to shake violently and this made matters worse. Panic had gotten hold of all of my passengers. I yelled out over the commotion and told them we would be okay. I really had no idea what would be the outcome of our situation, but I needed to be able to concentrate without a bunch of hysteria going on throughout the cockpit.

Momentarily, there was silence on board. I continued looking for an emergency landing spot. At that time, our plane was flying above a large housing development. I couldn't imagine making a safe landing on one of the streets running through this development. So, I kept searching for a better option. To make matters worse, the aircraft's engine seized up. This was no doubt due to the overheating caused by the lack of oil pressure. The planes' propeller ceased its rotation. As we glided without power, I knew every second counted. I absolutely had to find somewhere to land.

As my options were dwindling more and more, I was getting less and less confident any of us were going to survive this crisis. Suddenly, the thought came into my mind: *You're going to be okay*. All of a sudden, a peace came over me. At the time, I had no idea this was the Holy Spirit speaking to me and assuring me we were going to make it. When I think back on it now, how else could I have had such peace under such horrendous circumstances?

A few seconds after I received the encouraging thought, I spotted a small field running alongside the housing development we were gliding over. This seemed to be the spot I had been looking for. However, as I steered my aircraft towards this field I soon discovered I was facing a major obstacle. This field happened to be surrounded by power lines.

At the rate my aircraft was losing altitude, I had my doubts as to whether or not we would be able to make it over the high voltage wires. However, I knew I had no second choice. I had to go for it. I steered right towards the lines. The next thirty seconds was the longest time period I have ever experienced in my entire life.

As our plane glided towards the power lines, time just seemed to stand still. Then, there was an eerie silence. As we neared the high voltage wires, we all held our breath. I don't know exactly how much room there was between the landing gear of our plane and the high voltage wires surrounding the field. I really didn't want to see how close our plane was getting to them. All I could do was hope. As our plane finally glided over the power lines, we all gave a sigh of relief.

At that point, it seemed to me like everything was working out just fine. We made it. No sweat. However, as we descended onto the field I noticed there were very high sugar cane stalks and a number of small trees and brushes in our path.

I tried to steer away from the obstacles as much as it was possible. Then, I raised the nose of the aircraft in order to flare out for our imminent touchdown. In a split second the plane was atop the brush and its' landing gear snagged something causing it to violently lunge downwards

At this point, I remember seeing the cowl of the plane in front of me twisting and crumbling. (The cowl is the sheet metal covering the engine and the front portion of the aircraft). I was thrown violently forward in the cockpit. My head was jerked to the left side. As this happened, I saw the door on my side of the plane fly open and my sons being hurled out of it.

While all of this was taking place, my life flashed before me. I thought it was all over. Then, in an instant, the plane stopped moving completely. I was elated. We had survived. However, I wasn't so sure we were safe just yet. I detected a strong odor of fuel. The plane was leaking fuel profusely and I feared it could explode momentarily. I feverishly rushed to get everyone away from the wreckage as quickly as possible.

My sons and my niece were quite shaken up. They were hysterically weeping. Thankfully, none had received any injuries. The cane in the field had served as a cushion to break their fall. My girlfriend was the only one who had sustained any injuries during the crash. She had smacked her forehead on the dash of the plane upon impact. This resulted in her receiving a large bump over her eye.

I was uninjured, so I quickly tried to comfort everybody and get them as far away from the plane as I possibly could. From our position in the field, we could not see more than a few feet ahead of us. None of us had any idea which way we should go in order to get out of the field safely.

At the time, I was very concerned the heat from the planes' engine would ignite a fire. Between the spilling fuel and the dry cane all around us, we were sitting on a powder keg. I knew we had to get out of the field as swiftly as possible.

Amidst the chaos, I attempted to gather everyone together. I wasn't sure which way we should go, but I felt I had to at least get everyone away from the plane. If we stayed where we were, I figured we were all in danger of being burned alive.

I made a quick decision and started herding everyone in a southern direction. Within a minute, I heard a helicopter coming towards us. I looked up and there it was. What a welcome sight this was to my eyes. I thank God it was the U.S. Coast Guard. As the helicopter hovered overhead, one of the occupants motioned for us to head in an eastward direction.

I quickly followed his lead. As a result, we all made our way out of the sugar cane field in a matter of minutes. As we emerged from the cover of the tall stalks, we were greeted by news reporters, firemen and the local residents.

Plane lands safely

A single engine Cessna with five persons aboard had an engine failure last night but made a safe landing in a vacant lot at SW 123rd Avenue and 93rd Street. Pilot James McDonald, 30, of 9375 Fontainebleau Blvd., and his two sons, James Jr., 10, and Alan, 9, escaped uninjured when the plane went down, police said. Diane Riccobono, 24, of the same address; and McDonald's niece, Tammy Perry, 8, visiting from out of town, had minor injuries, police said.

Miami Herald 8-28-79

Apparently, after I had radioed a 'mayday,' someone had alerted the media. While the reporters were interviewing us, I was greeted by one of the locals. He just ‘happened’ to be a close friend of my former partner, Tony. During our conversation, this gentleman, whom I'll call Larry, took down my telephone number and offered to give it to Tony. He explained my ex-partner had been trying to get in touch with me but didn't know how to reach me.

A short time later, Tony contacted me. We arranged to meet at his home later that same day. Once we became reacquainted, he told me he had been having marital problems. This stemmed from the fact he spent a lot of time carousing about during the operation of his lucrative drug trading.

Immediately, I saw an opportunity. I made him a proposition. Since Tony liked horses and loved any form of self glorification, I knew he would be a perfect candidate to become my new partner. With a large influx of new money-which I knew he could provide-I figured I could expand my stable and promote my career as a trainer.

I offered to take Tony in as a silent partner. He readily accepted. From his point of view this was the perfect solution to his problems with his wife. After we made it official, he told his wife he was going to go legal and informed her of our newly formed partnership. She was delighted.

In the past, his wife and I had always had a good relationship. She respected my integrity and I guess she was hoping some of it would rub off on her husband. At any rate, she loved horses too and this made our union even more appealing. She informed me she was more than happy to become involved with horse racing through her husband's association with me.

I wasted no time making Billy an offer he couldn't refuse. At the time, he was building a new home and needed some cash. Since he did not think Newmarket Lady would ever recuperate and return to racing with her former abilities intact, he quickly agreed to sell his half of our stable for $20,000.

Tony got an awesome deal. At the time, neither of them knew it but Newmarket Lady alone was worth over $100,000. Since she had been sidelined for about six months, we could never have gotten that kind of money for her. However, I was optimistic.

After all was said and done, the end result was a blessing to me via my replacement for Billy. I was delighted to have a new silent partner. A few months later, Tony got a big return on his investment and his first taste of victory.

I had taken my time nursing Newmarket Lady back to health and it turned out to be well worth all of my effort. She made her way back into the limelight post haste. In fact, after I gave her a prep race at Gulfstream Park Racetrack, she was ready for her first win of the year.

On opening day, at Calder Racecourse, she won the feature race by nine lengths. This was quite a surprise; because this was her first long distance race ever. Up until that point in time, she had never raced at any distance longer than seven furlongs. Once again, God's grace prevailed and Newmarket Lady astounded me by her performance that memorable day.

H.B.J. Stable's
Rockin Rosy, 2nd
Cool Flower, 3rd
1 mile-1:39 4/5

Newmarket Lady

Calder Race Course

Frank Verardi, up
J. E McDonald, Trainer
May 9, 1980
Turfotos

I was especially delighted about this victory because I really wanted to impress Tony with my skills as a trainer. This turned out to be quite a showing. For me the victory was even sweeter, since rumor had it that Newmarket Lady was not capable of running in long-distance races and that my training abilities were not proficient enough. I figured I knew who was spreading all the rumors, but I didn't care. Bottom line, I was thrilled because I knew her performance on that day put all those rumors to rest for good.

If it weren't for God's intervention once again,

Newmarket Lady would not have even made it to Calder for that race. You see, I was stabled at Hialeah at the time. Therefore, Newmarket Lady had to be shipped to Calder via horse van.

The van arrived at Hialeah on schedule that afternoon. However, my younger brother, Louie, whom I had left in charge of loading Newmarket Lady onto the van for her trip to Calder, had fallen asleep in one of the tack rooms in our barn and wasn't aware the van had arrived.

Although the van driver had them announce over the track intercom it was time for Newmarket Lady to come to the loading ramp, Louie had not heard this. Strangely enough, someone (who I am thoroughly convinced was an angel sent by God) just happened to go to the exact tack room where Louie was fast asleep and awakened him. (this was a tack room never used by our stable before). Consequently, Louie and Newmarket Lady made it to the loading ramp just before the van driver pulled away. "Are they (angels) not all ministering spirits, sent forth to minister for them who shall be heirs of salvation?" (Hebrews 1:14)

However, I had no clue my heavenly Father had even bigger plans for Newmarket Lady and me. After her bang up performance that day, I told Tony our stable was ready for expansion. I figured it would be as good a time as any to bring some more stock into our stable via my new partner's bankroll. So, I started shopping for some new stock to fill up our barn.

Coincidently, Quitting Time's handlers let me know he was up for sale. (Not really because it was all in God's plan). At first, my new partner wasn't enthused with the idea of purchasing him. However, I was quite confident Quitting Time had great potential and eventually I convinced Tony to put up $10,000 as his half of the $20,000 purchase price for the horse.

I was quite confident I could advance his career in the same way as I had improved Newmarket Lady's status. Unfortunately, things don't always work out the way we mortals plan them. Shortly after we purchased, Quitting Time, all of my visions of grandeur regarding his and my future were brought to an abrupt halt. Due to an early morning training accident, he was forced to the sidelines by an injury to one of his ankles. Consequently, this put him out of action for almost a year.

Shortly after Quitting Time sustained his injury, I took the advice of a friend of mine and sent him to some veterinarian's farm for surgery. With him sidelined, my stable's future once again depended on Newmarket Lady.

I had hopes that I would have more than one horse in training capable of earning our meager stable enough money to keep up with our bills. However, this was no longer the case. My new partner wasn't happy with our unfortunate turn of events either. Through this unfortunate turn of events, he quickly discovered there are some unavoidable pitfalls in horseracing. Therefore, he became reluctant to invest any more money in our stable. Needless to say, that put a damper on my plans for expansion. My main goal suddenly became survival.

The future indeed looked bleak, but unbeknownst to me God still had a plan for me. I had no idea how blessed I would be by Newmarket Lady's future performances. Consequently, she went on and carried our stable to great heights. Her wins earned us purses that helped us to keep up on the bills for the remainder of the racing season in Florida that year.

At seasons end, we shipped our stable up to New Jersey. A few months later, Newmarket Lady chalked up a win at the Meadowlands Racetrack. I shall never forget what a surprise God had for me on that day. It was on September 3, 1980. She had just won the feature race that night. It turned out this was the biggest victory of both our careers.

After the race, I was standing in the winners circle. All of a sudden, God spoke to my heart in a way He never had done before. It was while I waiting to receive the trophy and have my picture taken.

I had just looked out into the crowd standing there in the clubhouse. As the fans stood there viewing the whole procedure, I lapped it all up. I gazed out at the spectators, and pondered what had just happened.

While I made my appearance there in the winners circle, I was wearing expensive clothing and very expensive jewelry. My girlfriend, Lina, stood beside me. She looked like a model right off the cover of Cosmopolitan magazine. She had just turned 20 years old. I was 32.

Along with us in the winner's circle, stood my best friend, attorney Lee Baxter, Lee's wife, Maggie, and my step mother Ursula. I was delighted to have so many loved ones at my side. This was indeed a most joyous occasion.

While someone was presenting me with a silver trophy, I marveled at the fact that when I was a teenager, I used to ice skate in the very meadows where the stadium and the Meadowlands Racetrack had been built. Back then, I had no choice but to skate in those frozen meadows. You see, I couldn't even afford to go to a skating rink. In fact, our family never could afford even the most minor of luxuries. Making ends meet was always our main objective. We barely had enough to get by. Therefore, I never dreamed I would someday be in this very spot making racing history.

There I was standing tall. I never imagined I would be experiencing such victory as a thoroughbred horse trainer in such a short time. In spite of my shortcomings, God had managed to help me to reach my goal much quicker than I ever dreamed was possible. It had only taken me a couple of years to make racing news. In fact, our victory that night landed me on the front page of the Racing Form. I was indeed a success.

However, I still had absolutely no idea this was all the result of someone else's plans and I was not the one in control of it all. I thought I was just 'lucky.' At that point, I was the proud owner and trainer of Newmarket Lady. While putting forth another one of her winning performances, she had just defeated some of the best fillies on the New York racing circuit.

Her victory had increased her value quite a bit as well. At this point, she was worth a small fortune. My place as a renowned trainer in horse racing now seemed very secure. I had no doubt from this night on I would have a reputation as an accomplished trainer.

My career possibilities are limitless, I thought to myself. And, I did it all on my own. I have the leading jockeys working for me now and I am the one calling the shots. Never again will I be deprived, I've got it made. I'm the one, now. I thought to myself. *I am the captain of my fate. I have taken on the world and I won. I started out as a pauper in the sport of kings, now I am king.* I boasted.

Newmarket Lady's victory had just enriched my kingdom with a whopping $25,000 purse.

With a horse like Newmarket Lady, I can write my own ticket now, I chuckled. *To top it off, I hadn't even planned on racing Newmarket Lady in this particular race. How much luckier can I get?*
I marveled.

Little did I know, luck had nothing to do with my circumstances-God was directing this. You see, I had entered Newmarket Lady into the race she had just won strictly as a favor to the racing secretary of the Meadowlands Racetrack. His name was Lou Rafferty. We had known each other for many years before he was promoted to this position.

Since Lou had given me five stalls at Hialeah Racetrack earlier that year, I felt I owed him. A few days prior to Newmarket Lady's big win, Lou had me paged to the racing secretary's office at Monmouth Park Racetrack. At the time, I had been training my horses there.

Once I entered the office, Lou greeted me and informed me he needed a favor of me. I didn't hesitate to offer to help him in any way I could. Then, he informed me he wanted me to run Newmarket Lady in a race he was trying to fill.

As it sometimes happens, they didn't have enough races scheduled to fill the card for the following night of racing at the Meadowlands Racetrack. (This was due to the fact some of the scheduled races didn't have enough horses entered. Therefore, it was the duty of the racing secretary to offer some ‘extra’ races. This procedure usually enabled the administration to find enough entries to put on some of those races in the place of the races which failed to attract enough entrants for the upcoming night of races).

Lou told me he wanted to put on a special feature race and he thought it would be a good spot for me to run my filly. At first, I thanked him for the consideration but declined. I explained I was pointing her towards another race-which was scheduled to take place about 10 days later. When he pleaded with me to run her as a favor to him, I relented.

At the time, I had no idea this was going to turn out to be the biggest victory of my short career as a thoroughbred horse trainer. In God’s economy, doing my friend this favor was going to result in a substantial gain for me. This should have been no shock to me.

As I thought back on it, I realized my whole experience with Newmarket Lady had been chock full of surprises. I often mused over the fact some horse trainers spend their entire careers and millions of dollars searching for a horse such as her and never reach their goal. This made every one of her victories taste even sweeter to me. Without the big money behind me, I had managed to accomplish what is truly a near impossible feat in horseracing.

I had something money can’t buy. I had Divine assistance, although I didn’t realize it at the time. All I knew for sure was the fact my moment in the sun had finally come. As I stood there and attempted to suck up the light from each individual ray shining down upon me, I was oblivious as to what was about to happen next.

All of a sudden God spoke into my mind something I definitely wasn't ready to hear.

"You think you know what life is all about don't you? But, you don't know a thing. This is not all there is. You have no idea what you're missing." He ominously warned me.

As soon as those words permeated my spirit, my heart sank. Immediately, I lost all of my joy. I suddenly came to the realization I was missing something. A heaviness, which I couldn't explain came over me. All of my life I had been searching for stability. I thought I had finally found it. But at that precise moment, I knew I had been missing it all along.

Where did I go wrong? Why should I be feeling down like this? I wondered to myself.

Although I usually had all the answers, this time I had no clue. Later that evening, the whole group of us, who had been in the winner's circle celebrating Newmarket Lady's victory, took a limo ride to Studio 54 in New York City. It was party time.

However, I didn't really feel like partying. Although I was usually the life of the party, I found myself searching for something else this night. For the sake of those who accompanied me I tried to act the part of a gracious host. But, as the night wore on I became more and more lethargic. I felt so empty inside. Never in my life had I been so confused.

Although Newmarket Lady catapulted me to heights I never dreamed I could reach, I still didn't have the peace and stability I had been striving for all of my life. Something was still missing. Even though I had reached the pinnacle of my career as a trainer and had acquired all of the material things I dreamed of, my life now seemed useless. This was not what I expected.

What happened? I questioned.

I thought I knew it all, but all of a sudden I couldn't find the answer to my life's meaning. The mystery of it all haunted me for the next several days. Eventually, I finally got caught back up in the rat race and managed to push my earlier experience into the back of my mind. I just wanted to get on with what now seemed to be my shallow existence. I did manage to console myself with the fact I had at least achieved success in the world's eyes.

As I think back on it, I am amazed I was able to totally ignore my unearthing experience and go on with my life as though this event never even happened. I guess my life in the fast lane distracted me that much. However, I often wonder why I never took the time to try and figure out why the best night of my life turned into one so void of pleasure. Why hadn't I put more effort into discovering who it was that had entered my innermost sanctuary and had spoken such chilling words into my spirit?

"He that loves silver shall not be satisfied with silver; nor he that loves abundance with increase: this also is vanity" (Ecclesiastes 5:10)

OPPORTUNITY KNOCKS

The following two write-ups were both taken from the front page of the Racing for Newmarket Lady had won the biggest race of my entire career. Notice they glorify James-not God.

Newmarket Lady 1st In Meadowlands Test

MEADOWLANDS, East Rutherford, N.J., Sept. 4—Veteran Don MacBeth guided H B F Stable's Newmarket Lady to a four-length tally in the feature here Wednesday night at a mile and a sixteenth.

The James E. McDonald charge circled the early leaders on the final turn and then went about her business while running the distance in 1:44.

The 4-year-old daughter of Noble Table from the Ridan mare Market Lady, who was stakes-placed on two occasions this season, including a third in the Eatontown Handicap at Monmouth, paid $11 in the field shortened to five fillies and mares after it was switched from the turf to the main strip.

Newmarket Lady has now won two of nine seasonal starts and the $15,000 winner's share of the purse boosted her seasonal earnings to $33,601.

In the pick six, no one among the 14,592 on hand correctly picked the 5-6-4-4-1-5 combination. A total of 68 tickets picked four winners and each was good for $214.40. There were 559 minor winners and they received $9.80. The handle for the pick six was $24,924 and for the program $1,803,198.

Bernon Sayler rode a double on the program. He scored with Fancy Farm's Squatters Rights in the fourth race and then came back in the eighth with Fred Hooper's Queen Ambra.

Squatters Rights, conditioned by Bill Cunningham, ran six furlongs in 1:12⅘ and paid $10.40. He started off a trifecta worth $1,120 when Circle H Stable's Susie Sue came on for the place and Glory B Stable's Steel Rock held on for the show.

Queen Ambra scored by a neck in the eighth event, a mile and 70-yard test for fillies and mares who had never won two races. She outgamed Tartan Stable's Demure in a stretch-long battle. Queen Ambra ran the distance in 1:43⅘ and paid $41. The exacta came back $268.20. Apprentice Kathy Moore was aboard Demure in her first eastern ride.

Newmarket Lady Heads Meadowlands Turf Test

By DOUG McCOY

MEADOWLANDS, East Rutherford, N.J., Sept. 29—H.B.F. Stable's Newmarket Lady, third in the Saddlebrook Stakes here last out, and Larry Kennedy's Fanny Saperstein, who came to life last time out when beaten less than a length by Record Acclaim, top a field of six fillies and mares in Tuesday's mile and 70-yard headliner on the grass.

Craig Perret will handle Newmarket Lady at 119 as the Noble Table filly seeks her third victory from 11 outings this season.

Buck Thornburg is slated to return on Fanny Saperstein at 115 as the one attempts to regain the form that made her one of the top grass running Jersey-breds in training last season.

Also expected to attract some support in the seventh race feature are Thomas P. Whitney's Chestnut Speester, third in a tough allowance event on the grass at Belmont last out, and Dogwood Stable's Keeler, who set the early pace in the Pardo Handicap at Delaware and a section of the Eatontown 'Cap at Monmouth in her last two outings.

Jean-Luc Samyn is slated to return aboard Chestnut Speester at 115 for trainer Phil Johnson while no rider has been named on Keeler at 117.

Also in the field are Henry L. Carroll's Quillascope, 115, Perret also named, and J. C. Perry's Dottie O., 110, apprentice Frank Lovato Jr.

Last time out in the mile and a sixteenth Saddlebrook, Newmarket Lady made a strong move while well out in the racing strip leaving the second turn but weakened slightly through the final furlong and had to settle for third behind English Trifle, beaten less than three lengths.

Prior to her Saddlebrook effort, the bay filly had rallied off the pace in an allowance event at a mile and a sixteenth and had drawn away through the final furlong for a four-length victory over English Trifle and Charming Cristal.

The last time Newmarket Lady ran on the turf was the first section of the split Eatontown Handicap and the James McDonald charge rallied to loom a threat in mid-stretch before tiring late to be third.

Interestingly enough, Newmarket Lady finished dead last in the very next race she competed in. Up until that point of my eighteen year career in horseracing, I had never had any horse I trained or rode finish last. I prided myself on that issue.

However, in Proverbs 29:23 God promises: "A man's pride shall bring him low". I found out the hard way that God's word does not return unto Him void. If He said it, it shall come to pass.

Unfortunately, like many of us humans, I was too busy at the time to stop and think about where all this 'strange' dialogue that I had been picking up in my spirit was actually coming from.

At any rate, during her winning performance in the Bristol Handicap, Newmarket Lady sustained an injury which eventually derailed her career permanently. After this catastrophic event, our stable was barely able to keep up with our financial burdens.

However, God wasn't through with me yet, so my career continued to take me to higher heights. He helped our stable to survive long enough for me to get Quitting Time back to the track and ready for action. In the summer of 1981, everything was in place for the final curtain. It was July of that year. I was at the Atlantic City Racetrack in Atlantic City, New Jersey. On this particular night I once again found myself in an all too familiar situation. The future of my stable, not to mention my career, was riding on the outcome of one single race which was taking place there.

I had entered Quitting Time in a cheap claiming race. I had hopes of making this race our big payoff. Up until this point, my partner and I had invested much time and money into this horse's career. However, due to his early morning mishap he had been out of action for about 14 months.

Even though things hadn't gone according to my plan, I thought Quitting Time would reward my confidence in his ability some day. He was a little speed ball who loved to run. Because of his spirit I felt he had great potential. He stood about thirteen and a half hands high. That's not very tall for a racehorse, but what he lacked in size he made up for with speed and determination.

Quitting Time was a three year old dark bay thoroughbred gelding. He had a white star on his fore head. He was stocky and had a short, thick neck. He was built like a quarter- horse. He had all the characteristics of a 'speedball.' His hind quarters were enormous. He was a very strong specimen and, whenever he was on the surface of any racetrack, he made it perfectly clear to his rider he was born to run and ready to race.

Much to my liking, Quitting Time was a people horse. He had a great personality. A few months before we purchased him I had witnessed his physical ability firsthand. On that occasion, he won the very first race he had ever competed in. It was a maiden special weights race. In that particular race, he had broken his maiden and had shown much speed. (For the benefit of the reader who doesn't know, a horse is considered a maiden until they win their first race).

From the first time I saw Quitting Time run, I was impressed with his character. Immediately, I knew he was my kind of horse. Although he was a gelding, he was no wimp. (Geldings are horses that have been castrated. Usually this helps to get the horse's mind off of any mares which might be around them and onto their original purpose- which is to win races).

Quitting Time's future had looked very bright to me. However, at the time I purchased him I had no idea my 'luck' was about to run out. I also had no idea how closely both our destinies were linked together. I never dreamed there was such significance to the name Quitting Time either. Only God could have imagined this whole scenario.

Although Quitting Time didn't have top notch breeding, I knew this would not affect his potential as a competitor. In fact, none of the horses I was able to claim had exceptional breeding. Yet, I somehow was able to bring out their hidden potential.

There is one reason for this- God had His hand on me. Unlike most thoroughbred horse owners, I had been able to profit heavily from my investments in horse racing. But, this was not because of my expertise. Everything I had achieved was due to God's grace. I now know, beyond any shadow of a doubt, I really had little to do with my success. Even though I was a former jockey and I know a good horse when I see one, my skills were not what had caused me to excel. Yet, I took it for granted. I had advanced my skills as a trainer to the point where I had no doubt I could get any horse in my barn to win races-regardless of their talents or lack of breeding.

However, in the case of Quitting Time my investment had been deteriorating. I figured if I could sneak in a quick win with him at the Atlantic City Racecourse we could recoup most of our losses. I figured if I ran Quitting Time in a claiming race for the meager price of $3,500, our problems would be solved.

I didn't normally gamble on my horses, but I couldn't see how Quitting Time could lose a race competing against the caliber of horses I pitted him against that night. To top it off, Quitting Time had trained up to this particular race magnificently.

I had personally worked him out in preparation for his debut at Atlantic City. Considering how he had trained with all of my 135 pounds in the saddle during his workouts, I figured he was unbeatable at the price he was running for.

As far as I was concerned, this was our golden opportunity to cash in. We were about to be rewarded for our efforts with some tax-free money. This was just one of the many perks in horse racing and I wasn't one to allow an opportunity to slip by. I went for broke.

Since my partner was a silent partner, I thought I was in the position of calling all the shots. In reality, it was the One who brought Quitting Time across my path was calling the shots. My partner had no choice but to put all his trust in my abilities and hope I could pull a rabbit out of my hat. At any rate, my partner didn't like losing. To top it off, this night was one of the few occasions when I had instructed him to bet his money.

On my recommendation Tony had sent his wife to the Atlantic City Racecourse that night. She flew in from their home in Florida. She wasn't traveling light. She had come to Atlantic City with a large amount of his money. She also had high hopes of having her picture taken in the winner's circle after the race.

I had no doubt this would have been the case. After all, Quitting Time was a much classier horse than the rest of his competitors. He should have whipped the field of horses he competed against that night while pulling the starting gate behind him. At least, this is the way I saw it.

However, shortly after the race began, I knew this wasn't going to be the case. Before the field of horses had traveled an eighth of a mile, I knew my gamble wasn't going to pay off. As the race unfolded, I was sure we weren't having our picture taken that night.

To my dismay, I observed Quitting Time trapped between horses and unable to get to the lead.
I knew he was the type of a horse who loved to run, but he definitely wanted to be on the lead. In fact, he should have been in the front of the pack from start to finish in this race.

However the apprentice jockey who was riding him failed to hustle him out of the gate. I couldn’t understand why this happened. But, I knew this was going to cost us the race. During the running of the race, all I could think about was that someone would probably claim Quitting Time for the lousy $3,500 claiming price. If this happened, our stable would have wound up losing all the way around.

As it turned out, I didn’t get to dwell on this thought for very long. In less time than most people can hold their breath for, the race was over. As the field came thundering down the stretch, I'll never forget the feeling of helplessness I experienced. Against all odds, I still hoped I would see Quitting Time making a bold move and gaining the lead during the stretch run.

To my utter disappointment, this was not the case. At that point, I asked myself how something like this could have happened. In my heart, I knew the answer. But, this didn't matter now. All that mattered was the final outcome of the race. We lost.

When they crossed the finish line, Quitting Time was somewhere in the middle of the pack. I didn't even bother to number his position. The fact was he had lost the race. In the process, I had just lost most of my 'case' money and possibly my horse.

After more than a year of hard work and preparation, I had missed out on cashing in. What hurt me the most was the fact I knew in my heart Quitting Time should have easily defeated those horses. Having to depend on a jockey to complete the final step in my plans never did sit well with me.

Since I was a trainer and a former jockey, I was

well aware of the fact it only took a small margin of error on my rider’s part to foil my plans. One bad choice during the running of a race could obliterate months and months of my hard work. Since the average horse race takes less than a minute and a half, this is a travesty to most horse owners and trainers.

Whatever the case may be, I was back at square one. My partner's wife stood next to me. I sheepishly glanced over at her and saw a befuddled look on her face. At this point, neither of us knew what to think. Both of our pockets were full of what now turned out to be worthless wagering tickets. We must have looked like two starving victims who had just missed their gravy train.

This scenario was definitely not what I had in mind. I’m sure she would have agreed with me on that. What now? I didn't even want to think about it. I was too stunned to even try. However, all was not lost. It turned out nobody had claimed our horse that night. I was quite thankful for this.

The bad news was I knew I couldn't run him back in any race at a New Jersey track and expect to get good betting odds again. Also, I was sure I wouldn't be taking Quitting Time home should his next race take place at a New Jersey racetrack. There was absolutely no doubt in my mind someone would put a claim in for him- especially should his next race take place in the $3,500 claiming range.

I know the jockeys talk about good prospects amongst themselves. I also had to consider anyone with an eye for a good horse would have been watching him in his debut race. This person would have pinpointed him as a hot prospect for a future claim. Since he came back from his race in sound condition, he would seem to be a winning proposition to anyone who was in the market for a sound investment.

After his race, he seemed to have plenty of potential left and since he now had a race under his belt, this made him more physically fit. Therefore, as long as he stayed sound, Quitting Time was now more capable of a winning performance. If he were to be claimed, this would add up to an early return for the investor.

Also, I had to consider the professional gamblers who watched him in his race. They would be just waiting to bet on him the next time he raced. At this point, I knew I had no control over the possibility somebody else could wind up cashing in on all of my hard work. To say the least, this was a disturbing thought to me.

After the valet unsaddled Quitting time, he was brought back to the stable area where I cooled him out. Within a couple of hours, I loaded him on a horse van. Then, I headed for the Garden State Parkway. It was now time for both of us to endure the long trek from Atlantic City to Monmouth Park Racetrack.

It was about a three-hour drive to Long Branch from Atlantic City. Unfortunately, there was no shorter route there. During the long ride back, my mind replayed the events leading up to the disaster I had just experienced. Not surprisingly, I came to the conclusion I should never have put a jockey I knew nothing about on my horse-even if my best friend did recommend him.

I couldn't have chosen a worse time to make such a boo-boo. Since this jockey, who had ridden Quitting Time, wasn't familiar with him, I definitely should not have been betting on him that night. I should have known better. In fact, I did.

During my career as a trainer, jockey errors had caused my horses to lose more than a few races. Some of those races were very important ones to me. Those losses had cost me hundreds of thousands of dollars in purses. Consequently, losing some of those races also prevented the value of my horses escalating. This resulted in even more substantial losses to me. (You see, it is not only the amount of races a horse wins which increases their value. The higher the class of the race the horse wins the greater bearing it will have on their value for future breeding purposes).

At any rate, in Quitting Time's case, I was aiming for the money we would have won for betting on him. I had my gun cocked and loaded, but it misfired. Now, I was just about out of ammo. He was indeed the best shot my three-horse stable had to get some cash flowing amongst us again. Now, my financial situation was beyond desperate.

Although I had failed before, this was the hardest defeat I had ever experienced. I thought Quitting Time was definitely our ticket out of debt. During our financial drought, our meager stable hadn't even had the opportunity to race a horse in months. To top it off, the other horses I trained weren't in any shape to be racing in the near future. In fact, at this point I wasn't sure either of our other two horses would be able to make it back to the races at all.

Our expenses were overwhelming us. The bills had been stacking up for some time. I owed the feed man, the veterinarian, the blacksmith, and the horse van transporters. After Quitting Time's loss, I had very little cash in my possession. I had a monthly mortgage payment on my home in Fort Lauderdale, along with a rock star's lifestyle. Speaking of rocks, I was truly between a rock and a hard place. To make matters even worse, I would have to deal with my partner and his loss. All I could do was wonder, *what next*?

Once we arrived at our barn inside Monmouth Park, I unloaded Quitting Time from the van. After I carefully inspected his legs, I concluded he might still have one more race left in him. I thanked God he had gotten through his race unscathed. I also thanked Him nobody had claimed my horse that night.

We might get another shot at it after all, I thought to myself. I tried to look at the bright side of it all. In a sense, we had a victory that night. Quitting Time would race again. I joyfully continued to unload all our gear from the van.

Afterward, I bedded Quitting Time down for the night. Finally my day was coming to a close. I left the track and was on my way to the place where I lay my head. Thankfully, I lived only a few miles from the racetrack. I had been staying with my best friends, the Lee Baxters.

Lee was an attorney, who had a practice in Colts Neck, N.J. I had known him for about 7 years. He also loved horse racing. In fact, I met him through his wife, Maggie. She also had a passion for those four-legged athletes.

Lee and I hit it off instantly. He was everything I always wanted to be. He was respectable, well mannered, easy going, honest, intelligent, and humble. He was also a very good attorney. He reminded me of Abraham Lincoln.

I remember how I envied Lee. Although he was an attorney, he seemed to have a lay back type of an existence. I hadn't yet learned how to live the simple life. Everything in my life always seemed to be on the fast track. (No pun intended).

I thought I liked being in that situation. I guess it was the challenge of just being able to keep up with the pace which kept me in that mode. At any rate, I had been living and partying as if any day could be my last one.

Up to that point in my life, I had already had two very close calls with death. Once, I was almost killed in a car wreck. On the other occasion I was in that small plane crash that I had already mentioned. Those near-death experiences made me realize I was not invincible. Formerly, I thought I was. At any rate, this inspired me to live life to the fullest. It truly shaped my whole philosophy on life; albeit not in a good sense.

Afterwards, I was always looking for new and better ways to enjoy my circumstances in life. I tried to indulge in as much of the finer things in life as I was able to afford. Strangely enough, I never gave a second thought as to what would have happened if I actually died in the state I was in.

While my girlfriend and I stayed with the

Baxters, all of us enjoyed much fine dining and partying in New York City. We had attended many plays, ballets, concerts, and whatever other entertainment New York City had to offer. Since Long Branch was only about a 45 -minute drive from Manhattan, we all made the trip there on numerous occasions.

As I pulled into the driveway behind the Baxter home that night, I looked forward to some peace and tranquility. At least for a little while, the madness would be stilled. Even though I had no idea what my next move was going to be, I no longer cared.

At that point, I was too mentally exhausted to let it concern me. Since everyone was asleep when I arrived, I quietly slipped in the back door and made my way upstairs to our bedroom. My girlfriend lay fast asleep upon the bed. I plopped down alongside her and was asleep before I knew it.

Usually, I awoke with the joy of facing a new day. I looked forward to meeting the challenges I would face. Somehow, I always knew I would succeed. I would not settle for defeat. No matter what obstacles appeared in my path, I had always found a way to overcome. Up to that point in time, I had always had the attitude that, if it could be done, I could do it. I always seemed to have all answers.

However, when I awoke the following morning, my exuberance was gone. I climbed out of bed and plodded into the bathroom. In an effort to fully awaken, I threw some cold water on my face, brushed my teeth, and made my way down the stairs and into the dining room. It was there I encountered Lee and Maggie. They both bid me a good morning. Then, Lee asked me about the outcome of Quitting Time's race the night before.

With bitter disappointment in my voice, I reluctantly relayed the events of the previous night to my two friends. After I finished, Maggie asked me what my future plans for Quitting Time would be?

"Quite frankly, I have no idea. I don't know of another jockey that I feel I can trust to ride him in his next race. That is, if he makes it to another race. My whole plan for him has been derailed. In fact, my career and my stable's future are in doubt right now. I don't know where I am going from this point on," I glumly replied.

Then, Lee said: "Why don't you ride Quitting Time the next time he runs?"

"You've got to be kidding! I am 135 pounds, and I haven't ridden a race in over 10 years. How could I possibly ride Quitting Time?" I sarcastically blurted out.

"You could do it, Jimmy," he said.

Lee wouldn't take no for an answer. I was startled. I didn't know what to make of it. At that point, I decided not to stay and have breakfast with Maggie and Lee. I had no appetite anyway. I was confused and not in the mood for further discussion on the matter.

I excused myself and hurriedly made my way towards the kitchen door. Before I departed, I did tell Lee I would consider his suggestion concerning me riding my horse in his next race. Actually, I was just trying to be nice. I had no intentions of doing so. Little did I know God had already ordained for this.

At the time, I was sure what Lee had just suggested was virtually impossible. I didn't realize it but God had just used Lee to plant a seed in my mind. It was a mere thought. But, it was about to turn into something much more

Although I had no clue God had a specific plan and I was about to carry it out. A short time later, He began watering the seed He had planted in my mind through Lee's suggestion. Suddenly, I found myself giving it serious consideration. *Maybe I can gain the victory I was denied if I try this. I have come too far to give up now. What do I have to lose by trying?* I thought to myself.

Anything is possible I began encouraging myself. Suddenly, I began to see some light at the end of the tunnel. The 'seed' had just been given a dose of God's miracle grow as His inspiring thoughts continued to bombard my mind. Before I realized it, determination was budding forth in my spirit. The Master was culminating His harvest in my mind with a dose of supernatural sunshine. Then, I thought to myself: *haven't I already done the impossible?*

As I continued my drive to Monmouth Park Racetrack that morning, I started planning on how I could shed the extra pounds my body was carrying. I drew on my former martial arts training. Focus. That is what my instructor emphasized the most. When I did so, I could break bricks and boards and defeat any opponent standing in my midst. If I really focused I could bring my body under subjection long enough to drop the necessary pounds and actually become a jockey again. Even if I only did so for this one race, it would be well worth my efforts.

At that point, Lee's suggestion suddenly turned into my life's goal. Nothing else I had ever done meant more to me now than winning a race with Quitting Time. I had been denied victory, but this never stopped me before. In fact my whole life seemed to be about overcoming defeat. I had faced defeat before and it never kept me from pressing on towards my goal. Just then, I got another thought: *What if I can't lose enough weight?* After all, I would have to lose about 20 pounds in order to be able to ride in a race again.

What if Quitting Time isn't healthy enough to participate in another race, I thought to myself? Then, I came to the realization I had no other options. Unless, I was willing to call it quits. However, this word wasn't even in my vocabulary. Although I couldn't be sure of anything in horseracing, I was sure I had to do everything in my power to try to bring Quitting Time into the winners circle. If not, I was sure my illustrious career in horse racing was destined to end in disaster.

During my 16 years of experience in the sport, I had learned never to take anything for granted. Horse racing is a gamble. In our case, Quitting Time and I would surely be going against the odds. However, my whole life I had been going against the grain. This never stopped me before. Why should I give up now? Against all odds, I somehow always managed to overcome whatever obstacles I faced in the past.

I did it then and I can do it now. I thought to myself. *That's it!* I'm going for it. I decided right then and there I was still up for the challenge.

As I drove up to the barn at Monmouth Park that morning, I saw my good friend, Budd Lepman, standing in the front. He was preparing to go to the track and watch one of his horse's in training. At that time, Budd had about 40 horses stabled at Monmouth Park.

As I exited my car, Budd bid me good morning. Then he asked, "How did Quitting Time do last night?"

"You don't want to know. That jock must have been on downers. I can't believe he got my horse beat!" I retorted.

"Unfortunately, he didn't fit Quitting Time the way you do Jimmy. Then again, maybe the horse didn't like that track." Budd apologetically explained.

I knew better, but I didn't want to discuss it further. Budd sensed that, so he bid me good-bye and headed towards the racetrack to observe his horses train. Meanwhile, I started off towards Quitting Time's stall. As I arrived there, my horse came to the front of his stall to greet me. He was a friendly little critter.

I placed his halter on him and led him out of his stall. Unfortunately, he didn't seem to be traveling too well that morning. I stopped walking him and proceeded to check his right front ankle.
Fortunately, I didn't find any abnormalities. Thankfully, he didn't have any heat in his previously injured ankle. (When an area of a horse's leg is warmer than usual, this is a sign of injury).

However, after further examination, I discovered he had some stiffness in his shoulders. This could have been causing him to walk a bit 'ouchy' that morning. Immediately, I knew I had to do something to remedy this condition. If not, the soreness in his shoulders would prevent him extending himself as he galloped. This would more than likely cause him to sustain further injuries as he went through his daily exercise routine.

When a horse is not one hundred percent, he tends to compensate for it. While the horse is in motion, this will usually cause the animal to put more weight on their uninjured legs. The added stress eventually takes a toll on the overall condition of the horse and compounds the problem.

Quitting Time couldn't afford another injury. If he sustained one, I feared he could quite possibly lose his desire to run. I could relate to this more than most people. I was in the habit of running 5 miles a day and I could remember times I had absolutely no desire to run. This was due to the fact I had soreness somewhere in my body.

Therefore, I never expected a horse to put forth much of an effort while they were experiencing any kind of soreness-especially since they were required to carry the weight of a person on their backs. Considering Quitting Times' deteriorating physical condition, it seemed as though we were in a race against time. It was only a matter of time before we would lose any competitive edge we had.

The situation was crucial and seemed to be leaning even more towards the impossible. I knew I had to make my next move count. Could I possibly beat the clock with Quitting Time? I didn't know for sure. But, I knew I had to give it my best. There would be no second chances.

Temporarily, I had lost the wind in my sails. But, my good friend Budd would once again come to my rescue. After I explained Quitting Time's condition to him, he led me to his tack room. (A tack room is the place where a stable will usually store their saddles, bridles, medications, bandages, and other materials needed to keep their daily operation running smoothly).

Once we were inside his tack room, Budd

proceeded to open a large chest. Then, he pulled a fairly large, black box out of it. Inside this box was a machine which resembled an automobile battery charger. As he opened the box, he explained to me that the machine was used to apply electrodes to a horse's muscles. The procedure of sending electrodes to the sore muscles caused them to relax. In turn, the horse's pain would ease up. He assured me most horses would eventually experience a full recovery after treatment. I was sure glad to hear that.

Then, Budd warned me there was no guarantee Quitting Time's problem would be totally alleviated by daily treatments. However, we both agreed it was worth a shot. I knew I absolutely had to give it a try. Together, we carried the machine to my horse's stall.

After we arrived there, my dear friend hooked up the various wires necessary to administer the treatment. Then, he gave me a demonstration of the machine's application. Once he was convinced I could operate the machine properly, he excused himself. I knew he had a busy schedule, so I didn't detain him any longer than necessary. Before he left, I gave him my heartfelt thanks for helping me once again.

This was another Godsend. The machine Budd loaned me was worth about $15,000.00. There was no way I would have been able to gain access to such a device on my own accord. Besides, at the time, I wasn't even aware such a device existed. I was truly blessed.

My troubles weren't quite over yet. Even if I could hold Quitting Time together for one more race, could I ride him to victory? In my heart, I knew there could be no guarantee. However, I also knew my horse would get the best ride possible with me in the saddle.

I'll do it! I can do it, I assured myself. At that moment, I realized there was no other logical choice. No other jockey would have as much determination as me to win a race with Quitting Time. To any other jockey riding him in a race would just be one more mount in their career.

However, as desperate as I was, I knew this would be my one and only opportunity to keep my career alive. My lifestyle was on the line. It was a do or die situation. If I were even 'lucky' enough to pull it off, I would probably only get this one last shot at keeping my dream alive.

Although I am an optimist, I am also a realist and I knew I still had to bear in mind I hadn't ridden in a race in about 10 years. I wondered to myself, *could I even be physically fit enough to accomplish my goal?*

To say Quitting Time and me were indeed quite the long shot was putting it mildly.

"The way of the wicked is as darkness: they know not at what they stumble." (Proverbs 4:19)

DESPERATION SPAWNS DETERMINATION

Although I didn't know for sure if I would actually get another opportunity to race Quitting Time, I was optimistic. If I could make the weight and ride my horse, I believed I could win a race with him. Since I didn't want to risk someone else blowing my chances for a desperately needed victory, I came to the conclusion I had to take control of this segment of the competition too.

I reaffirmed my decision. If Quitting Time did race again I would be the jockey in the saddle. In order to put my plan into action, the first thing I needed to do was to find the right race for him. The way I figured it the race had to be held at a track located out of the tri state area. It could not take place at a racetrack in New Jersey, New York, or Pennsylvania. If I wanted decent betting odds on Quitting Time, I would have to race him at a track where both of us were not known.

After I left the barn that morning, I went straight to the racing secretary's office. I knew I could find the information I needed there. In the racing secretary's office, they keep what are known as conditions books. Conditions books contain information on future prospective races. Those races and the tracks where they propose to run them are listed in these books. A conditions book specifies the types of horses eligible for a race. It also gives a specific price range of the horses who will compete; along with the price of the purse offered to the participants. It also lists the distance of the prospective race along with the weight each horse will be assigned to carry in the competition.

When I arrived at the racing secretary's office, I headed straight for the rack where I saw the conditions books for the various racetracks currently having their racing meets. The rack was stacked full with books containing the future races at Monmouth Park as well as conditions books from various racetracks throughout the rest of the country.

As I examined the rack, I saw a conditions book for Pimlico Racetrack in Maryland. Then, I saw a conditions book for Timonium Racetrack. This book caught my attention. It occurred to me that Timonium would have half-mile races and this would be advantageous for both Quitting Time and me. In those shorter distance races he wouldn't have to run so far, and I wouldn't have to ride him too far. Since I hadn't ridden a race in ten years, I knew it wasn't going to be an easy task for me to ride in a race farther than a half of a mile. I figured the jockeys who had been riding races on a daily basis, would have a physical advantage over me in that respect. However, I felt I was fit enough to ride in a half a mile race. Since Quitting Time was a speed ball, I figured I basically just had to hang on and allow him to do most of the work throughout the whole race.

I also believed the competition we would be facing would be softer at Timonium than the horses we would have to compete against at the Pimlico Racecourse. Therefore, I searched Timoniun's conditions book in hopes I could find a race for my horse at that track.

As I proceeded to browse through it, I came upon what I considered to be the perfect race for both Quitting Time and me. This particular race was a half-mile claiming race for 3 year-olds who hadn't yet won two races in their entire life.

I knew in this particular race Quitting Time would only have to face horses that had probably already run on numerous occasions and hadn't been capable of winning when competing against other horses which had a winning record. Those particular types of horses would not have won a race other than a maiden race in their entire careers.

Although Quitting Time had only won a maiden

race up to that point in his career, it was a maiden special weights race. This type of a race is more or less an allowance race for newcomers. The caliber of horses he had competed against and defeated were top notch competitors. Hence if he got into the race I was considering, he would be facing softer rivals.

The way I figured it the only reason Quitting Time hadn't won the second race of his career was due to his having been injured. Another reason he hadn’t chalked up another win could be contributed to jockey error. I had no doubt in my mind, as long as I could keep my horse sound enough to race, he would be a tough horse to beat in the race I planned to ride him in.

The claiming price for the race was listed at $2,500. This race was scheduled to take place 15 days later. I knew I would be racing against the clock trying to shed all of my unwanted pounds on such a short notice. However, I figured I had to at least give it a try.

According to the conditions book, Quitting Time would be assigned to carry 119 pounds for the race I had chosen. In order for me to be able to ride him, I would have to somehow reduce my body weight down to 116 pounds. I didn’t know if this was even possible, but I was about to find out.

I placed the conditions book in my hip pocket and left the secretary's office located on the backside of Monmouth Park Racetrack. Then, I drove over to the front side where the grandstand, the jockey’s room, and the administration building is located. My objective was to go to the jockey's room and weigh myself. I had to find out if my plan was at least feasible. How much I weighed at that time was to be the determining factor for my next move.

When I arrived at the scale, I was a little apprehensive. Once I stepped onto the scale, my apprehension quickly turned to delight. I weighed only 135 pounds. This had been my average weight since I quit riding in races years earlier. It didn't take me long to calculate. I would only have to lose 19 pounds. I would have two weeks in which to do it. In my estimation, my goal was definitely within my reach. That settled it. I would ride again. Suddenly, my spirit was overwhelmed by the fact I was getting a second chance to become a winning jockey.

I quickly hopped off the scale. I could hardly wait to get started. I walked briskly to my car out in the parking lot. On my way there, I was already formulating a plan which I hoped would enable me to lose those 19 unwanted pounds within the time frame I had to work with.

It didn't take much figuring. I decided to start out by sacrificing my lunches for the two week period. Instead of dining, I planned to exercise from noon to 1 pm. I also decided I would ride my bike to and from the racetrack each day throughout that time period.

Since I traveled to and from the racetrack several times a day in order to feed and water my horses, I figured I would get plenty of extra exercise. I also had hopes the bike riding would help me to get fitter and this would make it easier for me to ride Quitting Time. Although I was already pretty physically fit, I figured losing 19 pounds was going to have some affect on my physical strength. I had to do whatever was possible to offset this.

At that point in my life, I had been practicing the martial arts for over 10 years and I had been playing racquetball or tennis at least a few times a week. I also was accustomed to jogging an average of five miles a day. Since I also exercised my horses on a daily basis, I was relatively fit.

All things considered, I was in great shape. However, I realized I was also 33 years old. Therefore, riding Quitting Time in a race would require even more physical ability from me than I already had. In order to ride in a horse race, I knew I would have to use some muscles I hadn't used in years. Race riding requires an extreme amount of energy and fitness. If I were going to ride my horse, I wanted to be sure I would have all that it would take in order to get the job done.

I was an optimist, but I was also a realist. I had no doubts about the challenges I would be facing. In order to reach my goal, I would have to get everything right the first time. There was absolutely no room for error. I would not get a second chance at it.

I got into my car and drove home. After I arrived at the Baxters, I quickly exchanged my jeans for a pair of shorts, a sweatshirt, and a pair of sneakers. I planned to go bike riding. During my attempts for weight reduction, I wanted to make sure I would be burning up the maximum amount of calories.

I jumped onto my 10-speed bicycle and headed for the beach in Long Branch, New Jersey. It was a beautiful summer day. I remember how excited I was. I had a vision. I was going to accomplish something special with Quitting Time. However, at the time I had no idea this was the very plan of God all along.

After a brisk ride, I arrived at the beach. It was nice to smell the salt air and feel the gentle ocean breeze. As I rode my bike along the boardwalk, I remember the theme song from the motion picture "Rocky" started to come into my mind.

Earlier that year, I had seen the movie Rocky. In the film, Rocky was a struggling prizefighter attempting to make a nearly impossible comeback. I never dreamed that some day I would relate to Rocky in the way I now did. I was also prepping for the fight of my life.

While Rocky was working out getting into shape for his upcoming battle against all odds, "Rocky's Theme" played on in the movie. Rocky's Theme was now my anthem. I was determined. I focused on making a comeback. Somehow I would also win my upcoming battle against the odds.

I pedaled my bike faster. As I continued riding, I enjoyed feeling the ocean breeze flowing across my face. I heard the familiar sound of sea gulls scavenging for food. Their screeching sometimes drowned out the peaceful sound of the waves crashing along the beach.

Yet, it was all good. I basked in the moment. Meanwhile, the warmth from the gorgeous July sun was already causing me to burn off the unwanted pounds.

I couldn't help but appreciate the fact life that was really good. My life was a blessing. I had a new hope and a new purpose. Somehow, I just knew I would succeed. I knew in my spirit I was born to be an overcomer. By God's grace, I had made it this far. Surely there was more out there for me.

Several hours later, I pulled my bike into the driveway of the Baxters' home. I was sopping wet and loving every minute of it. I knew I had done well. I figured I had lost at least a few pounds that afternoon. Thousands of little droplets of sweat poured forth from my body. Each one signified my goal was that much closer.

Upon my arrival, a young trainer friend of mine, Mark, greeted me. It was obvious he had been waiting there for me and had something on his mind. I had known Mark for several years. He was not a very sharp horse trainer. After the time he had advised me to claim a horse which had broken down in the race it was in, I lost any respect I had concerning his ability as a trainer.

Mark never had been very successful in his chosen field. However, I always had a soft spot in my heart for him. Ever since we both had worked for Budd Lepman years earlier, I felt compassion for him. I could also identify with him, since I too had been struggling to make my mark in the sport of kings.

During our years of familiarity with one another, I did whatever I could in order to help Mark in his quest for success. It didn't work. Horse owners want results. They go with the winner. He couldn't produce. He always seemed to be a day late and a dollar short.

Previous to that afternoon, I hadn't seen Mark for some time and had lost touch with him. As I dismounted my bike, he stepped off the back porch and approached me. He stood about 6 feet tall and weighed about 180 pounds. He had black hair and brown eyes.

He had the appearance of a male model. However, I noticed on that day the clothing he wore was old and worn and he wasn‘t clean shaven. I assumed he definitely wasn't doing very well.

Before he ever spoke a word to me, I knew he had not come just for a social visit.

“Jimmy, I need you to do me a favor. I need to borrow a few dollars. I am flat broke,” he blurted out.

Then, he reached into his pants pocket and pulled out a few pieces of costume jewelry. As he handed it to me for inspection, he said:

“You can keep this jewelry until I pay you back.”

I didn’t need to examine it because I could see it was only junk jewelry. I had no plans of keeping it for collateral. Besides, after years of wheeling and dealing, I learned it was probably best not to lend anyone money. Should the borrower balk when it came to paying me back, I didn’t want to have to go through the changes of taking back what was mine. I had made it a rule not to lend anybody more money than I was willing give away. I always assumed I wouldn’t get paid back. If this turned out to be the case, I would have incurred no great loss. In the event the person did pay me back, good for them.

“Mark, I’m not doing that great myself right now. But, I can give you $100. Just pay me back whenever you get it,” I offered.

“Thank you so much, Jimmy,” he joyfully replied.

At that point, I put my bike on the rear porch of the Baxter residence and told him I would be right back. Afterwards, I went into the house to get the $100 I had planned to give him. When I came back out onto the porch, I handed him the money and he thanked me profusely.

”I’ll pay you back, Jimmy,” he promised.

Then he turned around, walked off of the porch, and made his way down the long driveway. I went back into the house and raced up the stairs into the bathroom.

I could hardly wait to feel the hot water caressing my body. Once inside the bathroom, I quickly shed what little amount of clothing I was wearing that afternoon.

I leaped into the shower and turned on the water. I stayed there under the shower until I had exhausted every bit of the hot water supply. Afterwards, I felt absolutely terrific. By this time, it was only about 8 p.m. and I was ready to retire. I felt I had a very productive day. I was totally at peace.

After a good night's sleep, I awoke the following morning chomping at the bit. I could hardly wait to get started. The vitality I had lacked the previous morning was fully restored into my life. I was anxious to go to the jockey's room and weigh myself. I could hardly wait to see how many pounds I had shed the day before. I was also anxious to tell my good friend, Budd, about my new plans for Quitting Time.

I hopped out of bed, and got dressed. After brushing my teeth, I felt like I glided down the stairs and into the dining room. Maggie and Lee were there getting ready to have their breakfast. Immediately, I told Lee about my plans to ride Quitting Time in his next race.

He was delighted. I thanked him for giving me the idea. I explained I appreciated having good, caring friends like Maggie and him. I truly realized the value of our friendship. Since the first day I met them, their encouragement had a favorable impact on my life.

At that point in my life, I knew everything which had happened to me would somehow work out for good. As I arrived at the barn that morning, Budd Lepman was pulling up in his pink and gray golf cart. (Pink and gray were Budd's stable colors.) The veteran horse trainer was just returning from the racetrack. He had been watching a couple of his horses go through their training exercises. Since the track was located about 50 yards from his barn, he rarely walked there.

After I cordially greeted my good friend, I informed him I had planned to race Quitting Time at Timonium Racetrack in Maryland.

“When”? He inquired.

“In two weeks,” I gleefully replied.

“I think I can hook you up with a rider for that one,” Budd volunteered.

“Don’t worry about that,” I quickly responded. “I’m going to ride Quitting Time myself.”

“Are you crazy Jimmy?” he questioned me.

At this point, I realized how astonished he was by what I had just nonchalantly declared.

“Those boys will eat you up down there,” he strongly suggested.

“Budd, I rode at half-milers before. I know how to handle myself at the ‘bush’ tracks,” I defensively replied.

I could tell by the expression on his face he wasn’t even a little convinced. However, I knew what I was capable of. Years earlier, I had ridden in a few races at a half-miler in Canada. (Half-milers are considered minor tracks. Some even call them 'bush' tracks. Bush tracks are much smaller than the major tracks. Major tracks are usually a mile or more in circumference. They are also much wider than the smaller tracks. The competition is fiercer at these half-milers and there is less space in which to maneuver a horse during the running of a race. Riders and horses have been known to crash into the hedges surrounding the racing oval during races. Hence the name ‘bush’ tracks).

Since I knew Budd was not aware of the fact I had ridden in any races at Blue Bonnett Racetrack, I tried to explain this to him.

“I've learned enough of the ins and outs of riding in races at the bush tracks. I am confident I can handle the competition at Timonium. As far as I am concerned, my biggest obstacle will be winning the battle of the pounds,” I confidently exclaimed.

He understood what I meant. After my explanation, he seemed to be more at ease about my plans for Quitting Time. Since I had worked with him years earlier, he knew I had been blessed with exceptional riding abilities. I believe he trusted my judgment concerning the things I had already experienced during my racing career as a jockey.

Budd also knew I was the type of person who would allow nothing to stop them once their mind was made up. Therefore, he stopped trying to dissuade me and offered to assist me in any way that he could. That was so like him. We ended our conversation on that note.

I jetted around to the other side of the barn where my horses were located. I was anxious to see how Quitting Time was doing. Once I arrived at his stall, I could see he was none the less for wear and tear. In fact, the shoulder treatment I had been administering to him seemed to be working. At that point, he was as full of energy as I was.

Later that morning, I went through my daily routine with a new found joy. Although the chores involved with the caring for three horses can be taxing at times, I always did enjoy it. However, this new challenge I faced with Quitting Time somehow brought more zeal into my life.

Once all my equine athletes were cared for that morning, I made my way over to the front side of Monmouth Park and stopped off at the jockey's room. It was time to check my weight again. I was eager to see how much progress I had made the day before.

On the way there, it dawned on me I would soon be in need of a racing saddle. In order to ride Quitting Time, I would have to use my own racing saddle. However, I no longer owned a racing saddle. I owned several exercising saddles, but did not possess a racing saddle. (The saddles used for exercising a thoroughbred, during their daily workouts, weigh about 10 pounds or more. The saddles used for race riding usually weigh two pounds or less).

Since I was a 'heavyweight,' I would in fact need the lightest racing saddle I could obtain. Hopefully,

I could get one which weighed a pound or less. I knew this would be a great help in enabling me to make the weight I would be required to carry for our upcoming race.

I wasted no time making my way to the jockey's room. Once I arrived, I got on the scale and weighed myself. As I observed the dial stopping at 131 pounds, I was even more delighted. Since the day before, I had lost four pounds. I only had 16 more pounds to lose. This was indeed good news.

As I pulled out of the parking lot and headed towards home, I contemplated my next move. Somehow, I had to line up a saddle for my ride aboard Quitting Time. I didn't know it at the time, but the great Planner had already supplied my need.

Before I got out of the parking lot, I crossed paths with John Maletto. John was an old time trainer and good friend of mine. Around the racing circuit in New Jersey, he was affectionately known as 'Pop'. He had been involved in many a race on his home turf in Long Branch, New Jersey. Although he had been training horses for many years, he had never trained a horse which developed into a stakes horse. Subsequently, he had never made it into the limelight of thoroughbred racing. Unfortunately, he had never realized his greatest expectations or the prosperity which comes with it.

However, Pop was able to etch out enough wins over the years to keep his meager stable afloat. He also managed to raise a pretty big family on this income. Most importantly, he was very well liked by all who had the pleasure to know him on a personal level.

Pop had nicknamed me 'lucky.' Earlier in my career, after I won the very first race I had entered my horse, Patriotic Petunia, into, he tagged me with that nickname. Many years later, I realized my nickname should have been 'blessed' because I truly was.

Within the first few years of my career as a

trainer, I had been blessed with the stakes filly Newmarket Lady. I managed to win more races training horses than I was able to chalk up during my short career as a jockey. At the time, I attributed this to the fact I had more control over the situation because I was training the horses I also partly owned. Little did I know who was really in control. He was totally responsible for any and all success I had attained.

At any rate, Pop and I were good friends and we had done numerous favors for one another over the years. He greeted me with his customary phrase.

"How are you doing Lucky?" he grinningly inquired.

"Same as you Pop. I'm still trying to survive in this game. I'm just another pauper in the sport of kings," I jokingly replied.

He laughed. Then, I explained the plans I had for Quitting Time. Before I even mentioned the fact I needed a racing saddle, he told me his son, John Jr., had a racing saddle I could use.

"You're more than welcome to borrow Johnny's saddle. In fact, you can use his saddle as long as you like he doesn't need it anymore," Pop offered.

I already knew John Jr., was no longer riding races. Years earlier, he had lost the battle of the pounds. I thanked Pop for his generosity. We conversed for a few more minutes sharing the latest racetrack news and he bid me goodbye. I told him I would try to live up to my 'name' and thanked him once again.

As I proceeded out of the parking lot, I mused about how wonderfully everything seemed to be working out for me. However, I wasn't quite out of the woods yet. For starters, I still had a few more pounds to lose. I knew it was going to become more and more difficult to lose weight. As I drew nearer to my goal, it would be harder to shed pounds.

Also, I was aware of the fact I could be disappointed in the end. There was always the possibility the race I planned on entering Quitting Time into wouldn't even take place. It was entirely possible the race could not go. (In other words, the situation could arise where not enough horses were entered into that particular race. If this turned out to be the case, the racing secretary would cancel that particular race and use some other race to fill their card for that particular day). On the other hand, the situation could also arise where more than 12 horses were entered into the race. In that case, Quitting Time could get placed onto the also eligible list. This would mean he would only get into the race if one or more horses scratched out of it. (Scratches occur when the trainer of a particular horse decides against racing his charge in that particular race for whatever reason).

Being the optimist I have always been, I made plans assuming the race would go. Even if that particular race didn't take place, I figured I could use the extra time in order to lose as much weight as was necessary before another race would come up. I was sure I would eventually get the chance to ride Quitting Time. However long it took, I was determined I was going to carry out my plan.

Once I arrived home, I quickly donned my exercising garb and took off towards the beach on my bicycle. After another enjoyable ride along the boardwalk that afternoon, I cruised back to Lee's in order to pick up my roller skates. I wasn't done yet.

Roller skating requires more physical effort than bike riding. Therefore, I also believed I would lose more weight by roller-skating to and from the racetrack. I loved to roller-skate anyway. So I actually looked forward to enjoying a good skate while I burned off some more pounds. After I exchanged my bike for my roller skates, I was off to feed my horses their dinner.

"A man's heart devises his way, but the Lord directs his steps." (Proverbs 16:9)

QUITE THE FRIEND

While I was on my way to the track, I was approached by Mark. At the time, I noticed he no longer bore the expression of humility he had the day before. On this occasion, he looked to me like someone who was up to something.

He was never one to beat around the bush. This time he was no different.

"Jimmy, I need to make some money. If you can get a couple of ounces of 'coke' from your partner, I have it sold already," he confidently proposed.

Before I had a chance to respond to his request, he offered to split any of the profits with me. I was taken aback. He had made this request because he knew my partner, Tony, was in the illegal drug business. He had met him at my barn on several occasions while we were racing in Florida.

Since Tony liked to impress people, he had let on that he was a cocaine dealer. Because he believed he was at the top of his game, he believed Mark would be impressed. Unfortunately, he seemed to think just because he was a major supplier of illegal drugs, he deserved the notoriety.

In order to help Mark get out of the financial jam he was in, I agreed to take him up on his offer. If I didn't help him, I figured he would just keep coming back to me to borrow more money. I didn't have the resources to keep giving him handouts. I also knew I didn't have the heart to refuse him should he ask me again.

I figured I could kill two birds with one stone by supplying Mark with the drugs. Not only would he profit from it, but I could make a few extra bucks for my trouble. I was hoping this could serve to keep me afloat until Quitting Time and I won our upcoming race.

I knew my partner would front me all of the coke

I could sell. Therefore, I wouldn't have to lay out any money. In my street wise mentality it looked to me like a win, win situation. I had no idea what I was getting myself into. However, this turned out to be one of the worst decisions I ever made.

"You got yourself a deal, Mark. As soon as I get the coke, I'll let you know. Just give me a couple of days," I confidently proclaimed.

He sported a grin from ear to ear.

"Okay Jimmy," he thankfully replied.

"I'm on my way to feed my horses. I'll see you later," I told him.

Then, I remounted my bike and rode it to the racetrack. Once I arrived there, I wasted no time feeding and watering my horses. After I had completed this task, I went to the jockey's room and weighed myself again. I weighed in at 129 pounds.

I had managed to lose another two pounds. But, I still had 14 more pounds to go. However, I felt much more confident because I had 12 days in which to do it. At this point, my goal seemed to be even more attainable to me than ever before.

Later that afternoon, I called the airlines and booked myself a flight to Miami. Afterwards, I called Tony and let him know I was coming back to Florida. I also let him know I had to have a meeting with him post haste. He instructed me to give him a call, once I had arrived there.

After caring for my horses the following morning, I left for the airport. Since I wouldn't have time to go through my exercise regimen I decided I would fast. I didn't expect to lose too much weight that day, but I had to try. I figured every little bit would help.

Less than 12 hours later, I had completed a round-trip mission to Florida and was back in Long Branch, New Jersey. As expected, Tony readily supplied the coke I sought after. However, the trip back and forth turned out to be an exhausting experience for me.

I didn't look forward to rising up at 5a.m. the

following morning. But, I knew I had a big day ahead of me. When I arrived home, everyone else in the house was sound asleep. I made my way to my bedroom as quietly as I could. I didn't want to awaken my girlfriend who was already fast asleep.

After undressing, I quietly slid into the bed next to her. I lay there in bed for a moment wondering just how many hours I could rest before morning as I drifted off to sleep. The next thing I remember is the sound of the alarm clock awaking me.

I hadn’t had much sleep, but I was invigorated. My girlfriend and I got out of the bed and wasted no time getting dressed. After brushing my teeth, I quietly made my way down the stairs. She worked with me as our groom, so she followed close behind me. We both exited the house through the kitchen door and mounted our bikes which were parked out on the back porch.

Together, we made our way through the deserted streets of Long Branch to the racetrack. We arrived there at about 5:15 am. As we pulled up to our barn, I noticed Quitting Time was poking his head out of his stall. I was delighted. He was as eager to go as I was.

While my girlfriend brushed him off, I went to our tack room and gathered a saddle and a bridle for him. By the time I arrived back at his stall, he was prepared for saddling. I gently put the saddle and bridle on him.

Then, I walked him out of his stall and on to the shed row. I took him for a couple of laps around the shed row. (Before mounting any of my horses, I always took them for a lap or two around the shed row. This allowed them to stretch out a little and more or less get the kinks out. In Quitting Time’s case, I knew this would be a big help to him. I wanted to give his shoulders as much of a chance to loosen up as was possible).

Afterwards, I mounted my horse and led him towards the racetrack for his daily workout. Once I got him onto the track I felt even more confident I would reach my goal. His actions made it clear that since his last race he was none the worse for wear and tear. In fact, he seemed to be more fired up than ever.

In order to loosen up his shoulders a little more, I jogged him for about a half a mile. He quickly took hold of the bit. This was characteristic of him. He was in his domain once again. He wanted to compete. He was now a little fitter than before and even more ready to go.

As usual, I had a difficult time restraining him. In order to control a thoroughbred, the rider has to communicate with his mount through the reins. A good rider develops sensitivity in his grip on the reins. This is known in horse racing as having ‘hands’.

A person with good hands does not over react to the horse they are riding. Over reacting only makes the horse pull harder at which time they tend to run faster and eventually burn themselves out. The object of hands is to make the horse want to run, while at the same time keeping the animal in control.

I was blessed with good hands. Over the years, numerous top-notch trainers had told me so. Even so, exercising Quitting Time was still a challenge for me. Whenever I did so, I found it necessary to keep his neck bowed. In that way, he was forced to pull against himself. This allowed me to keep him from running off and going too fast, during his daily exercise.

I galloped Quitting Time around the track one time. Monmouth Park Racetrack is one mile in circumference. That was the distance I normally took him for his daily workout. Although he had me and the heavier exercise saddle on his back, he had traveled well that day. I was grateful.

Upon returning to the barn, I dismounted and removed the saddle from off his back. Afterwards, my girlfriend gave him his morning bath. Then, I walked him around the shed row for half an hour. This was the normal procedure I used to cool him out.

However, he wasn’t cooled out after his 30 minute stroll around the barn. I knew I could attribute this condition to one of two things. Either the humidity in the air that morning or the stress from some soreness was causing him to perspire and preventing him from drying out. I hoped it wasn't the latter.

To my delight, he finally cooled out a short time later. Afterwards, I borrowed Budd's machine and proceeded to administer therapy to his shoulders. About an hour later, I massaged his legs with alcohol. Afterwards, I place some overnight bandages on his legs. (Overnight bandages consist of thick cotton and gauze wraps. The wrap is placed around the horse's leg just below the knee. Then, the wrap is covered with cloth bandages. This keeps the wrap in tact, in spite of the horse's activity in their stall during the night. Some horses have all four of their legs wrapped in this fashion each day. This is done in order to keep the animal from injuring itself in the stall at night, as well as for therapy purposes. Sometimes, a horse gets spooked and this can cause them to injure themselves. Any number of reasons could attribute to this. At any rate, the end result could cost the animal their racing career).

As soon as we finished up our daily morning chores, my girlfriend and I headed over to the jockey's room. I wanted to see how much weight I had managed to lose the day before. I was in for a disappointment. After I stepped onto the scale, I realized my lack of exercise the previous day had cost me. I weighed in at a little over 128 pounds. I had barely lost a pound.

I didn't gain any weight, but I still had 13 pounds to go and only 11 days in which to lose those unwanted pounds. I was in no position to slack off. I knew even a little lapse could cause me to miss my goal. I was determined not to allow that to happen.

Before I left the track that morning, I made it a point to pass by Mark's barn. I was determined to deliver his 'package' as soon as possible. When he saw me, his face lit up. He knew the purpose for my visit.

"How was your trip?" he inquired.

"Everything went according to plan," I replied.

"When can I pick it up?" he questioned.

"How about meeting me at my place in about an hour?" I suggested.

"That will be fine," he anxiously agreed.

After completing my other errands that morning, I went home so I could keep my appointment. As I rode my bike up to the back porch, I noticed he was already there waiting for me. As I dismounted, I invited him to come inside.

"Have a seat in the living room and I'll be right with you," I told him, as we entered the house.

Then I made my way through the kitchen and up the stairs to my bedroom. A few moments later, I came down and placed the package into his hands. As he took delivery, he explained he planned to meet his buyer later that afternoon.

"I'll have your money before dinner. How soon can you get some more of this?" he inquired.

That was so like Mark. He was always putting the horse before the cart.

"Let's talk about that later, a lot can happen between now and then," I cautiously forewarned.

"I'll call you later," he promised as he walked out of the kitchen and onto the back porch.

I followed close behind him.

"Later," I said, as he started walking down the driveway.

I followed his progress until he was out of sight. Something was telling me we were being observed. However, I didn't see any visible signs of this. I thought maybe I was just being too cautious. I turned around and went back inside. It was time to change into my exercise garb and get back to work. Later that afternoon, I rode my bike with a vengeance. Before I was satisfied with my progress, I had ridden along the boardwalk for a few more hours than I had originally planned. I was determined I wasn't going to allow a few pounds to stand between my goal and me. In order to insure I make the weight, I would do whatever I felt was necessary.

Since I had plenty of energy that afternoon, I put it to good use.

When I got onto the scale in the jockey's room the following morning, I was rewarded for my determination. I weighed in at 126 pounds. I had lost two more pounds. I was now only 11 pounds from my goal. I was pleased to know I still had 10 days left in which to lose those 11 pounds. I confidently smiled.

Mark didn't call me as promised. However, I wasn't moved by this. I knew that was the nature of the beast. Whenever I had any dealings with drugs, I always braced myself for the unexpected. Usually, I was not disappointed.

Since he hadn't called, I had decided to give him until noon the following day to contact me. If I hadn't heard from him by then, I planned to go looking for him. As it turned out, I didn't have to. When I arrived home that morning, he was already there waiting for me. As I dismounted my bike, he reached into his pocket and pulled out the money he owed me.

"Not here. You never know who could be watching. Wait until we're inside," I firmly instructed him.

As we entered the kitchen he apologized for failing to call me the night before.

"I didn't get to meet with my buyer, until late last night. I figured you wouldn't want to meet with me at that hour so I put it off until today. I hope you weren't worried. Anyway, the guy really loved the stuff and he wants to meet with the big guy to buy a few more kilos," he excitedly reported.

The moment he uttered his latest proposal, the thought, *this guy's a narc,* flashed into my mind. Undoubtedly, I smelled a rat. First of all, I knew the cocaine I had given him wasn't that great. I had taken out some of the original product for myself. Then, I had cut it with about a quarter of an ounce of manitol. (A white powdered laxative) This was my way of increasing my profit and paying for my airfare to

Florida.

Secondly, from experience I knew it was quite unusual for a dealer to go from selling ounces to selling kilos after only one deal. The real clincher was the fact this buyer supposedly wanted to meet the 'big guy'. I felt Mark was not street wise at all. I believed he had fallen for the bait. However, I hadn't.

"Mark, you better watch this guy, this sounds like a set up to me. Where did you meet this guy anyway?" I suspiciously questioned.

"I met him through a jockey I know," he sheepishly answered.

"If I were you, I would check this guy out because he sounds like a 'narc' to me," I advised him.

"I'll look into it, but I don't think he is a narc," he defensively replied.

Before our conversation had ended, Mark promised to ask around and let me know what he could find out about his new 'connection.' Afterwards, he headed out onto the back porch, and promised he would call me on the following day.

As I watched him walk down the driveway, my gut feeling was that he hadn't gotten the message. I could tell he didn't take the matter as seriously as I did. I didn't believe he could see past the dollar signs. I felt he was so sure his buyer was going to be a meal ticket for him that he was overlooking the seriousness of the situation.

I put my thoughts about the whole matter on hold temporarily. I knew there was nothing more I could do. I had warned Marc. Now, I focused on my plans for Quitting Time and me. As far as I was concerned, I had much more important matters to attend to that day. I needed to continue working off more of those unwanted pounds. That afternoon, I 'went for the gold.' In so doing, I burned up all of my energy reserves. As a result, I was in bed and fast asleep by about 8 p.m. that night.

A ringing phone awakened me from a very sound sleep. Clumsily, I answered it. In my stupor, I managed to gather it was Mark's voice on the other end of the receiver. He was quick to explain his jockey friend wanted to buy a few more ounces of coke from me. I just wanted to end the call as quickly as possible. I told him I would stop by his barn the following morning and hung up on him.

After I finished training my horses the following morning, I stopped by Marcs' barn. I had a few questions I wanted to ask him. When I arrived there, he was in a stall working on one of his horses. As I approached him, he asked me how long it would take for me to fill his order.

"Slow down, Mark," I abruptly ordered him.

"First of all, who is this for?" I questioned.

"Bobby," he blurted out.

From what I been able to gather, Bobby was his jockey friend. This particular jockey had won the Kentucky Derby at the tender age of 18. Unfortunately, life in the fast lane had led him to a cocaine addiction and some other bad choices. However, he was not the one who concerned me.

"What did you find out about the other guy?" I asked.

"So far, I haven't heard anything bad about him," he confidently proclaimed.

"Good, but please don't sell this guy anything else until I have had enough time to really check him out," I strongly suggested.

"Don't worry I won't," he promised.

"I'll get back to you on this other thing by tomorrow," I promised.

I didn't have to. That night, Mark called me up and explained to me he had inquired and found out the guy in question was okay. I trusted him enough to accept his explanation on the matter. Up to that point, I hadn't had a chance to check him out for myself. Or, maybe I was just giving him the benefit of the doubt. At any rate, I made an agreement with him to replenish his supply and wasted no time making the necessary arrangements.

I caught a flight out of Newark airport later that evening. Then, I basically just repeated the steps I took the first time I went to Florida to fulfill Mark's order. Once again, I returned the following day and was back in Long Branch in time to continue training my horses. Up to this point, it seemed like everything went rather smoothly.

Once I arrived home, I immediately set out to contact Mark. I didn't want to hold onto his package of illegal merchandise a moment longer than was absolutely necessary. As it turned out, I was not actually able to make the delivery until the following morning.

He contacted me early that day. During our short conversation, I arranged to meet with him at the track. After I finished exercising Quitting Time, I stopped by his barn and dropped off the merchandise to him.

After I left his barn, I proceeded to the jockey's room to weigh in. As was becoming my habit, I made my way to the scale upon my arrival. I was hoping I would find more favorable results this time. I stepped onto the scale. As I did, I recalled I had only eight days remaining. I was still hopeful this would be enough time to lose any more of the 'extra' weight I was still in possession of.

Once my second foot was planted firmly upon the scale, the spinning dial finally eased my mind. It stopped at 124. I had somehow managed to lose two more pounds. But, I wasn't quite there yet. I still had nine pounds to go. I knew it was getting crucial.

According to my calculations, it was going to take more than just an increase in my exercise to attain my goal. At that point, I knew it was time to take some extra added measures. I decided I would refrain from making any more trips to Florida. I couldn't allow anything to interrupt whatever routine I was about to come up with. I also came to the conclusion it was time to adjust my diet.

As reality set in, I came to the conclusion I had

to consider every option available to me. From past experience, I knew I could shave off a few more pounds just by altering my eating habits more drastically. I could no longer afford to eat whatever I desired. I had to cut back on any foods high in carbohydrates and fat. I decided I would eat more salad, fruit, and vegetables and completely refrain from eating meat.

Later that day, I realized I also had to consider getting a stall reserved for my horse at Timonium Racetrack. Once again, I thank God for my good friend, Budd. I asked for his help in the matter, and he abruptly made the necessary arrangements via a personal friend of his.

As I pedaled my bike homeward that afternoon, I pondered my next step. I had to arrange how and when I would ship my horse to Maryland. I wanted to have him there at least a week before the race was to take place.

I wanted to give him plenty of time to adjust to the racetrack. It was also imperative I see how he handled the surface of the track at Timonium. I was hoping it was not too hard. If so, it would probably aggravate his previously injured ankle.

When I arrived home, I placed a call to a horse trainer at the Atlantic City Racecourse named George W. Parsons. G.W. - as was his nickname-had been a personal friend of mine for years. Since we both lived in Florida, we very well acquainted with one another. In fact, we trained our horses side by side for a season and had both brought our horses to New Jersey that year in the same horse trailer.

G.W. had chosen to stable his horses at the Atlantic City Racecourse that summer. The horses he was training, at that time, were not able to keep up with the competition at Monmouth Park Racetrack. Since he wanted to win races, he wisely opted to race at Atlantic City that year.

Once I contacted him, I explained my plans to race Quitting Time in Maryland. Then, I asked him if he could assist me in getting my horse there. He was delighted to hear I planned to ride my horse in his next race and quickly agreed to help us get to Timonium.

We scheduled to make the move the following evening. G.W. picked me up at the Baxters' home as planned. Then, we drove to Monmouth Park to pick up my horse. A short time later, we were on our way to Maryland.

"A prudent man foresees the evil, and hides himself, but the simple pass on and are punished." (Proverbs 27:12)

BEGINNING OF THE END

As we left Monmouth Park Racetrack that evening, the sun was beginning to set. We drove on into the night. At about 11 p.m., we pulled up to the stable gate at Timonium Racetrack. Considering the precious cargo we were hauling, I was grateful the trip was uneventful.

To my surprise, the stable gate was located right next to a six lane roadway. To the right of the stable gate I saw the half mile racetrack where Quitting Time would soon carry me to victory. (I hoped). About 10 yards to the right of the racetrack, stood the dimly lit stable area. The small stable area consisted of about two dozen tightly packed rows of tin covered barns. In comparison to Monmouth Park and just about every other racetrack I had been racing at, everything at Timonium seemed to be a no frills version.

As G.W. brought his pickup truck to a stop, the security guard on duty approached us. Then, we presented Quitting Times' papers to him. After a careful inspection of the documents, the guard directed us to the barn where my horse would be stabled until race time.

G.W. wasted no time getting Quitting Time to his temporary residence. At that point, I knew he had a few more hours of driving ahead of him. Once he finally made it to bed, he would have to rise up at about 5 a.m. in order to tend to his own stable. I was sure he did not treasure the thought of this task, so I understood why he was getting a little anxious.

Once we located our stall, G.W. brought the truck and trailer to a halt. Then, he assisted me in unloading my horse from the back of the trailer. After we finished bedding down the stall, we unloaded all of my gear, hooked up the webbing to his stall, put 2 buckets of water inside, and filled up his hay rack with fresh hay. (Webbing is a shield placed in the front of the stall to allow the horse to look out at their surroundings while at the same time restraining them from escaping).

Once everything was in place, I told my dear friend how much I appreciated his help. At that point, he offered to drive me to a motel so I could also bed down for the night. Once this feat was accomplished, he wasted no time bidding me goodbye and abruptly made his departure to Atlantic City.

Meanwhile, I settled in to my new surroundings. The motel room was nothing to write home about, but it was clean and furnished with a television, a comfortable bed, a roomy bathroom and, thankfully, it wasn't too pricey. I was well satisfied with my temporary abode.

I didn't waste any time showering and making my way to the bed. I had left my car with my girlfriend in New Jersey. Therefore, I knew I would be skating to and from the racetrack at least three or four times a day in order to care for Quitting Time. Other than walking, skating would be my only mode of transportation during my stay in Maryland. With that in mind, I knew I needed to be well rested.

The following morning, I awakened at five a.m. and to my surprise I was well refreshed. I felt like I had just slept for ten hours. I was anxious to get to the racetrack and take my horse out for his morning exercise.

Within minutes, I had donned my roller skates and was on the six lane roadway skating to Timonium Racetrack. It didn't take me long to come to the realization of just how steep the hills on my route to the racetrack were. In order for me to get there, I had to navigate some pretty hefty inclines.

When I had traveled the same route the night before in G.W.'s pickup, I didn't get a true reading on this. I labored to climb the hills in my path. As I did so, the theme from 'Rocky' had been going through my mind and seemed to get more and more pronounced with every stride I took.

This enabled me to welcome the task ahead as a test of my endurance. I knew this labor could only enhance my physical condition which in turn would enable me to give Quitting Time a stronger ride when the time came. I arrived at Timonium Racetrack in less than 30 minutes. To my delight, I had managed to make the trip without resting in between hills. As I rolled up to the stable gate, I noticed the security guard wore an expression of unbelief. This is exactly what I expected. I was sure it wasn't every day he experienced a race tracker skating up to his security shack.

I quickly explained to him that I was a trainer and that I was from New Jersey; therefore, I did not possess a Maryland trainer's license. He instructed me to go into the office located right across from his booth. (Before being allowed inside the stable area, I had to apply for a temporary license). I went into the office and explained my situation to the clerk on duty. Then, I presented my New Jersey trainer's license and he issued a temporary trainer's license to me.

I stepped outside the office and took off my roller skates. I knew I wouldn't be allowed to skate inside the stable area. (Had I done so, a thoroughbred horse could get spooked and I didn't want to be the cause of any one of them getting injured in any way). I donned my riding boots and made my way, skates in hand, to the barn where Quitting Time was being housed.

When I arrived at his stall, I noticed he was full of energy. He was pacing back and forth. I was happy to see him in that state of mind. Apparently, he was none the worse for wear and tear. I wasted no time brushing him off in preparation for his morning exercise. After I finished this task, I gathered up my tack and saddled him up.

A few moments later, my horse and I were cautiously making our way towards the entrance gap of the racetrack. As he checked out his new surroundings, I was checking out the track's surface. As I expected, the surface was more tightly packed and was therefore harder than the track he had been training on. In one respect this was good because the horses we would compete against wouldn't be as strong as my horse. (Training on a deeper surface makes a horse fitter; sort of like running on the beach strengthens a person's endurance).

The flip side of this coin was the fact this particular surface would eventually take its toll on his sore ankle. Although I had to keep training him up until he raced, I wasn't sure his legs would be able to withstand the pounding. The way I saw it we were already in a race-a race against time.

After we had walked about thirty yards, I allowed Quitting Time to start trotting. As was his custom, he was getting anxious to run. However, before allowing him to break into a gallop, I planned to let him loosen up for at least a half a mile. He wasted no time taking hold of the bit. Though I wasn't pleased with the hard surface, it certainly didn't affect his passion to run over it.

As he broke into a gallop, I had to use all of my upper body strength to get him to bow his neck. As soon as I settled him down, another horse and rider galloped past us. To Quitting Time, this was the start of another race. I had quite a time convincing him it wasn't. I wasn't sure if that was due to the fact I was reducing and perhaps I was getting weaker, or if it was because he was getting more wound up. At any rate, I did manage to keep him under control and prevent him from injuring himself.

After I exercised him, I returned to the stable area where I gave him a bath, walked him to cool him out and then massaged his legs. Afterwards, I bedded his stall down and fed him. Once I was sure he was secured for the night, I left the barn and headed towards the administration offices. It was time to get my licenses in order.

When I arrived there, I was instructed to fill out the necessary forms in order to apply for a Maryland trainer's license. I explained I had planned to ride

Quitting Time, so the secretary told me I would have to fill out a separate form in order to obtain a jockey's license in Maryland.

At this point, I mentioned I was also part owner of Quitting Time. She advised me I could not own a horse and at the same time possess a jockey's license in the state of Maryland. Therefore, I had to circumvent that rule by selling my 50% ownership of him to my partner. In order to avoid being taxed for this transaction, I sold my share to my partner for one dollar. This was not an uncommon practice. Horsemen do it all the time. This kind of a transaction is known among horsemen as a 'paper' sale.

Once I finished filling out the paperwork, I was fingerprinted, and photographed. After they had processed everything, I was issued a trainer's license along with a jockey's license. I was elated. Since the time I had ridden my last race in Canada, 10 years had passed me by. During that period, I never once dreamed I would ever be riding in races again. I felt as though I had been given a new life. I had no idea this was just another step in God's plan. His underlying purpose was to lead me into a real new life by causing me to be born-again.

Although I was delighted, I still had no doubts my use of the jockey's license I had obtained was all contingent on me being able to lose enough weight. At that point, I decided it would be a good idea for me to take a trip to the jockey's room and weigh myself.

Upon my arrival there, I observed a couple of jockeys and a few valets milling around. I made my way over to the Toledo scale, stepped on it and watched the numbers spin around. They came to a halt at 122. I was glad to find out I had lost two more pounds since my last weigh in. However, I still had seven more pounds to go. Fortunately, I had seven days in which to lose those unwanted pounds so I wasn't really concerned.

I asked one of the jockeys I met who it was that presided over the 'jocks' room? He directed me to a short, gray-haired, gentleman. From his appearance, I assumed he was a former rider himself. I explained my situation to him and asked him to assign a valet to me. He promptly introduced me to one of the valets in the room.

My new valet also appeared to be a former rider.

"This guy will take good care of you," he promised, as he put his arm around my valet's shoulders.

I thanked him for his assistance. Then, I explained my situation to my valet and told him I would bring my silks and my saddle in to him the following day. He acknowledged. At that point it suddenly dawned on me I also needed a pair of riding boots. Though I owned a pair of exercising boots, I no longer owned a pair of race riding boots. (The boots used for race riding are much thinner than the boots used for exercising thoroughbreds. This is due to the fact normal boots weigh much more. In fact, exercising boots, weigh about five pounds. They are made of thick, heavy weight leather. Race riding boots usually weigh a pound or less. They are made of very thin, light weight leather. Race riding boots are about the same thickness as that of a leather jacket).

"Do you know where I could find a good tack store around here?" I inquired of my valet.

"What do you need?" he questioned.

"I have to get a pair of race riding boots," I replied.

"Sure," he said and proceeded to give me directions.

It took me about half an hour to skate there. I enjoyed my exercise on the way, along with the scenery, so the distance seemed shorter than the five miles I had traveled. As I made my entrance into the tack store, a friendly clerk greeted me. She was an elderly well dressed woman and didn't seem to be affected by the fact I had just skated into her store.

I explained my purpose for my visit. After I

mentioned I was in need of a pair of race riding boots in a size eight, her eyebrows quickly raised up. At this point, I knew I was in trouble.

"I don't believe we carry that size," she apologetically explained. "However, I will check out our stock in the back just to be sure."

While the woman was off searching her stock room, I browsed around and found a pair of white, silk racing pants in my size. Before I could search for a dressing room in order to try them on, the woman returned. By her expression, I knew my suspicions were correct.

"Sorry, we don't have anything in that size. However, we can order them for you," she offered.

"How long will it take for you to get them in stock?" I inquired.

"I could have them for you in three to five days," she promised.

"As long as it doesn't take any longer than that, I will place an order. But, I must have those boots no later than the fifth day. You see, I am scheduled to ride in a race five days from today. Without those boots, I won't be light enough to make the weight assigned to my horse in that race," I explained.

At that point, the woman told me she would call their other store and find out if they could provide her with the boots I needed in a timely manner. Once she got through to her associate store, she explained the situation. Afterwards, she quickly filled me in on the outcome of her conversation. "We can definitely have them here within 5 days," she confidently declared.

I agreed to those terms and gave her a down payment. I was relieved. I knew there were not many options left for me. I had to have those boots and there was no other place in the immediate area, where I could find them in a size eight. I knew I had to depend on that particular store to supply me with them within the time frame I had designated. If they failed to do so, all my efforts to ride Quitting Time would have been in vain. Trusting their promise to deliver them on time was a gamble, but I had no other choice at that point.

I left the store and skated back to my motel. Once I arrived there, I decided it would be a good time to swim off some more unwanted pounds. When I arrived at the pool, it was vacant. I was glad, because I knew I could do the laps I planned on doing without having to navigate around other people.

The water was crystal clear. It beckoned me in. I didn't need much coaxing. I plunged into the water and proceeded to do my laps. I took great pleasure in what I was doing. I thought of how blessed I was to be doing something I really enjoyed. I loved to swim. I loved my career. I loved my new purpose in life, and I loved my lifestyle.

As I plowed through the crystal clear water, with the bright, and beautiful warm sun beating on me, I thought of how other people were forced to work at a job they didn't like. During my entire career, I had always appreciated the fact I was not one of those people. I reflected back on my life and was grateful that although I hadn't started out with very many prospects in life, I had eventually been dealt a very good hand. I really appreciated this fact and in the only way I knew how, I thanked God for it; that is to say I often used the expression: “thank God”. Sadly enough, I didn’t know Him well enough to thank Him by living my life in a way that would have been pleasing to Him.

The following morning, I arrived at the racetrack at about 6 a.m. Although I usually started out a little earlier, I was not in a hurry to get there this particular morning. I wanted to make sure the gate crew would be at their posts before my horse and I stepped onto the racetrack.

My main objective this day was to take Quitting Time over to the starting gate. I had a two-fold purpose for this. My primary goal was to practice breaking my horse out of the starting gate. Strangely enough, I had never done so before. This was due to the fact I never saw the need to break him from the starting gate during any of his morning workouts. Since coming out of the starting gate puts more stress on a horse's legs, I avoided this.

My secondary goal this morning was to obtain clearance for me to ride Quitting Time in a race. Since I hadn't ridden in a race in over 10 years, this was a necessary procedure. The stewards at the racetracks do not want someone riding in a race who is not able to safely handle their mount once they come charging out of the starting gate. Therefore, I had to obtain their approval.

At about 7 o'clock in the morning, I managed to get my horse over to the starting gate. The starters loaded him without a hitch. This was a plus. Many times, racehorses are so keyed up they give the gate crew problems during the loading process. This can cause injury to a horse, the jockey, or one of the gate crew.

Once we were in place, the gate sprung open and we came bursting forth like water from a spout. I'll never forget the adrenalin rush this gave me. As we came thundering down the stretch, I remember rejoicing because we had passed the test.

I had allowed Quitting Time the pleasure of striding out at full throttle for half of a mile. He was in his element. Of course, once he got rolling, he didn't want to pull up afterwards. I stood straight up in the saddle and finally managed to get the job done.

After his workout, he was not showing any signs of soreness. I was delighted. I took him back to our barn and cooled him out. After performing the normal daily tasks on him, I bedded him down for the night. Then, I made my way over to the jockey's room.

I was anxious to see how much weight I had managed to shed, on the previous day. As I bolted through the jockey's room heading for the scale, I ignored my surroundings. I stood on the scale and watched as the dial swiftly spun around and stopped at 121.

At this point, I knew I still had six more pounds to lose. However, I was right on schedule. Even though it was getting harder to shed the weight, I was now thoroughly convinced I could do it. I was more determined than ever to do whatever became necessary to reach my goal. I was also quite sure than ever a few pounds were not going to stand between me and my greatest achievement thus far. I had come too far to falter now. I was not about to allow success to elude me.

The events of the next five days are only a blur to me now. However, one thing does stand out to me. I distinctly remember the day I went to the racing secretary's office to enter Quitting Time into the race. Afterwards, I was more anxious than I had ever been in my entire life. I guess this was par for the course; because I was so close to achieving the most important goal of my life. Yet, I knew I still had no control over the situation. I had to hope the race would go in order to get a chance at it. At that point, only God knew what the outcome would be.

All I could do was to wait until I could find out if the race would actually fill. However, waiting and patience never had been my strong points. At any rate, I was optimistic I hadn't come this far for nothing. The race would take place. I just knew it. Hopefully, I was destined to ride Quitting Time to victory. The overnights would come out later that afternoon and I would find out for sure.

Later that afternoon, I finally got my 'long' awaited answer. As I rolled up on skates to the stable gate at Timonium, I picked up an overnight from the box mounted on the wall outside of the security office. (An overnight is a one page publication put out by the racetrack. This publication lists the upcoming races 48 hours in advance. The purpose of this is to assist trainers so they can be informed what races are going to take place as early as possible. The handlers of the horses scheduled to run in a particular race must be notified in time to make any last minute preparations necessary. Sometimes, a horse will need to be given a certain medication prior to a race. Other horses may require certain drugs which help them with their daily training. However, some of these same drugs are illegal while a horse is racing and must be discontinued before a race. Those are the main reasons racetracks publish overnights).

As I read the overnight, my optimism was off the charts. Quitting Time's race had filled and he had made it in. It was all systems go. The race was on. My heart leaped within me. Although I was well aware there were three more obstacles I would have to clear, I knew I was up for the challenge.

First of all, I had to keep Quitting Time sound enough to race. In preparation for this race, I had worked him out earlier that morning. (A workout is when a rider takes a horse at full speed for a designated distance). He seemed to come off of that workout healthy, but I knew from experience his condition could change overnight. Until I walked him out of his stall the following morning, I wouldn't know for sure if he was experiencing any pain. If he were, my whole plan could go up in smoke.

Secondly, since my last weigh in I was aware I still had four more pounds to lose and only two days in which to do it. However, I knew there were ways to overcome this obstacle. I had planned to increase my exercise regimen. I also planned to use the 'hot' box if necessary. (The hot box is the steam room in the jockey's room).

The third obstacle was not under my control. I had to depend on the tack store making good on their promise to deliver the racing boots which I had ordered. If not, all my efforts would have been in vain. However, I was confident this too would work out. After all, everything had fallen into place so far. I just couldn't find it in my heart to believe it would end in defeat.

Later on that afternoon, I swam a few more laps than usual. Then, I skated a little farther than I had been skating. After dinner, I walked a few more miles. Once I finished my exercising, I felt great. Afterwards, I thoroughly enjoyed a nice, hot shower. Then, I turned on the television in my room in order to relax a little before retiring for the night. At that point, I wasn't so sure I would be able to sleep.

Although I was a little hyper, I did manage to fall asleep that night. The Lord knew I needed the rest. At 5:00 a.m. I woke up with total awareness. I was truly excited. Anticipation ruled my thoughts. At this point in time, I was almost finished with my life's greatest mission. I so looked forward to the day ahead.

I was about to ride in the biggest race of my career. At least this time, I knew I was in control. That is to say, I was about to ride a horse which I knew had the ability to win the race I was competing in. I was sure of that. For once, I didn't have to depend on some other trainer's competence. I knew the only way he would lose this race would be due to my error. I also knew I was not about to give Quitting Time a faulty ride. Both of us had waited for too long for this opportunity.

I wasted no time getting dressed that morning. Afterwards, I donned my roller skates and skated off to the racetrack. When I arrived, Quitting Time was waiting at the front of his stall to greet me. His workout the day before had made him a little more anxious too.

I fed him some oats. Then, I cleaned his stall, brushed him off and took him for a stroll around the barn. He seemed to be in great physical shape. As we made our way around the shed row, he calmed down. At this point, I knew we were ready to roll.

After a thirty minute walk, I placed him back in his stall and bedded him down. Afterwards, I set out for the barn where the groom whom I had hired to bring my horse to the paddock for his race was working. As I approached his work area, he greeted me.

"Are you all set?" he asked.

"We are as ready as we'll ever be," I confidently replied.

"I'll be over there to get Quitting Time prepared, as soon as I'm finished with my work in this barn" he promised.

"That will be fine," I said.

"I'll see you in the paddock," he enthusiastically replied.

"Not that we are sufficient of ourselves to think anything as of ourselves, but our sufficiency is of God." (2 Corinthians 3:5)

A LIFETIME ACHIEVEMENT

Confident in the fact I had made all the necessary preparations, I made my way to the stable gate. Once I arrived there, I donned my roller skates and skated to the tack store. I had one more task to perform. If I failed on this one, there was no way I could complete my mission. I still had to obtain my race riding boots. On my way, I must admit I was quite anxious. At that point, I couldn't think of anything else except my seeing a nice, shiny pair of size 8 boots being placed on the counter by the clerk at the tack store.

When I arrived there, I opened up the front door and skated inside. As I approached the counter, the clerk quickly announced my boots had arrived. Needless to say, I was quite relieved to hear those words. At that point, I would have been more than delighted to pay any amount she could have asked of me. After thanking her for delivering on her promise, I gathered up my 'trophy' and skated back to the track.

As I made my way to the jockey's room, I knew this was going to be a day to remember. When I arrived there, I made a beeline for the scale. As I stepped on it, the arrow spun around to 117. At this point, I was still a couple of pounds heavier than I wanted to be. However, I had already planned for this. I still had a few hours in which to drop the last few unwanted pounds. I had planned to spend the remaining moments until race time in the hot box. I quickly shed my clothing, grabbed a towel and headed for the steam room.

About three hours later, I heard the call for the jockeys to come for their weigh in. By this time, I had shed the last few pounds and was anxiously awaiting my weigh-in. I made my way to the clerk of scales. With all my equipment weighing four pounds, I weighed in at exactly 119. After my weigh-in, I managed to relax for about an hour before race time.

From my previous experiences in steam rooms and saunas, I knew only too well that subjecting my body to the intense heat would sap my strength. I figured I would need to have all the strength I could possibly muster up for the task that lay ahead. Therefore, I had planned to use the final hour before race time to rest my body. Everything went according to plan.

As soon as I heard the announcement for the jockeys to assemble at the saddling paddock, I put on my racing silks and helmet. Then, I placed some rubber bands around the wrist area of my sleeves. (These are used in order to prevent dirt and mud from making its way up a rider's sleeve during a race). I strolled out of the jockey's room and headed towards the saddling paddock. The other jockeys competing in our race had already begun filing out.

As we all paraded towards our destination, I noticed something. Although I was only five feet three inches tall, I was about a head taller than the rest of my colleagues. I was amused at the fact I was actually taller than someone else. During my lifetime, the racetrack was the only place I had ever experienced this circumstance.

I glanced around the paddock area and focused on the stall where Quitting Time was being saddled. He looked relatively calm, but alert. I knew he was ready to go and so was I. I could hardly wait to hear the paddock judge shout: "Put your riders up!"

As I made my way to the stall, my girlfriend greeted me. She had made the trip from New Jersey. She seemed to be more excited than I was. She had brought one of her girlfriends with her for the occasion and they were both as anxious as I was to get the show on the road.

We had barely exchanged greetings when the words I had longed to hear came forth. I will never forget how the adrenaline flowed as my mind absorbed the reality of what had already happened and what was about to happen. Anxiously, I grabbed the reins and a handful of Quitting Time's mane with my left hand and placed my right hand on top of the saddle.

At this point, the groom was quick to give me a boost up onto my mount. As soon as I was atop of him, I tied a knot in my reins and checked out the length of my stirrups. Our moment of truth had finally come.

Quitting Time was now more anxious than ever to do what he was born to do. So was I. Our moment of truth had finally come and we were ready for the competition. As far as I knew, the most important event of my life was about to take place.

The groom led us out of the paddock and placed us into the hands of the waiting outrider. (An outrider is a rider who uses a quarter- horse to help a jockey control his mount before and after the race.

This is called 'ponying'. Since thoroughbreds have a tendency to get a little rambunctious on the racetrack, ponying is a precautionary measure used to prevent the horses from running off with their riders and thereby burning themselves out before a race and possibly injuring themselves in the process).

Quitting Time wasted no time in making this outrider earn his pay. As soon as he took the first stride onto the racetrack, he attempted to bolt off. The rider took a stronger hold of him. As he did so, I rubbed my horse's neck and talked to him. My attempt to get him to relax didn't do much good. He was fired up. However, I didn't mind. At the same time, I was indeed thankful for the help I was receiving.

On the way to the starting gate, our objective was to slowly gallop Quitting Time for half a mile allowing him to loosen up. Although he fought us every inch of the way, we managed to accomplish our goal.

Upon our arrival there, the outrider was more than happy to hand me and my mount over to one of the gate men. They were already in the process of loading the first few horses into their stalls. The gate man, who was holding my horse by his bridle, walked him around in a circle. This distracted him from watching the other horses which were already in the gate and kept him from getting even more excited.

Finally, it was our turn to load. Several other gate men helped to complete the job. As we stood inside the gate, one of the gate men helped me to keep my horse relatively calm. Within seconds, the remaining horses competing in our race were loaded.

At that moment, I held my horse's head straight and grabbed a hand full of his mane. I anticipated the break to take place momentarily and I didn't want to be caught off guard. In an instant, the bell rang, the latch sprung and like water from a bursting dam horses and riders plowed through the gates which had previously restrained them.

Within two strides, I managed to position my super- charged thousand, pound dynamo alongside the leaders of the pack. Hoof beats sounding like so much thunder exploded all around us. Sand from beneath the leading horses' hooves was hurled into the faces of those unfortunate enough to be traveling behind us.

We had broken about third or fourth, but I didn't want to be that far back. I knew my horse was a front runner and more often than not, if a front runner doesn't make the lead, he doesn't run to his fullest capabilities. I didn't want to chance this happening to my horse, so I quickly urged him on in an attempt to capture the lead.

Quitting Time was my Apollo craft and we were shooting for the moon. Every fraction of a second was crucial. Any miscalculation on my part could abort our mission. I wasted no time getting him to accelerate. We shot past all but one of the horses which had been in front of us. By this time, we had already gone about an eighth-of-a-mile and only had three eighths to go.

We continued to bear down on the leader but he didn't seem to be faltering at all. However, Quitting Time seemed to enjoy the challenge and I knew he wasn't going to take no for an answer.

A few strides later, we took the lead. Within a few more

strides we were about two lengths ahead of the entire pack. At this point, I reached for a tighter hold of the reins. I knew I had to harness all of the energy my horse still had in reserve. Undoubtedly, we were going to need every ounce of it before the race was over. I sat completely still on his back and managed to get him to relax by easing off the reins thereby allowing him to take a breather.

After he had taken a few more strides, he began drifting out ever so slightly. This was not a good sign. Sore horses often fail to change their lead as they enter the turn for the upcoming stretch run. I knew I couldn't allow this to happen because we could be disqualified for drifting out into another horses' path.

At that point, we were in the middle of the course. As we approached the turn going into the stretch, I wanted to save as much ground as possible. I wanted my horse to be hugging the rail for the stretch run. I took a quick glance over my left shoulder in order to make sure there weren't any horses too close to us.

Once I was sure we had plenty of space between us and our closest rival, I eased my horse over against the rail. By this time, we were actually into the final turn heading to the top of the stretch. As we came out of the turn, Quitting Time started drifting off the rail towards the outside of the track again. I knew this was due to the fact his left, front ankle -which I was attempting to get him to change over to-was probably getting sorer from the extreme pounding it was taking. This was a direct result of him not having changed his lead up to that point.

At about the same time he started drifting out, I heard the pack of horses come charging up to the rear of us. The adrenalin burst through every fiber of my being. I knew I had to react quickly or victory would be snatched from us. In order to get him to change his lead foot and cause him to drop back in on to the rail, I took my whip and gently tapped him on the right side of his nose.

It was imperative I change his course swiftly. To my relief, he quickly responded by changing his lead foot causing him to drop back in on the rail. However, I knew our greatest challenge was yet to come. I was delighted to see he still seemed to be up for the challenge. The question in my mind was whether or not any of our rivals were?

At this point, I was expecting any of the horses that had spark left in them to be in hot pursuit of us. But, I was determined I wouldn't lose this race by allowing any of our competitors to close in on us. Therefore, I wasted no time in taking my whip and giving my horse a few brisk taps on his backside. In response, and to my utter relief, he fired his afterburners and increased his lead.

I took one last look over my right shoulder and saw the competition fading back. At this point, I knew there wasn’t a horse in the race that would be able to close the gap between us. I was certain we were about to get our picture taken. I tucked my whip in and sat still until we had crossed the finish line.

As I stood up in the saddle, I was exhilarated. Quitting Time and I were going to the winner's circle. Although I was reasonably sure someone would have placed in a claim for him, I wasn’t going to allow this to affect my elation and my subsequent celebration. I had waited a long time for this moment. I finally felt as though I had complete control over my life again. Every major goal I had pursued up to that point in my life was now accomplished. This was indeed the sweetest tasting victory I had ever experienced.

We had crossed the finish line three lengths in front of the pack. Afterwards, I discovered my horse still had plenty of run left in him and was traveling relatively sound. This added to my excitement. While I attempted to pull him up, he continued his course without missing a stride. At this point, I was grateful the outrider was nearby and that he wasted no time in assisting me.

On my way back to the winner's circle, I began

to ponder what had just happened. At that point, it seemed to me that I was finally in complete control of my future in horse racing. As far as I was concerned, I no longer had to depend on anyone else to help me to win races.

It gave me such an inner feeling of security to think I had just proven I could do anything I set my mind to do. In fact, I could do it all without anybody else's help. At least, that is what I thought. I envisioned a future without boundaries. I would call all the shots. I would make all the plans. No one else would even know what my plans were. And, I would never again lose a race because of someone else's mistakes.

Although I would still have to deal with having a partner, I had complete control. Besides, I had planned on buying my partner out in the near future. From then on, I could write my own ticket. In my mind the possibilities were seemingly endless. What a sense of freedom this gave me. Winning this race with Quitting Time was indeed a new beginning for me. However, I was soon to find out it was not in the sense I thought it would be.

Once we arrived in the winner's circle, I received some more icing on the cake. I found out my horse had not been claimed. At that point, I determined I was going to run him right back against the same caliber of competition he had just defeated. I knew I could win at least one more race with him at Timonium. I fully intended to bet on him again and I figured we could win another purse as well.

To top it all off, I was positive someone would put in a claim for him the next time he raced at that track. Since I knew his racing career wouldn't last much longer with that bad ankle, I knew I had to take advantage of this new opportunity.

The way I saw it I had nothing to lose should someone claim Quitting Time. Although I really had feelings for him, I didn't want to risk losing my meager stable simply because I wanted to hold on to a horse I liked. Unfortunately, he was now an even higher risk than before. At this point, I knew he could break down at any moment. I was grateful he had fulfilled his purpose and a new door had been opened for me, but it was time to move on.

Hopefully, I would soon be in a position to use the money I received from our winnings, the money we won from betting on Quitting Time, and the money we would gain from someone claiming him to restock our stable.

The way I saw it, I had already accomplished more than I had ever dreamed was possible. But, I also knew more challenges lay ahead. As long as I was involved in racing, they would pop up here and there like so many weeds on an unkempt lawn. I had to do whatever I deemed necessary in order to be somewhat prepared for the unexpected.

As planned, eight days after our big win, I raced Quitting Time again. We also won that race. However, this victory was short lived. Shortly after the start of this race, his ankle was getting sore from the pounding. In order to avoid the pain, he abruptly switched to his right lead. In so doing, his rear end swerved violently to the right. Unfortunately, this action caused him to cut in front of another horse in the race and this was considered illegal.

It happened so swiftly, I remember thinking he could have been going down. However, he managed to keep steady and regain his footing. Meanwhile, I just sat still on him in order to keep from hindering his stride.

Once Quitting Time straightened back out and regained his composure, he grabbed the lead on his own. At that point, I just reached for a tighter hold on him. I was trying to make sure he didn't stumble during the race. From past experience, I knew it was essential to keep a tired or sore horse together in order to prevent them from losing their rhythm. Consequently, this would cause them to stumble.

In spite of what had just happened, as long as my

horse still felt like running, I was going to give him the best ride I could. He didn't disappoint. As in his previous race, he stayed on the lead and finished well in front of the pack. I was euphoric. This only confirmed what I thought I already knew. I was sure I was in complete control. We had accomplished our purpose again.

I had hoped Quitting Time would manage to come out of this race in good condition. Unfortunately, as we crossed the finished line and I stood up in the saddle, he changed over to his left, front lead and nearly stumbled again. Immediately I realized his career had come to an end. He slowed down and bobbled slightly allowing me to pull him up. This was another sure sign he was experiencing major problems. Usually, it was next to impossible to pull him up by myself after a race.

Jogging back to the winner's circle, I saw the tote board flash 'inquiry'. I knew our latest victory was about to be snatched from us. The rider, whose horse we had cut in front of, claimed foul. The stewards reviewed the film of the race and this was all it took. We were disqualified and placed last. This meant we not only lost the money we had bet, but we were deprived of the purse money as well.

However, there was some good news mixed in with the bad. I found out someone had claimed Quitting Time. Considering his present condition, I was not at all sorry to hear this news. In one way, it was still a victory for our stable. At least the money we would receive from the claimant would give us the finances we needed to carry on.

Although I knew I had no control over the previous events, I was still able to console myself with the idea it would have been much worse had no one claimed my horse that day. I was sad Quitting Time and I had to depart under those circumstances, but I knew it could have been worse. That's horse racing.

After I finished writing Quitting Time, our Father led me to place photos throughout the book corroborating the events described within. I wasn't sure if this was His idea or mine. So, I prayed and asked Him to confirm to me if it were indeed His will to do this. Shortly after, He led me to look at the photo of the first win I had while riding Quitting Time. Then, He pointed out to me our wining number for that race was the five. In biblical numerology, this signifies God's grace. This was His way of showing me He gave me the grace to do something I had always longed for-to achieve my first victory as a jockey.

Next, He pointed out the horse which followed me as I crossed the finish line was the number two. The number two in biblical numerology signifies Jesus. As

He put it: “Jesus was pursuing” and my time was coming.

After that, He pointed out to me that the second victory I achieved, while riding Quitting Time, took place eight days after that first win. Eight is the number signifying new beginnings. Although I had no idea at the time, it was the end of my life as I knew it. It was time for me to begin my new life in Christ.

Next, He pointed out I was assigned the number two for that race. Consequently, even though I won that race too, I was disqualified. In effect, my new beginning was to be in Jesus. At that point, God in His sovereignty had disqualified me from pursuing my own goals. I was never allowed to race again. “Therefore if any man be in Christ, he is a new creature: old things are passed away; behold all things are become new.” (2 Corinthians 5:17)

"Better is little with the fear of the Lord than great treasure and trouble along with it." (Proverbs 15:16)

BLINDSIDED

While I made the long drive back to New Jersey, I anxiously pondered my future in horse racing. I was very excited about the different opportunities opening up to me. At that point, I figured I could get back into the saddle as a jockey at my own discretion. Since my first love had always been race riding anyway, I was ecstatic.

As I mulled over the circumstances leading up to my present situation, I joyfully pondered that thought. Although I had experienced some lean years, everything seemingly had worked out for my good. I was now in a position to ride as well as train thoroughbred horses.

Although the furthest thing from my mind was the fact I would some day become a jockey again and achieve my first victory on a horse which I was training, this was God's plan all along. Although I wasn't aware of it yet, He was responsible for the it all and He manifested it in His own perfect timing.

At any rate, I was overwhelmed by the fact I had just achieved the one thing which had eluded me for all those years. I had finally won a race as a jockey. Now, I felt like I had achieved total victory in life.

Through it all I learned one thing for sure- anything is possible. But, I didn't quite grasp the fact I never knew what was going to happen next. I guess this is because I didn't yet know I was not the one who was in control.

Unfortunately, I thought I had finally found the solution to all of my problems. All I saw was success. I figured I could ride horses for other trainers and earn even more money to finance my stable in the process. Eventually, I could be in total control of my stable and my life. At least that's how it looked to me.

Over the years, I had made some good connections in horse racing. More importantly, I had proven myself to be a winner. As is in any competitive sport, winning is essential to advancement. I had proven beyond a doubt I could win races.

At this point in my career, I figured my good friend, Budd Lepman, would be more than happy to help advance my quest to become a leading jockey once again. If I asked him, I was sure he would use me to ride some of his horses.

With someone like him behind me, I had no doubt my career as a jockey would really take off. This time it would be different. I wasn't going to be the downfall guy. I was going to be the star. I was ecstatic. I thought I was still actually going to accomplish what I had started out to do years earlier. At this point, I felt sure I could live out my dream and someday win the Kentucky Derby.

Although I really enjoyed training thoroughbreds, the thrill of competing while riding on one of those magnificent four-legged athletes, was the pinnacle of adventure to me. To become a successful jockey was my greatest unfulfilled desire. But, this goal was no longer out of my reach. I figured all I needed to do was to put some time and effort into it and everything else would fall into place.

As a trainer and an owner, I always had to put my money on the line. Therefore, I hadn’t been able to store up any funds for my future. As a jockey, I could ride other people’s horses and let them worry about paying the bills. My overhead would be minimal.

I thought my golden opportunity had just arrived. I looked forward to getting started. I was anxious to begin rebuilding my racing stable too. I figured having some strong competitors of my own to ride could only enhance my career as a jockey. The way I saw it, I was going to be the sovereign king of my own domain. It didn’t look like there was anything to stop my rise to power. I could hardly wait to put my plan into action.

After I arrived back in New Jersey, I stopped by Budd's apartment. I wanted to present him with a picture of Quitting Time's and me winning a race. As he answered the door, my exuberant friend cheerfully greeted me.

"Congratulations," he said as he heartily shook my hand.

Then, he turned to some gentleman who was already there visiting him.

"This is Jimmy McDonald.-He's the best! He got tired of those pinheads getting his horses beat so he just took one of his horses off to Maryland, rode it himself, and won the race! Incredible! And, that was the first race Jimmy has ridden in 10 years," Budd joyfully boasted.

Then, he introduced his friend to me. The gentleman, Mr. Morgan was one of the horse owners Budd trained some horses for. As far as I was concerned, I couldn't have been in a better place at a better time. We spent the next few hours discussing various experiences we had, during our racing careers.

Finally, I realized it was about time for me to head home and get ready to go to work. At that point I bid everyone goodbye and left Budd’s apartment. Although there were several ways I could have driven home from there, I decided I would take the scenic route which took me along the Jersey shore.

As I was driving, I began to analyze what had just taken place. I was surprised at the fact Budd was so excited about my latest feat. He was like a father to me. During my childhood, I never received such recognition and accolade from my own dad.

I really appreciated Budd and I was very thankful for the way he had introduced me to Mr. Morgan. In fact, I couldn't have had an agent do it any better. I knew his praises for my accomplishments with Quitting Time had left its mark on this horse owner. I had no doubt in the near future I would be riding in some races on horses this man owned.

To say I was enthused with my life would be an understatement. Everything seemed to be going even better than I ever could have planned it. Little did I know this was because someone much greater than I had been calling the shots all along. I wish I really knew Him at that time. Unfortunately, I only knew about Him and I wasn't even really sure of His existence as of yet. I had no idea I was about to find this all out through some very painful events.

Suddenly, the God who had been blessing my socks off threw a curveball at me. Once I arrived at the racetrack, I experienced the most earth shattering news imaginable. It certainly turned my world upside down. My dreamlike welcome back to New Jersey was turned into a nightmare. In an instant my illustrious career came to a screeching halt.

As I entered the clubhouse at Monmouth Park Racetrack that morning, I saw Mark. He briskly approached me and from his demeanor I knew he was the bearer of bad news. Immediately, I surmised this all had something to do with his selling cocaine to the guy that I told him to stay away from.

"Hi Jimmy, I have some really bad news," he blurted out.

"What's up?" I hesitantly asked.

"I sold some of the coke you gave me to the guy I was telling you about and I found out you were right. He is an agent. I also found out the police are looking for me. I have been told they have a warrant for my arrest. They are charging me with selling cocaine to an undercover agent," he whimpered.

"Great. This is just terrific," I sarcastically replied.

"What am I going to do?" He pleaded for an answer.

At this point, I was more concerned with what I was going to do. Bells and whistles sounded an alarm in my inner sanctum of self grandeur. Immediately, I knew my gig was up. What I had just heard utterly annihilated every ounce of joy I once possessed.

I suddenly realized that although I had spent much of my life accumulating fame and fortune, none of this could help me now. My mountain of sin had just erupted and was spewing the lava of its consequences throughout my life. This was going to get ugly.

I had no doubt Bobby (Mark's jockey friend involved in the transaction) would turn on me. I also figured Mark wouldn't hold up under pressure. I could foresee my career going down like the Titanic as it hit the iceberg.

“I found out Bobby has already agreed to testify for the state," Mark whined.

At that point, I didn’t need any further confirmation. My suspicions were well founded. I knew it was all over. I just knew they would both be making a deal with the authorities in order to save themselves. This could only mean one thing. I was heading for a ride up the river.

As far as I was concerned, the only way I could possibly avoid this death sentence would be for me to hide Mark from the authorities for a while and hope for a miracle. Although I was on the ropes and reeling, I was quick on my feet and started to put my plan in motion.

"First of all, you need to get out of New Jersey until we can find out how much they have on you. We can get a lawyer and have a bond set for you. Then, we can figure out how to fight the charges," I cautiously advised Mark.

At this point, he was up for anything and quickly agreed to my suggestion. Abruptly, we left the racetrack together. I instructed him to pack his luggage and get ready to flee the state. I arranged to pick him up a short time later. Then, I dropped him off at his apartment and headed home.

Once I got there, I wasted no time making a reservation for Mark on a flight to Michigan. He was scheduled to fly out of Newark airport later that afternoon. I was only too happy to drive him to the airport in order to make sure he didn’t miss his flight.

While we were on our way there, I asked him what his plans were. He assured me he had some friends in Michigan who would help him out. He told me he planned to hide out there until we figured out what to do next.

Before I dropped him off at the airport, I told him I would help him out in any way I could. Then, I told him to stay in touch and gave him several phone numbers where I could be reached. I assured him I was prepared to use whatever resources I could muster up to assist him. However, I could tell by his frightened disposition he probably wouldn’t ever call me again.

I had a gift of being able to read people pretty well. From what I had observed of Mark’s behavior that day, it left me with the impression he was fearful of me. I believed it was because he figured I would use my friends from Brooklyn to snuff him out so he couldn't testify against me.

Knowing some of the people I had been associated with, he had good reason to fear. I could understand this because during the years we had been acquainted I had foolishly let him know too much concerning the escapades of my friends from across the river.

Consequently, Mark was well aware of their ways of dealing with people whom they considered to be a threat to their way of life. Due to my indiscretions, he had some firsthand insight into the Sopranos long before the hit show had ever made its debut.

Even though harming my friend was the farthest thing from my mind, I knew it was in the forefront of his. I had no doubt he was scared stiff. Therefore, I knew once he left New Jersey he would avoid me like the plague. I figured the only time I would see him again would probably be at my trial as a witness for the prosecution.

Considering the prison time he would be facing, I fully expected he would do whatever necessary to save himself and his so-called career in horse racing. No matter if this meant putting me on the spot. If he was convicted of the charges he was facing, his career in horse racing would be over. Even though he didn't have much of a career, I knew this was his only passion in life. I also knew he would not very likely be giving this up, along with his freedom, just because we were friends.

Unfortunately, I was right on target. A short time after Mark's departure from New Jersey, Lee used some of his legal connections and found out they were about to issue a warrant for my arrest. He informed me I was going to be charged with possession of cocaine, distribution and conspiracy. When I heard the bad news, I immediately arranged to meet with him and discuss my options.

Although I didn't think there were any options, I realized Lee had pulled more than one rabbit out of the hat for me before. And, nothing was impossible. Without a doubt, he was an excellent attorney and I trusted his judgment implicitly. At this point, I was up for anything.

Later that day, we met at his home.

"I'm sorry to hear about the situation you are in right now. I'm sure this has put quite a damper on your current success," Lee apologetically greeted me.

"That's putting it mildly," I replied.

"You'll overcome it. You're a survivor," he encouraged me. "Meanwhile I will arrange for you to have a meeting with a very, sharp colleague of mine. Doug Sawyer is his name. He will be glad to represent you. I cannot represent you on this since you were living in my home at the time of the alleged crimes, Jimmy," he apologetically explained.

"I would rather have you defend me, but I understand your situation and I trust your judgment completely," I sheepishly responded.

"Doug will be at his office until 3 pm. today," he informed me.

"I'll be there within the hour," I anxiously replied.

As I drove to my planned destination, I couldn't

help thinking of the precarious position I had placed my good friend in. By trying to help Mark, I had jeopardized Lee's career as well as mine. I was saddened at the thought. I could not help thinking what a fool I had been not to realize my crazy lifestyle would some day end up in disaster.

I knew what I did was illegal, but I really believed my actions were justified because I was just doing a friend a favor. At the time, I still wasn't aware my circumstances were a wake up call from God. All I could think was that it could all have been avoided if only Mark hadn't ignored my advice. Playing the blame game wasn't going to solve the problem though. It looked to me like I was going to be paying the ultimate price for it all. At that point, I felt as if the rug was being pulled out from underneath me. Everything I had cherished the most was in danger of being taken away. I didn't think I had even a slight chance to overcome the odds this time.

Why, oh why did I have to push the envelope again and again I torturously berated myself?

During our initial meeting later that afternoon, I had a long conversation with Doug. He assured me he could win my case in court. Although this was good to hear, I had my doubts. However, I had no other choice. I had to trust his judgment.

Right then and there we settled on his fee. Then, he told me he had to do some research before he could give me any more advice. Afterwards, he recommended I surrender to the authorities and post my bond. My bail had been set at $50,000.

At this point, I told him I would prefer to wait and turn myself in to the New Jersey police after he finished his research. Before I surrendered, I wanted to sort things out for myself and make sure I would be able to post my bond. After our meeting I wasted no time making my departure out of New Jersey. I figured it was safer for me to do my sorting out from afar. I also wanted to first find out if Doug could arrange for me to put up my home in Fort Lauderdale, Florida, as my bail bond. If this were the case, then I would surrender to the authorities.

I didn't want to have to use any of the cash I had on hand to post my bail. In fact, I didn't have enough cash to post the whole bond anyway. Besides, I figured my arrest was going to affect my ability to race my horses and this was going to hinder my potential to earn an honest living anymore. In light of all this, I thought it would be wise for me to hold on to every penny I had for as long as I could.

About a week later, Doug informed me he had arranged for me to post my home in Fort Lauderdale as collateral for my bond. After stressing to the max, losing much sleep, my appetite, and wishing I were never born, I was slightly encouraged by this news. At least I would be able to post my bond without having to spend what little money I had to stay out of jail.

However, my confidence didn't last for long. Shortly after posting bail, I received the confirmation my career was probably over. The racing commission had officially suspended me pending the outcome of my case. At this point, I was very apprehensive about my future.

All I could think about was how hard I had worked to establish myself in life and how many years I spent risking life and limb to forge my career. Now, in an instant, it could be taken from me by someone I had considered to be my friend. To top it all off, it didn't look like there wasn't anything I could do.

Duh! This was a God thing. However, I still didn't have any incline He was trying to make me realize my situation was an object lesson about my life. I did not at that time or at any other time ever have control over my life. I only thought I did.

At any rate, until I was exonerated of the charges I faced, I wouldn't be allowed to set foot on any racetrack in the entire United States. *How could this be happening to me*? I questioned myself. Unfortunately, I wasn't yet ready to receive the truth about myself.

I had been living the lifestyle of royalty for years on end and now my gig was up. I still had a mortgage on my home to pay, horses to feed, and numerous other bills and expenses. How would I survive? I had gotten myself into a position where I could no longer earn enough money to sustain the lifestyle I had become accustomed to living.

I became bitter and angry. I didn't know it at the time but the enemy of my soul was using my circumstances to blind me to the fact that this was nobody's fault but my own. I was trying to rationalize myself out of it.

In my warped sense of reasoning I felt the authorities were depriving me of my livelihood. Legally, I was blackballed and, because of the 'establishment', I was in danger of losing everything I had worked for all of my life. I was between a rock and a hard place and I didn't even think I was at fault.

I couldn't control my feelings at the time. As far as I was concerned, the whole world was against me now. But, I was bound and determined I was not going down without a fight. I didn't realize it, but the upbringing I had received from my step-father had influenced me in a negative way. His perverted interpretation of justice was instilled in me at an early age and I reacted accordingly.

Please don't misunderstand me, I'm not saying I'm not totally responsible for my actions. I am saying I learned my definition of right and wrong from example- the wrong example. As long as I could remember, my step-father was involved in some form of criminal activity. My mom didn't condone this, but she loved him and so she accepted his behavior.

Mom and all us kids lived with this man for years. Eventually she married him. In order to please her, he always tried to teach my brother, my sister, and me to be honest. However, I saw too much going on behind the scenes. He would bring home the booty from many of his crimes and would go into detail explaining his escapades to mom. Although I was in another room most of the times this took place, I was listening intently to his every word.

From what I had seen and heard, my step-father only seemed to get ahead when he was successful in his criminal endeavors. His legal profession was that of a book binder. However, it seemed he barely eked out a living from the pay he received when he was working honestly. With his weekly paychecks, he could barely provide us children and my mom with food and clothing. I figured that was his reason for turning to crime again and again.

Amazingly, he never got caught committing any of the crimes I knew about. As I witnessed his lifestyle, it had a great influence on my philosophy of how to go about getting ahead in life. Although I didn't realize it for most of my adult life, my observations had seriously corrupted my judgment.

Unfortunately, my life took much the same path as his. When I worked hard and tried my best to make an honest living, something always seemed to get in my way. Whenever I had a setback, I would blame it on the 'system' and get involved in some form of criminal activity. I had been taught no one was going to give me anything, so I had to take it or do without.

Since I had been raised in a poor environment, I also figured I would be doomed to stay there all of my life. In my mind, the only way I could get ahead would be to take what I wanted from the world. As far as I was concerned, I had little education and no worldly connections. Therefore, I had virtually no shot to achieve my American dream legally. I hate to admit it, but I really believed I had no recourse in life but to turn to crime in order to prosper.

At this point in my life, I figured I had tried to get my piece of the rock legally and that didn't work. Now, I was ready to do whatever was necessary to survive. I had no clue that I had surrendered to the enemy of my soul and accepted the rationalization that no matter how hard I tried I couldn't overcome the 'world' system.

I thought back on how I left horseracing years earlier because I had no control over my future. Afterwards, I took the risk and managed to overcome the odds. I was able to come back and establish myself as a respectable horse trainer.

Although I committed many crimes in order to finance my career, I quickly abandoned that lifestyle. As soon as I was financially able, I pursued a legal, legitimate profession. I never really wanted to be a criminal. I just wanted to achieve the American dream. The way I saw it my career was my one and only chance at being a legal success in this world. Now, I had to resign myself to the fact that the boat had already sailed.

While I was on top, I figured I would never again be living a life of neglect. Although I had managed to overcome my status in life for years and years, I was now being forced back to square one. I had gone farther in my life than I had ever dreamed I could, but I had to face up to the fact that I had broken the law in order to do it.

However, I wasn't ready to give up the control I still thought I had over my life. I still had plan B. I wasn't through yet. I had overcome the odds before. As long as I was breathing, I believed I still had a chance.

God had other plans. He was about to knock me off of my high horse. (No pun intended). He had put me into the limelight in the sport of kings. Now, He would give me a taste of being a beggar fighting for his life. He had moved me into an early retirement. He was about to show me what life is really all about. My real quitting time had finally arrived.

In order to bring me to the place where I needed to be, God was manifesting His promise recorded in the Bible concerning reaping and sowing. The harvest had begun. In human terms, my life was a nightmare. The only sensible thing I could have done would have been to throw in the towel.

However, being the optimist I am, I took it all in stride. (Again no pun intended). In my mind, I believed I could still resort to the one thing which had given me an opportunity before. Crime did pay. I could cash in one more time.

Instead of turning to the One who could really help me in my desperate need, I turned to my partner, Tony. Since we were always very successful in our criminal activities before, I knew I could make lots of money with him. I planned to use my ill gotten gains to pay for my legal defense. In the process, I could somehow keep my lifestyle and my future intact.

Believe it or not, I still had hopes I could beat the case against me. If it all panned out, I planned on going back to doing what I loved best. Hopefully, I would get another shot at earning my living legally again. Meanwhile, I was quite willing to break the law some more.

"The wisdom of the prudent is to understand his way; but the folly of fools is deceit" (Proverbs 14:8)

SINKING DEEPER

Within a few months of my suspension from horseracing, I had managed to rip off over 500 pounds of marijuana, and a few kilos of cocaine. The marijuana had a street value of about a half million dollars and the cocaine was worth about a quarter of a million. Tony and I had robbed several drug dealers in the process and we were on a roll.

Although I knew how deadly the consequences of this game I was playing could be, I had little fear. In spite of the fact the people I was robbing were armed on a level equal to most military squads, and wouldn't hesitate to kill me, I jumped in with both feet whenever the opportunity presented itself. As I think back on it now, only God could have preserved my foolish flesh through it all. Not only did He spare me, He also spared the people I ripped off from being harmed. It was only by His grace I didn't hurt anyone in the process of our heists.

I believe this was due to the fact, that most of the time my victims never even saw me. Most of my 'scores' were achieved through cat burglaries. As time passed, our heists increased in value. My flawless execution of these crimes was earning me some notoriety within the circles of the criminal element.

As with any of my pursuits in this life, I strived for excellence. I would have it no other way. I prided myself on being a cat burglar par excellence. I think this mindset was the result of my childhood idle, Alexander Monday.

It Takes a Thief, a television series from the 1960's, was my favorite program as a teen. The smooth style of Alexander Monday intrigued me. Some of the crimes he committed in the series were classics. Although I never dreamed I would one day be emulating him, I received quite a thrill every time I managed to pull off a major heist.

Even though I always was one for pushing the envelope, I knew my ‘luck’ was bound to run out. So, as soon as we had sold our stolen drugs and gathered up enough money, I decided to stop my criminal activities altogether. At this point, I figured I had enough money to survive until my upcoming trial was over. I thought I would just enjoy my ‘mandatory’ vacation and concentrate on winning my upcoming battle in court.

In the following months, I met with Doug several more times. He seemed quite optimistic. After thoroughly reviewing my case, he told me we would more than likely overcome the evidence presented against me in a court of law. Even if both of my accusers were there to testify against me, he figured we would still be victorious. He was sure neither of my accusers would come across as a credible witness.

Needless to say, I was quite relieved to hear this. In fact, until he told me that, I was seriously considering having one of my finger pointers taken for a one-way ride. In fact, my partner's mob-connected son had already offered to have this snitch snuffed out. Someone had already followed the potential victim around and we were aware of where he could be easily reached at any given time.

I am amazed when I think back on how far I had fallen. Up until this point in my life, I had never deliberately hurt anyone. I had always been totally against this. However, in my distorted frame of mind I was seriously considering taking my partner's son up on his offer to “alleviate the problem”. Thank God, the good news I had just received led me to abandon all such plans.

By the grace of God, I had found out there was a better way to alleviate the problem. It was a gamble, but I figured I would rather take the chance of winning in court than to be responsible for someone's death. At that point, I had enough confidence that my lawyer would beat the system for me.

I was not disappointed. He did a masterful job defending me. He destroyed the credibility of both of my accusers and in the process made me look like a saint. He was everything I had hoped for and more. The jury in my trial returned a swift verdict of not guilty.

I still remember what an awesome experience it was when I heard those two crucial words: NOT GUILTY. At that moment, I felt as though I was given my life back. I had overcome. It was like I had been born again.

My step-father had been there with me during my entire trial. After we received the verdict, he congratulated me. Then, he strongly advised me to stay on the right track. He told me I had been given the chance of a lifetime with a brand new start and I couldn't afford to take any more chances. He warned me I should try to play it straight from that point on.

I assured my step-father I had all intentions of walking the straight and narrow path. I knew beyond any shadow of a doubt how fortunate I had been to overcome the case the state had presented against me. I wasn't about to tempt fate any more. I planned on focusing totally on training my horses and had absolutely no desire to do anything else.

After my trial in New Jersey, I returned home to Florida. The following day, I went to Calder Racecourse and applied for a jockey's license. During my 'vacation,' I had managed to keep the weight off. I figured I would take advantage of the edge I still had of being able to ride my own horses in their upcoming races. Once again, it looked to me like I was in complete control of my future.

This was short lived and proved to be fallacious. God wasn't through with me yet. He wasn't about to just let me take up where I had left off. The day after I applied for my license, I was informed I was no longer eligible to race in Florida or in any other state. According to the stewards, I was still under suspension in New Jersey, Pennsylvania, and Maryland.

They claimed I had falsified my applications when I applied for my jockey's license, my trainer's license, and my owner's license in those states. I was infuriated, because I knew the authorities were just messing with me. They just wanted to keep me from racing as long as they possibly could. Those suspensions were bogus. I hadn't done anything wrong.

According to their explanation, I had lied about selling Quitting Time to my partner before I raced him at Timonium. Although what I did was commonly done between owners and trainers all the time, I was being penalized. Supposedly, there were more allegations against me but I was never given the rest of the details concerning this.

Shortly after learning I couldn't be licensed, I called my friend, Lee. After I explained the situation to him, he told me we would have to set up hearings in all of the states where I was suspended from racing. Then, we would have to make arrangements to appear before the racing commission in each state. He informed me this process could take months and months. Obviously, this was going to cost me.

I told him I didn't care how much money it cost. I just wanted him to launch a counterattack - immediately. I was not going to stand for this. In order to get back into my chosen profession, I planned to do whatever was necessary to beat the 'system.' I wasn't about to give up my fight now. I was determined I was going to have it my way.

Herein lay my problem. I didn't realize it was God I was fighting against. I was not going to have it my way any longer. Money was not going to solve my problems. The way I saw it, my battle was with the racing officials and this was going to cost me dearly. However, by this time I didn't really have much money left to work with.

Being one who always had an answer to the problem, I quickly came up with what I thought was the solution. Since I couldn't fulfill my dreams legally, in my angry, corrupt state of mind I decided I would go back to crime again. Somebody was going to pay for my legal fees and it wasn't me. At this point, I was determined I was still going to reach my life's goal of success and prosperity.

I spent the next few weeks looking for a score. I had filled my partner, Tony, in on my situation concerning the racing authorities. He was glad to hear I was ready to team up with him once again to do some more rip offs. However, he told me he didn't have anything lined up at that time. But, he promised he would get to work on it.

As the days passed by, I got more anxious. Before I knew it, the days had turned into weeks. Since Tony hadn't been able to set up any heists for me to pull off, and my lifestyle hadn't changed, my cash was dwindling fast. Fear set in. The fear of losing my earthly possessions was always in the forefront of my mind.

Yet, I wasn't about to give back what I had thus far taken from this world. I decided to do some scouting on my own. During this process, I found what I had considered to be a worthwhile target. I had come across a person whom I had assumed to be a drug dealer. My 'mark' lived in Boca Raton, Florida. I found out he had a huge safe in his house. It was located in the master bedroom. I assumed he kept a lot of valuables in it.

While doing some surveillance on his home, I found out how many people were living there. I also found out he did not have a burglar alarm. Even though I liked the plan I had come up in order to pull off this crime, for some reason I really didn't feel comfortable with it.

While my partner, Gary, and I made attempts to execute my plan, I sensed something was telling me this wasn't going to turn out good for me. Although I had pulled off many heists in my lifetime, I never got this gut feeling before. So, I kept putting it off.

Meanwhile, my partner began to become more anxious than me. He needed money more desperately than I did. Therefore, he just wanted to do the score and get it over with. I told him I was waiting for what I would consider to be a better opportunity to come along. In spite of his efforts to convince me otherwise, I put him on hold.

During the waiting period, my partner's son, Nick, contacted me. He informed me he had a couple of contacts in Florida he wanted me to meet. Among other things, these guys were involved in the illegal drug business. He told me they were willing to set up some scores for me to do. I wasted no time telling him I was very interested.

A few hours later, he set up a meeting between us. After our first rendezvous, I felt quite comfortable with these guys. One was named Vinny and the other Louie. They explained to me they were involved in the drug trade and would wait for the right opportunity to come along. Once they found the right victim, they would put the ball in my court and depend on me to do the rest.

I could tell they were professionals and I had no doubt they had the right connections. It would only be a matter of time before they would get into the right position and set someone up. However, I had no idea how long it would take for this to happen. I was never one to pass up an opportunity, so I didn't care what the time frame eventually turned out to be. I would definitely be available at their beck and call.

Besides, I figured working with these two would give me more reason to postpone my scheme to rob the man in Boca. As it turned out, we came to an agreement between us three that same day. They had promised to call when the time was right. I was looking forward to this. We ended our 'meeting' on this note.

After our initial introduction, a few weeks passed by. I still hadn't heard from Vinnie or Louie. Therefore, I contacted them. They told me they were still trying to work out the details of something they had planned.

Although I didn't know exactly what they meant

by that, I didn’t think it was my place to question them. Since I didn't want them to think I was in too much of a hurry, I acted unconcerned about it. Therefore, I told them I was just touching base with them and looked forward to hearing from them.

In reality, both Gary and I were getting unbearably anxious. I didn't know how much longer I would be able to spend my money without bringing some in. On the other hand, he was eager to make enough money to be able to move into a place of his own. He and his girlfriend had been living with me for quite a while and they both wanted to get a place of their own.

Actually, I really wanted them to move out of my house more than they wanted to move on. Since he had no job and no income, this was not an option. If we were successful pulling off my plan in Boca, I figured they would both be in the position to make the move. Otherwise, they would be staying with me indefinitely.

Eventually, push came to shove and I decided we should just go ahead and do the score in Boca.
I wanted to get Gary out of my hair and I figured I could make enough money to hold me over until something better came along.

I told Gary we would go there on the following night. He was excited. Later that evening, I gathered up two pairs of gloves, two hats, two bandanas, some burglar tools, a flashlight, and one revolver. I placed all this equipment into a duffel bag and put it into the trunk of my car.

As planned, Gary and I left my home at about 6:00 p.m. We were finally on our way to Boca Raton. This had been a long time coming. Although I had mixed feelings, I was sure it would all work out in the end. I was looking forward to putting my problems behind me for a while.

In my wildest dream, I could never have imagined what was about to happen. As I was walking down my driveway towards my car, I heard an inaudible voice in my mind saying:

"You're getting greedy!"

At the time, I had no way of knowing this voice was the Holy Spirit from God Himself. Instead of acknowledging this fact, or inquiring where this voice was coming from, I just tried to justify my intentions.

"I'm not greedy. I just need to make a few bucks to help pay for my expenses. I can't wait until the last minute to do something. I'll run out of money. Then, I'll never be able to get back on the racetrack," I defensively responded to the inner voice.

According to my perverted rationalization, I was right. So, it didn't really matter what I had just heard. I really should have realized this was the same voice that had spoken to me while I was in the winner's circle at the Meadowlands Racetrack back in 1980. Unfortunately, I didn't.

As I think back to that monumental event, I am amazed at how incredibly blind I was. I had absolutely no clue as to what was going on in the spiritual world. In fact, at that point in time, I didn't even know for sure the spiritual world existed. All I did know was the fact that I was still fighting to get my piece of the rock. As far as I was concerned, this world never gave me a thing and I wasn't about to give up any of the ground I had already gained.

Even though I still had $10,000 in cash in my safe deposit box at the time, I was sure what I had wasn't enough. Before I got back into the position to earn my living legally again, I figured I would need some more money. At the rate I spent money, I was heading for bankruptcy. Throughout my adult life, this had always been my greatest fear.

I had come too far in life. I couldn't bear to go back. Unfortunately, it never once occurred to me I should have tried to curb my style of living. Then, I would have had enough money to pay all my bills for another year. Had I done so, I wouldn't have had to resort to crime to supplement my income until the time came when I could win some races again.

I was blinded by the god of this world and had no idea what this would someday cost me. Later that night, Gary and I pulled off the robbery as planned. We got away clean. Afterwards, I had no reason to believe we would ever get caught for this crime.

However, on our way home from Boca Raton, something strange happened to Gary and me. First, I started getting feelings of remorse for our victims. This never happened to me before. I told him about the way I was feeling. Strangely enough, he told me he also had been getting feelings of remorse for our victims.

At the time, neither of us had a clue we were feeling this way because the Spirit of God was convicting us of our sin. God was preparing me for the work He planned on doing in my calloused heart. Unfortunately, I was so far out there it didn't take very long for me to suppress those feelings of guilt and move on.

After all, I had accomplished my purpose. I figured I now had enough money to hold me over for quite some time. As far as I was concerned, I was a success. I was in control of my life once again. I had overcome one more time. I really had no idea I was my own enemy and had just played into the hands of the enemy of my soul.

Once we arrived at my home, we counted our take. All my feelings of remorse faded away as quickly as the morning dew under the warm rising sun. We had managed to steal about $250,000. About $6,000 of our haul was cash. However, along with the cash we had also managed to steal tangible goods worth a small fortune. The first thing which entered my warped mind was:

"It's time to party!"

I quickly concocted another great plan. Since most of our haul was in jewelry, coins, and collectible firearms, I would go to Brooklyn, New York. I would then sell our stolen goods to Nick. I wasted no time calling him and consummating a deal. We scheduled to meet each other the following day.

After I met with him, I planned to party with one of the girls I knew in New York. Once again, I thought I had it all figured out. After our phone conversation, I called the AmTrack train station to make reservations for my trip.

I booked a cabin for myself on a train going to the city. I planned to rest on the way there so I would be vitalized and ready to party after I had taken care of 'business.' I was back in the fast lane and ready to boogey.

The following morning, I awakened at 6:30 a.m. My girl, Tracy, and me got out of bed and dressed quickly. In a matter of minutes, we were on I-95 heading north towards the AmTrack station in Fort Lauderdale. Everything seemed to be going according to plan. We were right on schedule. I just didn't know whose schedule. I had no idea what God had planned for me that day.

Once we arrived at the AmTrack station, we went inside to purchase my ticket. As we approached the sales clerk, I was totally unaware we were being watched. Stationed in the office were two undercover agents. They were working with the Broward Sheriff's Office, and the DEA. The officers were looking for people, who were purchasing tickets and happened to fit their profile as drug couriers.

For some strange reason, I decided to use a fake I.D. to purchase my ticket that morning. I didn't need to do that. I had my real I.D. in my wallet and I wasn't wanted for anything. I really had no reason to use bogus I.D. that day. Once again, God was at work. I purchased my ticket using a bogus state of New Jersey driver's license.

After buying my ticket, Tracy and me walked out onto the platform to await my incoming train. Once we arrived at the north end of the platform, we placed my two bags of luggage on the ground in front of us. We leaned back on a large, round support beam which was directly behind us. We were kissing and bidding one another goodbye. She was in the process of promising to make me a chicken cacciatore dinner upon my return.

We were both oblivious of the fact the two undercover agents were creeping up on us. While we were in the midst of a kiss, I remember feeling someone tapping me on my shoulder. As I opened my eyes to see who it was that was disturbing us, the agents identified themselves and explained their business.

According to what they told me, there was a problem in South Florida in regards to drug smuggling. They further explained, as a result of this, the authorities were doing random searches at the various disembarkation points throughout the state. I quickly told them I wasn't interested in their problem and wished to be left alone.

They didn't care. The told me they wanted to see some ID. At that point, I knew they were going to want to search my bags as well. I had no plans of allowing them to see the guns, and the stolen goods I was carrying. I knew they had no legal reason to search my bags so I tried to just brush them off. I presented one of the agents with my fake ID. While I was taking this ID out from my wallet, one of the agents noticed my Florida Drivers license in my wallet bearing my picture. It was obvious to them something was amiss. Immediately, they became more persistent.

They continued trying to coerce me into cooperating with them and insisted I allow them to open my luggage. I refused their request. At this point, they told me I wasn't going to board my train unless I gave them access to my luggage.

Suddenly, I noticed the train approaching the station platform. I was hoping the agents would give in and allow me to board the train as long as I didn't grant them permission to search my luggage. Then, one of the agents noticed I had a lock on my luggage and asked me if I had the key for it. I told him I didn't have the key with me.

In reality, I held the key in the pocket of my jeans. If I didn't present them with a key, I hoped they would give up on me. I also figured, if they didn't let me go, they would probably break open the small locks on my luggage. I was sure, if they did this, I would have grounds for having the evidence they found suppressed in a court of law.

Once again, I thought I was planning ahead. Should I wind up getting charged with a crime, I wanted to give my lawyer something to work with. Although I thought I had all the answers, the One who really does was about to put a stop to my charade.

Eventually, the agents did break open my luggage and found my cache of stolen goods. Immediately, they called in the serial numbers on the stolen guns to a police dispatcher. A few moments later, they traced the weapons to their original source.

After receiving this information, the agents arrested me. However, I figured this was not the end of the story. I could still bond out of the county jail and could probably beat the case once it came to trial. I figured there would definitely be some holes in any case they came up with.

Speaking of holes, I had no idea o the hole I had gotten myself into. This time, it was way too deep for me to climb out of. Furthermore, God was planning on taking away my shovel. He was about to show me just how difficult my life could become.

Within a few hours of my initial arrest, I had posted a $50,000 bond and was on my way home. Along the way, I stopped somewhere and contacted Vinny and Louie. I arranged a meeting with them. Believer it or not, I was ‘off the chain.’ I didn't want to waste any time plotting out my next crime. At that point, I was more determined than ever to beat the system. I knew I would have even more attorney’s fees to pay now and I wasn’t going to be left short.

I was hoping Vinny and Louie would be

instrumental in helping me to somehow get that money. We met the following afternoon and they told me they were sorry to hear about my arrest. They had gotten the details of my arrest as they were broadcast on the 5 o'clock news the night before.

Actually, I hadn't planned on telling them anything about my arrest. I felt so stupid because I had gotten caught on what I thought was a fluke. I cared more about their approval of me than I did about my arrest.

However, my getting arrested hadn’t affected their opinion of me. In fact, Vinny and Louie didn't seem to be concerned at all about my ability to pull off crimes successfully. In fact, they had already planned out a crime for me to commit.

Before filling me in on the details of their plan, Vinny asked me what had happened to cause my arrest. After I gave him the details, he told me he too was confident I could have the evidence against me suppressed in a court of law. Then, he explained he had a personal friend, Jack Morgan, who was a very good criminal lawyer. He encouraged me to hire him to defend me. I agreed to meet with Jack in order to discuss my case with him. Vinny told me he would set up an appointment for me.

Once we finished discussing my case, Vinny filled me in on the details of his plan. He explained to me one of their out of town buyers was due to arrive in Florida within a day or two. This buyer was scheduled to rendezvous with a connection of his.

He promised, once the buyer arrived, he would inform me where I could catch up with him. The plan was for me to intercept this guy before he was able to make his purchase. He predicted our potential victim would be carrying well over $100,000 in cash.

I had a new hope. If this plan worked out, I would have more than enough money to fight the battles that lay ahead of me. As our meeting came to an end, Vinny told me I should stick close to my phone for the next couple of days. He said he didn't want me to miss this opportunity when it came. At that point, I promised him I would be right at home awaiting his call.

I was always a man of my word. I anxiously waited…and waited. Then, the call came. When I answered the phone, I was relieved to hear Vinny's voice on the other end of the receiver. I figured this meant I was going to get a green light. I was right on point. He informed me his buyer had arrived in Florida and I should get ready. He promised to call me as soon as he learned the exact location of where our potential victim would be arriving.

About an hour later, I received another phone call from him. It turned out to be just the call I had been waiting for. He instructed me to meet him at some diner.

"Come ready for action," he instructed.

Within the hour, we met in the parking lot of some diner. Vinny explained he would take me to the house where our victim would be staying. The rest was up to me. I agreed. Together, we drove there. Once we arrived at the house, I observed the surrounding homes and the area in general. To my delight, it was a quiet, poorly lit, residential area.

As we drove back to my vehicle, he explained he would periodically cruise by the area I would be working in just in case I needed something. Then, he instructed me to meet up with him later that night if the mission was a success. At that time we could split the take.

A short time later, we arrived at my vehicle. I opened the trunk and took out my gun, gloves, facemask, and some handcuffs. A few moments later, I lay on the side of the home where my potential victim was due to arrive. I periodically surveyed the area for signs of activity. I wanted to make sure there wasn't anyone else around who could possibly be a witness to the crime I planned to commit.

Within minutes, my potential victim arrived. He jumped out of his vehicle and very swiftly proceeded to make his way towards the front entrance. Before I had the chance to rise up and get to him, he was right in front of the very well lit doorway of the home. To make my attempt even more difficult, someone had already come to the doorway to greet him.

At that point, I dare not chance a confrontation. I had no idea whether or not the greeter was armed with a gun. I backed off and considered my options. I was very disappointed, but not defeated. I observed the victim was carrying a suitcase into the home. I assumed it was full of cash.

At that point, I determined I was not going to let this opportunity escape my grip. Somehow, I would get into the home and take that money. I was in desperate need of cash and I figured I wouldn't get too many more opportunities to get my hands on that much money. I absolutely had to somehow capitalize on this one.

I prowled around the premises for hours in an effort to find out how many people were in the house and what specific rooms they were in. During my investigation, I learned there were a total of four people inside the house. Before making my move, I decided I would wait for them all to go to sleep. After a few hours, most of the lights inside the home went out. Only a night light in the kitchen remained lit.

I patiently waited for everyone inside the home to get into a deep sleep. When I figured everyone inside was sound asleep, I quietly made my way into the home. With my pistol drawn, I made my way into the room where I had seen the victim place his suitcase earlier that night.

I was fully aware, at any given moment, someone could awaken and a gun battle would ensue. I was so desperate I didn’t care. I was prepared to do battle if necessary. I wanted the money that badly. I was willing to take that chance.

By the grace of God, no one in the house awakened. I was able to get in and out of the house undetected. In the process, I made off with the suitcase full of cash. In an effort to get back to my car, I walked about a half mile. Then, I saw a car coming towards me. It was about four in the morning, so I figured it was either Vinny or a cop. I hid on the side of someone's hedges until the oncoming vehicle was close enough for me to identify. Once I realized it was my partner in crime, I flagged him down.

He slowed down to a stop and I quickly got into his car. When he saw the suitcase I tossed into the back seat of his car, his face lit up with a big smile. He knew my mission was a success. Joyously, we drove back to my vehicle. Along the way, I filled him in on the specifics as to how I completed the rip off.

Once we arrived at his house, I took the suitcase out of my car and we went inside. As we both entered his dining room, I opened the suitcase and poured its contents onto his dining room table. Neatly packed bundles of money came pouring out of the bag. Both of us were all smiles. Our take was well over $100,000 that night.

After we had split up the money between us, he told me he had managed to set up an appointment for me to meet with Jack Morgan the following morning. It looked as though I had pulled another rabbit out of the hat. I had plenty of money and an opportunity to overcome the system via my new attorney.

I felt like I had some room to breathe again. Although I knew having a good lawyer was no guarantee I would win the trial I was facing, I was grateful I was fortunate enough to have found someone good so abruptly. I was fully aware I would have had to shop around and hope I could come up with a good lawyer to handle my defense had Vinny not known Jack was a winner. If this were the case, I may not have been able to find one before it was too late. Since I didn't know any criminal lawyers in Florida and had no idea where to start, I really thought this latest development was quite a stroke of 'luck'.

Although my friend, Lee, could have helped me

to find a good lawyer, I didn't dare plan on telling him about my arrest. I was too embarrassed. My pride just wouldn't have let me. After only recently winning the legal battle of my life, how could I possibly tell my best friend I was arrested again and facing the possibility of life in prison? At this point, I really felt like the fool I was.

"Be not deceived; God is not mocked; for whatsoever man sows, that shall he also reap." (Galatians 6:7)

PIPEDREAMS TO NIGHTMARES

As I walked into Jack's swank office, he introduced himself to me and informed me he had already obtained the police reports concerning my arrest. In the very short period I conversed with him, I felt comfortable I could count on him to defend me. I believed he was sharp enough to help me beat the system one more time.

Just when I was gaining confidence all was not lost he gave me some disturbing news. In the initial police reports, he had read that the victims of the crime claimed they could identify me. All the precautionary measures I had taken should have been enough to prevent this from happening.

During the robbery, I wore a bandanna which covered my face up to the bottom of my eyelids. I wore a hat which covered my head. As if that weren't enough, I disguised my voice. I couldn't understand how anybody could have put the finger on me. This should not have been possible.

However, one of the victims we robbed claimed she would recognize my big, brown eyes anywhere. I didn't guess that in itself wouldn't be too damaging, but there was more. Jack had learned the victims stated my partner had actually called out my name during the course of the robbery. I was shocked.

I thought back on it for a moment. Then, I realized my partner did indeed call out my name in the presence of the victims. At one point, the owner of the home had hesitated to open his safe for me. This caused my partner to become discouraged and he lost it momentarily.

After several unsuccessful tries at opening his safe for me, Mr. Jones had claimed the dial on his safe was stuck. He claimed it wouldn't work properly because the safe had been damaged in an earlier robbery attempt.

At that point, my partner was really getting nervous and he blurted out: "Let's just get out of here, Jimmy. He can't open his safe."

I hadn't even given that incident a second thought. After all, we didn't leave any clues as to who committed the armed burglary. I didn't think the police could possibly connect me to the robbery with only a first name.

Although I had no clue the desperate plea of my accomplice to abort our mission would be instrumental in my downfall, this apparently was the case. Yet, in spite of the evidence against me, Jack assured me we had a good ‘chance’ of winning. I wasn't so sure. Still, I agreed to give him a retaining fee to start working on my case.

However, I didn’t pay him on the spot. In the back of my mind, I knew I still might want just decide to take flight. A few days later, I opted to do just that. I changed my mind about fighting it out in court. After I had considered the possibility of how much time I was facing, I decided I didn’t want to ‘chance’ it.

I arrived at this decision mainly because I figured a legitimate career was out of the question for me anymore. Therefore, I decided I might as well resign myself to a life of crime. Being on the run wouldn’t really matter one way or the other to me now. Once again, it was quitting time.

At that point, I decided I would never again try to make my living legitimately. My darkened mind was convinced it was a waste of time. I had tried and tried to pursue an honest career only to face bitter defeat. As far as I was concerned, life had just dealt me its last batch of lemons. In my warped mind, I rationalized I could still make lemonade - but this time it wouldn’t be legal.

I was still determined to pursue my dream of financial independence. I wasn’t about to be deprived of the luxurious lifestyle I was accustomed to living. I planned on using my crime connections in Florida and New York to their fullest potential. I figured I could live quite comfortably by doing business with either one of my partners-in-crime.

After our latest escapade, I wasn't pressed for money anymore. This made it easier for me to sit back and wait for my partners in crime to set up some more scores for me to do. While I was waiting for them to set up our next crime, I planned to buy myself a nice sailboat. I wanted to just relax in some place far away.

A few days later, I made my run for the New Jersey shore. Since I had spent much time trying to pursue my fortune through horse racing, I was very familiar with the area. Upon my arrival, I started shopping for a sailboat. It didn't take long for me to find the boat of my dreams. It was a 32 foot Pearson. The boat was in excellent condition and sea worthy enough to take me around the world.

Once I purchased this sailboat, I figured I could rent a slip somewhere along the Jersey shore and just enjoy the good life for a while. In order to get familiar with my vessel, I planned to do a lot of sailing that summer.

Since I wanted to be close to New York, the Jersey shore was the perfect place for me.
I knew my friends in New York would eventually set up some crimes for me to commit. I also wanted to be close to the Newark airport just in case I wanted to go back to Florida to do a score for Vinny. It was my erroneous belief that living on board a sailboat would be the perfect hideaway for me.

I rented a slip for the summer in Sea Bright, New Jersey. I planned to eventually sail around the world. I tried to stay optimistic about life. But, I was deeply affected by my losses. I tried to drown out my sorrow with liquor and partying but I still had a very empty feeling inside

Everything I had worked so long for was gone. My career was over and I was a wanted man. I had no future - at least not in the legal sense. Worst of all, I had to look over my shoulder constantly. I didn't know how long I would be able to avoid being captured by the authorities. I didn't want to even think of what would happen if I were.

A short time after my arrival to the Jersey shore, I got together with a couple of my New York crime connections. Since most of the cash I had on hand was now depleted, I figured I had better get busy. We began plotting some crimes. I'm not going to give the devil glory by going into the details concerning the crimes we committed that summer. However, I will say that I made enough money to live quite comfortably for a long while.

Eventually, I got back together with an old girlfriend of mine named, Betty. She had been living in New Jersey. She came to live with me on my sailboat. We went to Studio 54 in New York about five times a week. We ate dinner in the finest restaurants and enjoyed the New York night life together. We were party-minded creatures.

In the daytime, we basked in the New Jersey sun and sailed along the Jersey shore. At that point in my life, I had temporarily succeeded in my efforts to silence my deepest woes. I carried on as though I didn't have a worry in the world. As far as I was concerned, life was good and I was determined to enjoy as much of it as I could, for as long as I could.

However, that wasn’t as long as I had hoped it would be. Before I knew it, my worst nightmare became a reality and my stint in paradise came to an abrupt halt. One night as my girlfriend and I were preparing to retire, we heard footsteps on the deck of my sailboat. Immediately, I sensed the sounds I heard up on deck were being made by the authorities. They had finally caught up with me.

My suspicions were quickly confirmed. One of the policemen, who were on board my boat, shouted out my name and announced their intentions to arrest me. I was ordered to toss out all the weapons I possessed and come up onto the deck with my hands raised in the air. I responded by opening the hatch and climbing out. I was greeted by several shotgun-wielding policemen. They quickly placed me in handcuffs and ordered my girlfriend to come up on deck.

Since my girlfriend had committed no crime, she was soon released from police custody. Shortly after I was booked at the local police station, I was transferred to the county jail in Freehold, New Jersey. I was scheduled to be held in the county jail until I was given an extradition hearing.

After I was processed into the county jail, they placed me in a cell with about twelve other men. When I arrived at my new home, all the other men were sleeping. It was about five in the morning. Once I entered the bunk area of the large cell, I made my way to the only empty bunk. I was exhausted. All I wanted to do was sleep. I was hoping I would awaken later and discover this was only a bad dream. I plopped down onto my bunk.

As I lay on my back looking up, it suddenly dawned on me. *If I'm so smart, what the hell am I doing in here? After all I have accomplished with my life, why am I at square one again?* As these thoughts flooded my mind, I realized all my efforts to achieve my American dream were in vain.

I had managed to steal millions of dollars, and outwit some of the slickest schemers I ever met. I even managed to survive my dealings with organized crime. All of this while also managing to elude police detection for years. Yet, now I was on the verge of losing everything. Most importantly, I was losing my freedom.

At that moment, I knew I was absolutely helpless. I finally realized this time that I had really come to my quitting time. I couldn't go on doing the same things anymore. I needed help desperately. I had absolutely no one to turn to...except God. At that precise time, I prayed: "*God, if You are real, please change me. I don't want to be the same person any longer. I'm sorry for all I've done wrong. Now, please help me if You can. If I get out of prison someday, I don't want to go back to my old ways."*

In my wildest dreams I could not have imagined praying that prayer was actually the best thing I did in my entire life. I had no idea I was opening up the way for the God of all creation to come into my life and straighten out the enormous mess I had created. I had no clue about what He had in store for me.

After I prayed that prayer, I fell asleep. When I awoke, it was life as usual. I got comfortable with my surroundings, made a few friends, and tried working every angle I possibly could in order to get out of jail. Nothing worked. This time, I couldn't help myself, nor could anybody else. I realized I was definitely no longer in control of my life. Strangely enough, I thought this was a bad thing.

About 10 days later, I found out different. It was at that time I was introduced to the reality of the One who was in control. While I was in the process of being extradited from New Jersey to Florida, my heavenly Father finally opened my eyes and revealed the truth to me.

I was being transported via a twin engine plane and the trip seemed to be taking forever. We had been hopping from state to state picking up and dropping off prisoners along the way. I grew more and more impatient with each stop we made.

While I was sitting shackled in my seat for the second day, I suddenly got this thought: *Take a look under your seat and you will find something to read.* I had no idea where this thought came from, but I figured it wouldn't do me any harm to look. As I felt around under my seat, I latched onto a book.

As I removed it from under my seat, I saw its title: "Where Flies Don't Land" Although I thought this was a strange title for a book, I felt compelled to read it. The book was written by a man named Jerry Graham and it was about his life.

As I read it, I discovered Jerry was a heroine addict. According to his own testimony, he was way out there. He had pimped out his girlfriend, robbed his family, and did much evil over the years. Suddenly, everything caught up to him and he was in the county jail awaiting trial for his crimes. He was a three-time loser. If he were convicted of the crimes he was charged with, he would never see the streets again.

While he was in the county jail, he met a man who told him how Jesus had helped him. The man assured him Jesus could indeed help him as well. He didn't have any other options, and decided to give Jesus a try. He did the smart thing and gave his life to Jesus. He was soon delivered from his heroine addiction.

For some strange reason, the prosecutor in Jerry's case decided to make a deal with him. Needless to say, he was overwhelmed with joy. He accepted the terms the prosecutor set forth and eventually was released from jail. Afterwards, he went on to start a boys' ranch for troubled youth. He stayed clean and eventually wrote the book I was reading.

I was astounded. I always thought drug addicts were beyond help. Heroine users topped my list of losers. After reading Jerry's life story, I realized Jesus had to be awesome. I didn't think I was any worse off than a heroine addict. Therefore, I figured there was still hope for me too. At that point, I had no doubt Jesus was what I needed.

Right there in my seat, I bowed my head and asked God to forgive me for all of my sins. Then, I asked Jesus to come into my heart. It was quitting time for the 'old' man. I had finally come to the conclusion I could do nothing better than to surrender my life to God.

Immediately afterwards, I knew in my heart everything was going to be alright. I had a peace which I had never experienced before. I realized I still had to face the music. I didn't expect to be set free like Jerry Graham. Yet, I no longer cared about the difficulties which lay ahead. I knew my life was now in God's hands and I was certain Jesus could make it better. Only God could have given me such reassurance at such a desperate time in my life.

After I prayed that prayer of submission, I only wanted one thing in my life. To be all God wanted me to be was now my only goal. Throughout my life, I always went after anything I wanted wholeheartedly. I pursued God's will in the same way. I knew the only way I could learn God's will was to read His word. The Holy Spirit inside me was inspiring me to dig into the Bible in order to find out more about Jesus.

Since I didn't have a Bible, I figured God would provide me with one. It didn't take long for me to experience our loving Father's helping hand in action. I received a Bible within 24 hours of my arrival at the Palm Beach County Jail. Immediately, I started reading it diligently.

The more I read my Bible, the greater my hunger for it grew. I just couldn't get enough of it. As I read it, I realized how real God was. Once I was sure He was real, I was determined to get to know Him better.

More importantly, I was determined to do whatever He required of me. During my lifetime, I had no problem pitting my self against the authorities. In fact, I had outfoxed them most of the time. But, I wasn't about to deliberately disobey God. From what I had already learned, He was behind those authorities. I realized, if I wanted God on my side, I could no longer be at odds with them either.

As I read on, I learned of the spiritual war mankind is faced with every day. Then, I learned Jesus is the only way to victory over the spiritual forces of darkness. I never did want to be a loser, so I knew I could not let go of this golden opportunity to be an over comer. Best of all, I learned it was God who gave me this victory. In spite of my mistakes and shortcomings, He had already caused me to be victorious in Jesus.

One day, I came to the passage where Jesus was asking Peter and the disciples if they were going to turn away from following Him. This was in the Gospel of John Chapter 6 verse 67. Though some of the others had ceased following Jesus because they considered it too hard a task, Peter was not about to follow suit. He had realized there was no other place to go.

I was determined to be as resolute as Peter. I too realized, if I turned away from following Jesus,
I had nowhere to go but down. During the next few months, I grew spiritually in leaps and bounds. Unfortunately, it seemed to me that nobody else could understand what was happening in my life. I tried to tell my family what Jesus had done for me. They all seemed to think I was going through a weird jailhouse experience. They were sure that it would eventually pass away.

4Since my family had known me all of my life, they could not believe I could ever be changed. In fact, they were right. I could never have changed - at least not on my own power. However, I knew I had been changed. This change was supernatural. That is why no one who hasn't been born again can understand it.

However, in the Bible it clearly states,
"Therefore if any man be in Christ, he is a new creature; old things are passed away; behold all things are become new." (II Corinthians 5:17) I knew God had changed me in a way beyond human comprehension. I was not the same. I also knew there was no way I could convince the judge in my case, my lawyer, my family, my girlfriend, or too many other people that I had become a different person. But, I didn’t care.

I figured that was all up to God. In His time, He would show them. If He deemed it necessary, He would make a way for them to see the change in me. If not, it really didn't matter. I had the peace that passes all understanding and I knew God was in control of my life. As far as I was concerned, everything else was just incidental.

I must confess there were times I wished the judge hearing my case could understand what I had become in Jesus. It would have made life easier for my lawyer, my family, and me. However, the judge's only duty was to see that I was punished for the crimes I had committed.

Because the judge could only judge me according to my past record, it was no surprise he refused to give me a bond. Before going to trial, I had three bond hearings. Though my lawyer tried his hardest, the judge refused to grant me a bond in all three of those hearings.

Within six months of my arrest, I had gone to trial and was convicted of armed burglary and armed robbery. I was facing a life sentence. Since there were issues being raised concerning the legality of the evidence used to convict me of those crimes, I had high hopes my conviction would be overturned by a higher court. My lawyer agreed we had a good chance at it. He quickly filed an appeal for me.

While awaiting my appeal, I was sentenced. The judge gave me two life sentences. My family was devastated. I wasn't. I knew there was no way God would allow the authorities to overstep their legal bounds and imprison me for life.

First of all, I was sentenced under the Florida guidelines. This meant I shouldn't have been sentenced to more than seven years for the crimes of which I had been convicted. The state had just instituted a new point system. According to their own guidelines, my past record only caused me to be appointed with enough points to warrant such a sentence.

Secondly, I knew God was well aware the evidence used in my trial had indeed been obtained illegally. All things considered, I didn’t believe for one moment I was going to be imprisoned for life. After my sentencing, I was returned to the county jail to await my transfer into the state of Florida's Department of Corrections.

In spite of the latest turn of events in my life, I continued to seek God by reading His word as much as I could. Although my physical life was utterly decimated, I continued to focus solely on getting to know Him better. I had absolutely no doubt in my mind this was what really mattered the most. I wasn't about to allow anybody or anything to keep me from my pursuit of my Creator. Thankfully, He had kindled a fire in my soul which has yet to be quenched.

"An inheritance may be gotten hastily at the beginning, but the end thereof shall not be blessed." (Prov. 20:21)

AWAKENING

It was about 3 a.m. and I was far from being sleepy. But, I was not in some nightclub partying. This would have been quite normal for me. I loved partying. As far as I was concerned, living life in the fast lane was the only way to go. However, my love of pleasure had led me right into my present lifestyle. I was being held prisoner in the Palm Beach county jail.

A few days earlier, I had become a convicted felon. I had taken one too many gambles. The result was a total catastrophe. My high-flying pursuit of happiness had taken the ultimate nosedive. The master pilot had stalled his aircraft and none of his training, connections, or fancy moves could help him to recover. It was too late. I had pushed beyond the limits. When my craft could no longer respond to my maneuvers, I pushed it some more.

After all, I was no quitter. I had always taken pride in the fact I would never give up. I had always managed to achieve my goal - whatever it was. Now, my life was in a tailspin and I had absolutely no control over it.

Gone were the expensive racehorses I had owned and trained. Along with these, my career, home, sailboat, fancy cars, expensive jewelry, and just about all of my other earthly possessions. In spite of all this, I was enthused about my future. I had stumbled onto something of much greater value and I was earnestly pursuing it at the time.

Although most people would have considered suicide as a valid option to escape my present circumstances, I was seeking new life. Actually, I was trying to put my old self to death - but not physically. I knew what I needed was a drastic change of character.

I had recently learned what I really needed was to allow the Spirit of God to work on me and in me. Although I was newly born again, I had already been given everything I needed - for free. I was in awe. Up until that time in my life, nobody had ever given me anything for free.

Once I surrendered to God, He had freely given me all the tools I needed to become acquainted with Him in a personal relationship. Even though I was in the Palm Beach County jail in West Palm Beach, Florida, I could spend intimate time with the God of all creation. This was the most awesome experience of my life.

As I sat in the well lit day room of the cell block I was being held in, I relished the moment. My cellmates were fast asleep. At the time, I'm sure the officer on duty that night was probably wondering what in the world was keeping me up. On the other hand, I was oblivious to his or her presence. I was enjoying the peace and quiet during those wee hours of the morning. This was a rare moment indeed and I was taking full advantage of it.

I had chosen to spend my 'quiet' time reading my Bible. As I was reading and meditating on the passages, I sensed God's Presence like never before. Although, I had absolutely no idea what He had in store for me that morning.

As I read the Gospel of John Chapter 15, I came upon the seventh verse. I read the verse. Then, I repeated the verse to myself. All at once I grasped the truth of that verse of scripture for what it was. It seemed to ignite in my spirit dispelling the darkness that had held me captive all my life.

Like a baby eaglet forcing it's way out of the egg and into the world, I had labored diligently until I was able to break through the walls of unbelief that had surrounded me. I made my entrance into a new realm of existence. All of a sudden, I was soaring like an eagle. As this verse of scripture permeated my spirit, I received my very first revelation from God's Word.

John 15:7 states: "If you abide in me, and my words abide in you, you shall ask what you will and it shall be done unto you." As I meditated on that verse, in the deepest core of my being, I suddenly realized it was totally the truth. I had just struck the mother load.

At that very moment, I knew beyond any shadow of a doubt that the verse of scripture I had just ingested was not written only for an elite few. Although it had been thousands of years since that scripture was written, this applied to me then and there. I knew it could not have meant any more to those who first heard those words from the very mouth of Jesus. I had absolutely no doubt the promise was just as applicable to me as it was to them.

"Wow!" I thought. *"God, You have given me a blank check! I do abide in You because Jesus is my Savior! Your words abide in me; because I have read much of Your Word. Therefore, I can ask what I will and You will do it. Isn't that right"?* I questioned God.

He abruptly answered me - not verbally, but in my spirit. He assured me it was exactly the way I had understood it

"Okay," I testily requested. "I want an appeal bond so I can go home to be with my newborn son."

"Call your lawyer and have him arrange a bond hearing for you," God countered.

I was on cloud nine. I had just received a miracle from the Great I Am. I could hardly wait until I was able to get through to my lawyer late that morning. I knew that I knew that I knew I was going home soon.

A few hours later, I reached my lawyer at his office. After I had a short conversation with him, I instructed him to file a motion on my behalf to have a bond hearing. He reluctantly agreed. To put it mildly, Lee was skeptical. I understood why. After all, the judge handling my case had been against me throughout the whole judicial process I had gone through. Why would he change now?

Since I had lost my trial and had been convicted of armed burglary, it wasn't logical to assume the judge was going to grant me a bond. Considering I was given a life sentence, human logic would defy any odds of this ever happening.

Nevertheless, I assured Lee I had just heard from God and I knew things were about to change. Although I knew he didn’t share the same sentiment, I didn't care. I knew beyond any shadow of a doubt that God had spoken to me. My lawyer reluctantly agreed to file a motion for a bond hearing later that day.

To his surprise, I was swiftly granted that request. Hours before my bond hearing was scheduled to take place, I was taken to the holding cell in the Palm Beach County courthouse to await the procedure. As I sat there with a handful of other prisoners, I suddenly heard the opening of a door down the hall. Then, I heard footsteps. To my surprise, I looked up and saw Lee outside the bars right in front of me.

"Hi Jimmy," he cautiously greeted me.

I stood up and approached him.

"Listen, Jimmy, don't get upset if the judge denies your bond again today," he pleadingly requested.

The moment I heard those words, the Spirit came upon me and with all boldness I looked Lee right in the eye.

"You just get in there and do what you have to do. God will do the rest. I know what will happen today,” I confidently proclaimed.

After my outburst, he was quite taken aback. I must admit, I was almost as shocked as he was. I could hardly believe what had just taken place. I had never experienced a move of God's Spirit on me like that before. However, I knew it was a good thing.

I also knew I was indeed going to cash in on the blank check God had given me. My next day in court was not going to be like the earlier ones I had experienced. In horseracing I had always been one to agree there is no such thing as a sure thing. Yet, I just knew this was a sure thing. I had no doubt God was going to be in that courtroom with me and that He was for me. He was going to do the impossible. Things were going to be different.

A short time later, the bailiff escorted me into the courtroom. Once everyone was finally assembled together, the judge came in and began to announce the purpose of the proceedings. He confirmed my conviction and sentence for the record.

"The law says while you await your appeal I must set a bond. I hereby set your bond at $100,000", the judge sternly declared.

Shortly after those words left the judge's mouth, the prosecutor leaped up and strongly objected. The judge was not fazed. He finalized his decision with the drop of his gavel and ended the proceedings.

I was ecstatic! Lee was in shock. My girlfriend, who was also in the courtroom, was dumbfounded. Before any of us had time to compose ourselves, the bailiff escorted me outside of the courtroom.

Lee followed us out and asked the bailiff to give us a moment.

"I don't believe the judge just made that ruling. It is not a law that he must give you a bond while you are awaiting the outcome of your appeal. In fact, it is totally discretionary for the judge to decide whether or not to set a bond in such cases," Lee explained.

"God was responsible for that ruling," I enthusiastically assured him.

At that point, he got a little sarcastic.

"Oh yeah, and just how are you going to come up with $100,000 for your bond?" he retorted.

Once again, the Spirit gave me boldness.

"The same God who got me the bond will provide me with the money," I boldly proclaimed.

Just as I believed God was going to see to it that I was granted an appeal bond, I trusted He would indeed provide me with the money to post that bond. At the time, I had no clue as to how or when this would take place. Truth of the matter is I didn't even have enough funds to buy a bus ticket from Palm Beach to Miami at the time.

Later that same night, as I lay on my bunk

reading my Bible, God spoke to my spirit again. I don't even recall exactly what it was I was reading in the Bible at the time. But, I'll never forget what He promised me.

"As soon as you are ready to stand on my Word, I am going to open the doors for you," He graciously assured me.

I was astounded. I was never expecting to hear those words. Needless to say, I was elated that I did. Before God gave me that promise, I was digging into the Bible with the expectation of getting to know Him. After I received His promise to release me from prison, my incentive to learn more about Him became even more intense.

I wasn't sure how long it was going to take me, but I was determined to learn how to stand on God's Word to speed up the process of my release. Once I accomplished this, I knew what He had told me would indeed come to pass. There was not a doubt in my mind that God had another miracle waiting just for me. At just the right time, He would deliver on his promise.

About a week after I had my bond hearing, I was transferred from the county jail. I had been placed into the state prison system. I was hoping I could have posted my bond before I was turned over to the department of corrections. I was hoping my miracle would be manifest right there in the county jail. It didn't happen.

When I learned I was being transferred to Lake Butler, I was more than a little disappointed. While I was being held in the county jail, I was able to see my family on a weekly basis. I was able talk to them over the phone daily. However, since the reception center was located in central Florida, I knew once I arrived there I wasn't even going to be allowed to call my girlfriend at all. Worse still, I was sure I wasn't going to be able to receive any visits from her or my family.

I wasn't happy with this latest turn of events, but I knew God was faithful and I figured He would work even this out for my good. By the time all this took place, I had read enough of God's Word to realize following Jesus isn't always easy. I had already learned that, in order for a follower of His to grow, God allows His children to go through trials. In light of this, I believed what I was going through was only a test.

After being packed like a sardine into a small van with about ten other inmates, I was transported to Lake Butler. It turned out to be the most uncomfortable journey of my entire life. Not only was the van overloaded, all of us passengers were in shackles for the entire trip. It seemed like our journey would never end.

About seven hours later, we finally arrived at the reception center. It was about 11 am. Once we were all unloaded from the van, we quickly learned our hosts had no intentions of giving any of us a lick of southern hospitality.

All of us inmates were treated with disdain. The red neck guards seemed to enjoy making life difficult for us. I felt I deserved the treatment I was receiving, so I humbly accepted it. After all, God had forgiven me, not man. I expected no mercy from the authorities. I wasn't disappointed.

Yet, I was at peace. I knew what really mattered. I had read Romans 8:31: "If God be for us, who can be against us?" As long as God was for me, I knew I could overcome any circumstances I faced. In man's eyes, I was a loser. I had no rights, no say, and no freedom. In God's eyes I was special.

I made up my mind I wouldn't let their treatment of me influence my faith. I knew my name was not only written on the commitment papers the judge had signed. My name was also written in the Lamb's book of life. The Judge of all judges had personally made that entry. I had victory in Jesus and the peace of knowing absolutely nothing could change that.

I also remembered I had read: "But as many as received Him, to them He gave power to become the sons of God" According to God's Word, I was a joint-heir with Jesus Christ. I knew what I had. I also knew no one could take it away from me. Everything else was just incidental to me now.

However, this in no way stopped me from doing everything in my power to break the physical bonds I was under. While I was at the reception center, I did everything I could think of in order to raise enough money to post my bond.

At one point, my younger brother, Louie, told me he had the $10,000 I needed to post my $100,000 appeal bond. He had even promised to bring the money to my attorney's office in New Jersey later that same day. I was elated. I didn't think it would take my brother very long to drive from Staten Island, where he was living, over to New Jersey. I really believed I was mere hours away from freedom.

After our phone call had ended, I was counting the hours until my release. Since we both had a very close relationship, I had no reason to doubt Louie was going to do what he had promised me.

While I awaited a call over the PA system at the reception center beckoning me to the front office, I decided to go out to the recreation field for a walk. While I was walking, I was communing with the Lord. I was thanking Him for His faithfulness and for such a quick delivery on his promise. I was absolutely overjoyed.

Suddenly, this verse of scripture popped into my mind: "Confidence in an unfaithful man in time of trouble is like a broken tooth, and a foot out of joint." I was dumbfounded. I knew that particular verse of scripture was found in the book of Proverbs in Chapter 25 and verse19. Once that verse of scripture entered my mind, I knew exactly what God was saying to me.

My dearly beloved brother was going to let me down. I hoped against all logic I was wrong. I hoped I was misunderstanding what I had just heard. I even tried to convince God my brother would never let me down like that. Yet, He gently assured me it was so. However, He encouraged me that even this shocking turn of events would turn out for good.

Our heavenly Father consoled me with the promise He still had every intention of bringing about my release. Until that time came, I knew I just had to patiently endure. This was quite a hard pill to swallow. Patience was definitely not one of my virtues. At the time, I had no idea God was preparing me for the long haul and was about to give me more patience than I could ever dream existed.

As I was forewarned, my brother failed me. He never showed up at my lawyer's office. I was devastated. I couldn’t understand how my own flesh and blood could abandon me in my greatest hour of need. As much as it hurt me, I loved him enough to determine I would never hold it against him. I understood he was still lost and blind. Therefore, my beloved brother was subject to the god of this world. All I could do was pray for him. I did.

I tried to focus on the task at hand. I continued my quest for the knowledge I would need in order to convince God I could stand on His Word and was ready to be released from prison. I had hopes I could accomplish this feat before I was shipped from Lake Butler on to another prison.

To my disappointment, my efforts weren’t enough. I was eventually transferred to the Baker Correctional Institution in North Florida. This really upset me. Baker's location was even further away from where my family lived. I had expected I would at least be assigned to a prison reasonably close to home.

When I arrived there, I was quite surprised. Except for the high, barbed wire fence and the gun towers surrounding the compound, Baker had the appearance of a college campus. Unfortunately, some of the inmates I was to meet there quickly changed any misconceptions I had about the place.

Once I was processed into the institution, I was

assigned to my dormitory. A short time later, I had my first encounter with one of the undesirables from the inmate population. It wasn't good. Considering what I had already experienced in the county jail, I didn't expect it would be.

I had just unpacked my belongings and was attempting to take a hot, relaxing shower. The shower was hot alright, but definitely not relaxing. During the entire time I was bathing, some other inmate had been lusting after my body and proclaiming to the other inmates in the dorm how he was planning on making me his 'boy.'

As this evil doer rambled on and on, I couldn't help but become more and more uncomfortable about being in the nude. I dried off and hastily put my clothes back on. Meanwhile, the big mouth had gotten the attention of the entire dormitory. All eyes were on him and me.

At that point, I knew I had to act. I didn't want to get into a fight and go to lockup on my first day there. Yet, I didn't think I had much of a choice. I knew I had to show the rest of the inmates I was not a coward. If I didn't put up a fight, I was sure others would be trying to take advantage of me and I would have more problems than I could have imagined.

I decided I had to make an example out of the guy who was harassing me. In order to do so, I figured it would be best for me to move out of view of the officer stationed inside the dorm. I walked over to the water fountain located in a hallway outside the showers. This area gave the officer a limited view.

I was still naive enough to hope if I walked right up to my tormentor and showed him no fear, he would cease from his verbal attack. No such luck. Instead, the attack escalated. He stood toe to toe with me, raised his right hand and pointed his finger in my face. As he did this, he declared I was surely going to be his boy. This was a big mistake on his part.

At that point, I decided I had had enough. I

struck him on the side of his jaw with a hammer blow. He fell back against the wall. I could see the expression of unbelief on his face. Afterwards, I expected he had gotten the message and would leave me be.

Not quite. He quickly regained his composure and leaped at me grabbing my legs just below the knees. As he did so, I wrapped my arms around his body in order to prevent him from slamming me onto the floor. He quickly attempted to lift me up over his head and do exactly that.

His plan failed. I was not about to let him succeed with that maneuver. While I was holding onto my attacker for dear life, a group of other inmates grabbed hold of my attacker and me. Then, they separated us from one another.

A short time later, the authorities came rushing into the dorm and took hold of my attacker and me. One of the officers, a sergeant, inquired as to what had been the cause of the fight. Once they had sorted the whole matter out, the officers decided to take my opponent to lockup.

To my surprise, the other inmates had backed up my side of the story. Therefore, the officers released me and instructed me to go to my bunk. I wasn't even given a disciplinary report for the incident. So went my formal introduction to the inmate population at Baker CI.

"Be anxious for nothing, but in everything, by prayer and supplication with thanksgiving, let your requests be made known unto God. And the peace of God, which passes all understanding, shall keep your hearts and minds through Christ Jesus." (Philippians 4:6-7)

THE PRESSURE COOKER

Being in a hostile environment didn't affect me as much as being away from my loved ones. I figured I would not see any of them for a while. This put a burden on my heart. Therefore, I determined I would work harder on raising the money for posting my bond. This was a task which seemed to be getting more difficult by the day. However, I knew I couldn't let that bother me. I had to stay focused.

God hadn't run out of miracles. At any time, I knew He could provide me with everything I needed. I felt sure my situation was simply the result of His testing me. As I read my Bible more and more, I became more focused on his will and less occupied with my surroundings.

The Baker Correctional chapel was very well equipped. There was a cassette tape room where the inmates had access to numerous tapes containing sermons and teachings by some of the best Christian ministers. Since the chapel was open on a regular basis, I spent much of my free time there. Whenever I wasn't working in the kitchen, my assigned job, I could be found in the chapel.

I constantly listened to and learned from such awesome preachers as Kenneth Hagin, Chuck Swindoll, and Charles Stanley. When I wasn't in the chapel or at work, I spent every spare moment I had saturating my mind with God's Word. I also read a lot of materials pertaining to the Bible.

Eventually, all this had a profound effect on my thinking process. While this was taking place God was busy creating circumstances that allowed me to get my feet wet in spiritual warfare. During such times, I did indeed learn how to apply the Word of God to the situations I found myself in. Most importantly, I learned His Word does not fail.

I didn't know it at the time, but I couldn't fail either. You see, Jesus promised the Holy Spirit would comfort, teach, and reveal the truth to God's children. In the Gospel of John, Chapter 14 verse 26 Jesus said, "But the Comforter, which is the Holy Spirit, whom the Father will send in my name, He shall teach you all things, and bring all things to your remembrance, whatsoever I have said unto you."

God was manifesting this promise in my life. Since I had accepted Jesus as my Saviour, God had given me the Holy Spirit of promise. This is awesome. The very same Spirit who raised Jesus from the dead lived in me and this Spirit had created a hunger in me for God's Word.

In 1 Peter 2:2, God instructs His people, "As newborn babes, desire the sincere milk of the Word that you may grow thereby." Just as a baby needs to be fed in order to grow, a spiritual child needs the nourishment of the Word of God. Just as a baby relies on its parents and they provide for that child, God had been providing me with everything I needed. I was indeed becoming what He had created me to be.

When it pertains to the welfare of their children, good parents will overlook nothing. The Father of creation didn't either. Once I learned this fact, a team of wild horses couldn't have pulled me away from my Bible. The more I read it, the stronger my faith became. Therefore, I kept digging.

Eventually, I began to find out what an awesome teacher the Holy Spirit is. I was enjoying my spiritual journey so much, I pretty much lost track of time. If I hadn't missed my girlfriend and my newborn son, I wouldn't have even cared about being incarcerated.

About six months passed by. One day, I was speaking to my lawyer over the phone. By that time, I had exhausted every possible avenue of coming up with the $10,000 deposit I needed to post my bond. Then, Lee caught me totally by surprise.

"I am going to borrow $10,000 from the bank

and use the money to post your bond," he suddenly announced.

According to him, our mutual friend, Budd Lepman, offered to co-sign for the loan. I was overjoyed, amazed and quite shocked. I could hardly believe what I was hearing. Apparently, God had stirred up the hearts of two of my friends and my delivery was in the works.

Budd was like a father to me but I knew it was God's prompting which was causing him to go out on a limb and co-sign for a $10,000 loan. In Proverbs Chapter 21 verse one it reads, "The king's heart is in the hand of the Lord, as the rivers of water; He turns it wherever He wills." I was witnessing this firsthand.

Lee instructed me to call him back the following day. He also told me to line up a bondsman for him to contact. I thanked him profusely and agreed to follow his instructions. After our call ended, I called another friend of mine, Vinny.

Once I got him on the line, I explained I had just spoken to my lawyer and he was planning on posting my bond. Upon hearing this news, he was elated. He immediately offered to put his home up as collateral for my bond.

If I had any doubts about God being behind the events taking place, this offer completely squashed them. After all, how many people would offer to put up their home for someone other than a family member?

I thanked him very much for his offer to help. Then, I asked him the name and phone number of a bondsman he was well acquainted with. I had hoped I could have Lee contact him on my behalf. After supplying me with the number I requested, he instructed me to call him back as soon as I had heard from my lawyer again. I agreed to do so.

"I'll see you soon," Vinny encouraged.

Then, we ended our phone call. After receiving all that good news, I was so excited I could barely think straight. It all seemed too good to be true. But, I knew I wasn't just having a dream. No, this was a dream come true.

The following day as I spoke to Lee, I informed him I had found someone to put up collateral for my bail bond. I was so excited. I was finally getting the results God had promised me all along. However, I had no way of knowing it, but more testing was on the way. I wasn't quite out of the woods yet.

During our conversation, I gave Lee the information concerning the bondsman which Vinny had given me. Then, he informed me he should have the loan from the bank within 24 hours. He promised he would make all the arrangements to have me released as soon as he received the money for the loan.

We ended our conversation on that happy note. When I called him the following day, he told me he had gotten the loan from the bank. Then, he promised me he would contact the bondsman and have him contact the judge.As we ended our conversation, Lee promised me he would fill me in on the progress of everything when I called him the following day. At that point, I joyfully agreed to call him as instructed. Afterwards, I opened my Bible and started reading it. As I did this, I came across Philippians 4:19. This verse states: "But my God shall supply all your need according to His riches in glory, by Christ Jesus."

I thought on that verse for a moment. Then, I realized I had just experienced that promise. *"How awesome is the God I serve?"* I thought to myself. I was in awe.

At that point in my life, I realized I was not just some schlep trying to overcome the world system on my own. No! The God of all creation was on my side now. I had the real powers- that-be working on my behalf for a change. As God's Word had promised me, I was now an over comer.

When I called Lee the following day I did not receive the news I was expecting. Instead, he informed me the bondsman would not post my bond. Turns out he wanted us to put up more collateral, before he would agree to do so. I was shocked. What an utter disappointment. Vinny's home was worth about $250,000. I couldn't understand why that wasn't enough collateral. Lee was very apologetic, but that didn't console me much.

I was dumbfounded, but the Holy Spirit quickly reminded me of what I had read in my Bible the day before. After that word of encouragement, I was sure God would complete the work He had begun on my behalf. In my spirit, I knew He was going to continue helping me. I had no doubt He was eventually going to free me from my physical bonds. I had no idea how, but I just knew He would.

When I regained my composure, I told Lee I would call Vinny and find out what other options we had. After we terminated our call, I made haste to call Vinny. Once I got him on the phone, I explained my situation. To my surprise, he told me not to worry. He promised to talk to a mutual friend of ours, Tony, for me. He explained he was sure Tony would agree to put up his home as added collateral for my bond.

“I'll call Tony and have him call the bondsman," Vinny promised.

As we ended our conversation, he instructed me to call him back the following day. Once again, I thanked him for helping me. I must admit I was quite surprised God had come up with the answer to my latest problem in such short order. Still, I knew I wasn’t totally out of the woods yet. Anything could still happen. I needed a little insurance.

After I hung up the phone, I went to my bunk and removed my Bible from the drawer where I kept it. I opened it up to Philippians 4:19. Then, I prayed and told God I was standing on His Word. He promised to supply all my needs, so I was taking Him up on it.

Since I knew He knew my needs, I fully expected Him to fulfill them. I asked Him to manifest His promise in my situation. Afterwards, I had no doubt

He would.

However, the testing still wasn't over. When I called Vinny the following day, the first thing he told me was Tony could not post his home as collateral for my bond. His wife wouldn't allow it. Of course, I was very disappointed.

Thank God, Vinny wasn't through yet. He explained Tony also had a condominium, which his wife was unaware of. Although he couldn't put up his home, he promised he would use his condo for the rest of the collateral I needed. Once again, I was shocked. God came through again in a way I never could have imagined.

As we terminated our conversation, he told me to call Lee and have him contact Tony. He also instructed me to get back to him on the following day. I hastily agreed.

Immediately, I made a call to Lee. I explained the latest development in my quest for my physical freedom. He was also delighted at the good news I passed on. He promised to get in touch with Tony and afterwards contact the bondsman. Then, he instructed me to call him once I was released. We ended our conversation on that high note.

However, later the following day I was still in prison and hadn't heard from anyone. Needless to say, I was getting a little weary. Discouragement was fighting hard to overcome my optimism. Thank God, it's just not my nature to quit. I was determined I wouldn't give up. In my heart, I knew God hadn't given up either.

I made a phone call to Lee's office in Farmingdale, New Jersey. Once I got him on the phone, he quickly explained the situation to me. It seemed Tony had filled out the necessary paperwork for the bondsman. Then, the bondsman had attempted to post the bond. When the judge received the necessary paperwork, he refused to sign the order for my release.

"The judge said he thought you would run, if you were released on bond," Lee apologetically explained.

I was livid.

"How could the judge do this? He can't prevent me from posting a bond, which he himself set, can he?" I demanded.

"He is the judge. He can do a lot of things to hinder your release. Right now he wants me present at a hearing. However, I'm going to call him and see if I can convince him otherwise", Lee promised.

After he had said all he could to encourage me, he told me to call him back the following day. I told him I would and that I was going to pray concerning the judge's decision. Then, I assured him God would somehow work it all out. At that point, we ended our phone conversation.

After I hung up the phone, I walked over to my bunk and just sat on it. I just wanted to cry. I was so close, but so far. At that moment, the Holy Spirit urged me to read my Bible. I opened up my locker drawer and took it out. As I opened my Bible, I turned right to the page where my eyes locked right onto Proverbs 16:7.

In that verse of scripture it states, "When a man's ways please the Lord, He makes even his enemies to be at peace with him." Wow! It hit me. I had read that verse just recently. This was the solution to my problem. Had I already forgotten this verse of scripture in the confusion?

No matter. The Holy Spirit hadn't forgotten and He just reminded me where the answer to my problem was. I quickly went into prayer and brought that verse of scripture to God's attention. Then, I asked Him to manifest this word of His into my situation as promised.

After I prayed, I was confident I wasn't going to be denied my freedom much longer. I knew God was about to deliver on His promise to me. I finally felt at peace. I knew He had heard my prayer and I was sure I qualified for that promise. I was doing my very best to please Him and I had no intentions of going back to my old ways. He knew my heart and knew full well of my intentions.

I also knew God had seen what the judge was doing to me. I was sure He didn't want him to prevent me from posting my bond. After all, hadn't He been the One who had provided me with the means to post it in the first place? I knew he hadn't brought me this far just to disappoint me.

I was right. The following afternoon, I called Lee at his office. He was quick to give me the good news. He joyfully informed me he had spoken with the judge earlier that day and he had agreed to sign the order for my release. He also told me the bondsman was in the process of having me released.

My time had actually come. I can't begin to explain how excited I was. I was about to be a free man again. I wouldn't be totally free, but at least I would be out from under the supervision of the Florida Department of Corrections.

Lee instructed me to call him after I got settled in. I agreed and we ended our conversation. After I hung up the phone, I picked it back up again and dialed my mother's phone number. I could hardly wait to give her the good news.

Once I got her on the phone, I told her I would see her that night. She was overjoyed. Our conversation ended on that happy note. Then, I left my dorm and went walking around the perimeter of the compound. As I strolled, I praised God for His faithfulness. I felt like I was walking on air.

Later that afternoon, I was called to the front office and released from custody. I'll never forget the joy I felt as I left the prison. My greatest joy lay in my knowing I had God in my life now. Having my physical freedom was great, but knowing I was about to go out into the world for the first time as a child of God was even greater. This just added icing to the cake for me.

Indeed I was seeing everything in a different light. Now, I could really appreciate God's creation. Although I had always appreciated creation before, even the little things seemed so important to me now. I now had a personal relationship with their Creator. He was on my side. I was His chosen. I was in total awe of him.

I was also joyous because I knew I was finally going to be able to prove, to all who doubted it, that I was a new creature in Christ. I felt compelled to show the world around me-especially my family this truth. Most importantly, I wanted to show God I would be as faithful to Him as He had been to me. (As if He didn't already know exactly what I was going to do).

At any rate, I was anxious to serve God out in society. I knew I could never repay Him for all He had done for me, but I sure planned on giving it my best effort.

At the time, I had no idea how much opposition I was going to face. Like most other Christians, I thought mountaintop experiences are followed with more of the same. I soon learned such is not the case. Before I knew it, I was down in the valley again. But, at least this time I knew I wasn't alone. Thankfully, I knew I could stand on God's Word and He would give me the desired results as long as I qualified for the promise. Otherwise, I would have had no hope of standing up to the enemies' onslaught which I had encountered.

"if from there you shall seek the Lord your God, you shall find Him, if you seek Him with all your heart and with all your soul." (Deuteronomy 4:29)

OUTSIDE THE BOX

Once I arrived at my mom's, I quickly realized why God had taught me to stand on His Word. Many temptations lay ahead of me. If God had not prepared me, I would have undoubtedly fallen into the snares awaiting me. There is absolutely no way I could have otherwise passed the tests I was faced with. Without the knowledge of God's Word, I would have been no match for the wiles of the devil.

For example, I never expected my mom to react towards my situation as she did. Immediately upon my arrival, I was faced with strife in my own family. Of course, the Word of God promises this very thing. "And a man's foes shall be them of his own household." (Matthew 10:36) I was also tempted with peer pressure, discouragement, and fear.

At the time, my girlfriend and I were trying to put our lives back together. However, we couldn't even afford our own place. We were forced to live with my mom. The problem was my mom was living in a one bedroom apartment.

Needless to say, this led to some unpleasant conditions. To top it off, my girlfriend and me had a six month old baby boy to care for and mom quickly made it clear she didn't really want the three of us staying there with her.

This was fine with my girlfriend. She didn't want to stay there with my mom anyway. To compound the problem, my sister and my girlfriend didn't get along. Unfortunately, my sister was living in an apartment downstairs from my mom at the time.

All of these circumstances combined to make our situation very uncomfortable. My girlfriend was looking for any possible way out of the apartment. After just having spent 14 months behind bars, I just wanted to settle in and enjoy some long awaited peace.

Regardless, I wasn't about to let my

circumstances dominate my feelings. I was simply looking to serve God and enjoy my newfound freedom. Meanwhile, the devil was steadily trying to put an end to my resolve.

The day after I was released on bond, Vinny and Tony paid me a visit. They congratulated me on my release and then quickly tried to get me back into crime. They informed me of a score they were planning for me to carry out.

As we concluded our 'reunion,' they told me they would call me the following day with more information on the victim. They were really gung-ho on it. However, I really wanted no part of it. But, I knew I had to be more than diplomatic about it. Therefore, I didn't turn their proposition down initially.

At the time, I was afraid to tell them I had given my life to Jesus. I figured they would think I had flipped out. If that happened, I knew there was always the possibility Vinny and Tony could change their minds about putting up their property for my bond. If I made the wrong move, I figured they might even get the bondsman to cancel my bond and I would be back in prison.

I didn't know how to deal with this situation, but I knew someone who did. I prayed and trusted Vinny and Tony would change their minds about the score they planned. I even hoped a situation would arise which would make the score look less desirable to them.

Meanwhile, my girlfriend asked me what I had planned to do. Understandably, she just wanted me to get some money so we could move out of my mom's apartment. When I told my girlfriend I didn't know what I was going to do she said: "Maybe their offer to do a rip off is God's way of helping you to get started again."

"That isn't God!" I emphatically responded.

At that point, I grabbed my pocket Bible and turned to Philippians 4:19.

"Read this," I boldly instructed her.

After she read the scripture, I explained how God

had taught me to stand on His Word.

"The Word of God worked for me while I was in jail and it will not fail me now that I'm out. I trusted God and His promises to get me out of prison and He delivered. Now, I'm going to stand on His Word just the way He taught me. He will provide all of our needs," I confidently insisted.

At this point, I knew I needed to find a job quick. Unfortunately, I didn't have a lot of options. I wasn't very skilled. I could no longer depend on my talents concerning thoroughbred horse racing. I had no idea what kind of work I could possibly do to earn a decent living. I prayed.

A short time later, I recalled from my former dining experiences that waiters made pretty good money. Whenever I ate out, I tipped my waiter at least 20% of the bill. The Lord then encouraged me with the idea I could learn how to serve tables relatively easy. Since I knew what I expected from a good waiter, I didn't feel I would have too many problems giving people what they wanted insofar as service goes. This seemed to be my best option for earning quick cash.

I began to scan the local paper for job opportunities. At the time, I had very little cash on hand. Therefore, I figured I would not have enough money to carry us through until I could bring home my first paycheck. Thankfully, I had one option. I decided I would sell the one piece of jewelry I had left.

Since my girlfriend had sold all of the other valuables which I had left her, I considered the fact we still possessed this ring to be the work of God. After I had been arrested, my girlfriend had been very stressed out and had used various drugs to help her cope. The only valuable she hadn't sold or pawned was this ring. It was made of gold. It was in the shape of a lion's head. It contained a number of diamonds encased in the gold and it had rubies in the eyes. My girlfriend knew this had been my favorite piece of jewelry. Perhaps that was the reason she had held onto it. However, I had no reservations about selling it.

My girlfriend and I took the ring to a pawn shop. The owner there offered to give me $300 for it. I felt it was worth much more. At any rate, I knew I had to sell it so I did. When I thought about it later, I realized getting $300 from a pawn shop for my ring was actually a blessing from God.

Once we had the cash, my girlfriend and I felt a little more at ease about our situation. Yet, I knew this wouldn’t last for long. I had to find a job as quickly as possible. When we returned to my mom's later that day, a friend of my sister's was visiting her. This particular woman lived in the apartments across the street from my mom's.

In fact, this woman actually managed the building across the street from my mom’s. She was looking for new tenants. After we were introduced, the woman told me my sister had informed her that my girlfriend and I needed an apartment. When I acknowledged the fact, she told me she had a vacancy in her building.

Actually, I wasn't ready to move just yet. I explained to her I didn't have much money and I wasn't even employed.

"That's okay, come and see the apartment and we'll talk," she insisted.

My girlfriend was quick to accept the invitation. I figured we had nothing to lose, so I agreed to go along. On our way to the apartment, we passed through the courtyard of the building. I noticed there was a swimming pool located in the center of the complex. At that point, I figured this was going to be expensive.

Once we arrived at the apartment, the woman opened the door leading inside. We stepped inside and I quickly noticed how dinghy the apartment looked. When I commented on it, the woman told me she would supply us with all the paint we needed in order to liven the place up.

While we toured the one-bedroom apartment, I

calculated what it would cost for us to settle in. In my estimation, there was no way it was feasible for my girlfriend and me to pull this off.

As I was pondering this thought, the woman asked: "What do you think?"

"Right now, I couldn't even afford to turn the electricity on and we don't even have any furniture," I half heartedly explained.

"No problem," she replied.

She flipped the light switch up and to my surprise the lights went on.

"The power is still on. We will leave it on until you can afford to have it switched over into your name. As far as furniture, we have plenty of used furniture in some of the other apartments here. We will give you whatever you need," she offered.

"How much do I need to move in?" I asked.

"One month's rent and one month's security, but you can just give me $100 down right now and the rest of the money in payments," she replied.

I was absolutely amazed. God had swiftly provided our needs in a big way. I wasted no time giving the woman the $100 deposit. Afterwards, she gave me a key to the apartment and told me I could start painting as soon as I liked. Needless to say, my girlfriend was elated.

The following day, I saw an ad in the local paper for a waiter in an upscale seafood restaurant. This particular restaurant was located in Sunny Isles. It wasn't too far from where our new apartment was located.

I called the number listed and was given an appointment for an interview later on that afternoon. When I arrived, the maitre d' greeted me. He informed me he was the one in charge of hiring new employees. As it turned out, he was an avid horse racing fan.

As soon as the he read my employment application and discovered I had been involved in horse racing, he befriended me. I knew I had landed the job.

After a long discussion between us concerning horse racing, my new 'friend' told me to come in the following day. Right on the spot, he had scheduled me to start training for the server's position.

Once again, I was amazed at God's provision. He had truly made His Word come to pass and He did it in a faster time period than I could ever have imagined. Everything was falling into place. What a difference a day makes - when God is on your side.

However, I still had more trials to face. Later on that same day, Vinny called me and told me everything was set up for the score Tony and him had been working on. I was completely caught off guard. I didn't know what to say. All of a sudden, the Holy Spirit spoke to me.

"Just tell Vinny you don't think you should attempt to work with him just yet; because you feel you could be under surveillance," He suggested.

I knew that thought had to come from God, because I didn't have a clue what I could do to remedy my dilemma. So, I did just what was suggested to me. I also told Vinny it would probably be better if we were careful about contacting one another for a while. I explained I wanted to wait until I could be sure whether or not this was the case. Something must have clicked in Vinny's mind. He told me he appreciated my concern and agreed I should check things out before we attempted to pull anything off. He agreed I could possibly be under some sort of surveillance.

He promised he would check back with me in a few days and we ended our conversation on that note. To my delight, I never heard from Vinny or Tony again. The Lord had worked everything out for me once again. I was so appreciative for all He had done in my life. I was so happy. I felt I could finally just live a 'normal' life with my girlfriend and our newborn son.

This newfound peace did not last for very long. I didn't realize it at the time, but I had made a big mistake with my choice for a mate. I had allowed my fleshly desires to cloud my better judgment. I hadn't considered the fact that my girlfriend was almost 15 years younger than me. I also hadn't considered her spiritual condition. Unfortunately, I wasn't aware it really mattered. I could not have been more wrong.

It was my sincere desire to live my life for Jesus. My main purpose in life had become to do whatever God willed. I was very passionate about serving Him. However, my girlfriend didn't share the vision. Since she wasn't born again, she had no desire to change her lifestyle. She enjoyed partying and wasn't through sowing all her wild oats just yet. Unfortunately, she hadn't yet reached the point in her life where she felt she needed to change.

To top it all off, shortly after my release from prison I had made my girlfriend pregnant again. She had absolutely no desire to keep our second child. In her mind, having two healthy children was not a blessing it was an intrusion into her lifestyle.

She made it clear to me she was afraid and didn't want another child. I could understand her fear. After all, she didn't know whether or not I would have to go back to prison someday. If so, how could she survive?

At the tender age of 19, my girlfriend felt as though she had totally lost control of her life. She didn't really want the responsibility that was being placed upon her. I sympathized with her plight, so I consented when she told me she wanted to get an abortion.

I accepted the rationalization, that if it were aborted, the child would only be going back to God. *If this child never has to face the cruelties of this world, it would be better off,* I reasoned with myself. Then, I prayed about it. I honestly don't remember if I was just praying to try and get God's stamp of approval on our plans.

Meanwhile, my girlfriend wasted no time scheduling an appointment to have the abortion. I agreed to take her to get the procedure done. However, on the day I was supposed to take her to the doctor, the Holy

Spirit convicted me so heavily I just couldn't bring myself to do it.

I tried to dissuade my girlfriend about having the procedure. However, she had already made up her mind and in no way agreed with my proposal to keep the baby.

"You've got three boys already. Why do you want another one?" she pleaded.

"How do you know this child isn't a girl?" I confidently retorted.

"You only make boys," she replied. (I already had three sons at the time).

At that point, the Holy Spirit came on me and with all boldness I blurted out:

"We are going to have a girl, and we are going to name her Faith. I'm going to show you what faith in God can do!"

My girlfriend was shocked by the words she had just heard. God must have touched her heart too. She accepted the fact I wasn't going to allow her to have an abortion. At that point, I thought the matter was settled. As time went on, I found out differently. I could sense she resented the fact she had agreed to carry the baby to full term.

During the next few months, we had numerous spats. She wanted to go partying most of the time. I really didn't want to go to clubs anymore. Besides, we definitely were not in a position to spend what little money we had on partying. I tried to explain this, but my girlfriend liked to get high and didn't care.

If I had allowed it, she would have smoked pot on a daily basis. As far as I was concerned, I didn't want to smoke marijuana at all. Eventually, I came to the realization we were both headed in different directions. For example, I never wanted to miss a worship service. On the other hand, my
Girl friend didn't really even want to go to church. Each time I tried to get her prepared to go to church, she would strive with me. Her pet excuse was she didn't

want to attend church because she didn't have a sufficient wardrobe.

I couldn’t understand why she wasn’t grateful for what we had. I sure was. On a regular basis, she complained about what we didn't have. I tried to solve the problem by getting her some new clothes to wear to church. I figured this would make her happy. She still complained. Considering what God had already done for us, I couldn’t understand why my girlfriend had such little faith. I didn’t like the fact she was always focusing on the negative. After all, I was an optimist. I absolutely believed as long as I continued following God, our standard of living would eventually improve.

Meanwhile, it seemed like we never had enough to make ends meet. No matter what I did, we just couldn’t stay ahead of our bills. I was making decent money serving tables, but we never seemed to be able to make financial progress. We always seemed to be one paycheck away from poverty.

As if my financial situation wasn’t already tough enough, I had a bitter disagreement with the owner of the restaurant where I was working. This resulted in me quitting my job. At the time, I figured I wouldn’t have any trouble finding new employment. I had turned out to be quite a competent waiter.

Unfortunately, I had failed to realize the tourist season in Miami was coming to a close. I couldn't have picked a worse time to abandon a well paying position and begin a new job search. Most of the tourists were already in the process of going back up North for the summer. Most restaurants were cutting back on their wait staff. My prospects were few and far between.

After I realized the predicament I was in, I prayed and asked the Lord to provide me with my needs. The following day, I went on a job interview and was hired on the spot. I was delighted because I had been hired to work in what I had heard was considered to be a classy restaurant.

However, I was not aware this particular place

had changed hands earlier that year. Unfortunately, the new owners of the restaurant hadn't kept up the standard of excellence the original founders had established.

When I reported to work my first day, I began to suspect things weren't up to par. After examining the menu, I realized it was going to be hard to make good money serving tables there. The food was inexpensive and the restaurant also offered an even cheaper 'early bird' menu.

When I met the wait staff, my suspicions were confirmed. I could tell by their demeanor the servers there weren't very experienced. Most of them were youngsters still in school. I couldn't picture any of them working in a fine dining atmosphere. When we opened for business that evening, I took note of the absence of a maitre d' at the door. It didn't look promising.

During the first few days I served tables there, I earned less money than I had earned working any one of my worst days at my previous job. I knew I was in big trouble. My worst fears were coming to pass. I knew there was no way I could possibly keep my new job and still manage to keep up with all of my bills.

Before I got myself into too deep of a hole, I took my situation back to the One who could remedy the problem. I prayed. After I presented my case to our Father, I received the peace only He can give. I didn't know how, but I knew He would fix things for me.

The following day as I prepared to start my shift as a server, I sensed something good was about to happen. I didn't have a clue as to what it was. I just knew it in my spirit. As I was picking up my guest checks from the cashier, people had already started to come into the restaurant. I noticed some of the people making their way towards station three.

At that point, the cashier informed me I was on station three that evening. I looked at my first guest check and proceeded to fill in the date in the box provided for it at the top of the check. It was March the third. So, I wrote three and three at the top of the check.

After I filled in the date, I wrote down the table number where my guests were seated. They were seated at table number three. I noticed there were three people seated at my table. So, I wrote three in the space provided on the check for the number of guests.

Then, I asked the cashier what my server number was for that evening. She told me I was server number three. As I wrote the number three in the space provided for it on the check, I got the thought the number three would have significant meaning to me. As I walked over to table three, I thought about how this could be possible.

When I arrived at table three, I greeted my guests. They were two women and one man. As I greeted the gentleman, I asked him if he frequented the horse races. He acknowledged he did. Then, I showed him all the number threes at the top of his guest check. For some strange reason, I felt compelled to suggest to him the number three might be his lucky number the next time he goes to the track.

Afterwards, I gave each of my guests the menus and took their drink order. Shortly thereafter, they placed their drink order. With order in hand I made my way over to the bar. When I arrived, I was still preoccupied with what all those number threes meant to me.

A few moments later, I received table threes drinks and brought them over to my guests. After I had placed everybody's drink in front of them, I proceeded to take their dinner order.

Once my guests had placed their order, I went into the kitchen. After I placed my order with the chef, I picked out three dinner salads for my guests. I placed the salads onto a tray and went back into the dining room.

As I came out of the kitchen, I noticed a group of people walking over towards another one of my tables. I walked over to table three and delivered the salads to my guests. Afterwards, I turned around and headed towards my newly seated table of guests.

As I arrived there, I noticed there were five guests. I also quickly took note they were seated at table five. At that moment, I realized the five was also going to have significance to me. *The three and five are going to be my numbers,* I thought to myself. However, I had no idea why I thought that. But for some strange reason, I just knew it.

To put it mildly, I was taken aback. After a moment or two, I continued to serve my tables. It was difficult to stay focused on doing my job that night. I just couldn't seem to get this idea of the three and five out of my mind.

The rest of the evening seemed to pass by more quickly than normal. Nothing else relating to the events which took place earlier happened that night. On my way home after my shift, I couldn't help but wonder what my earlier experience was all about.

When I arrived home, I explained the whole experience to my girlfriend.

"I think the Lord is trying to bring me to the racetrack in order to bet on the three and five, but I'm not sure. I have no idea when I should go much less what race I should bet on. What do you think I should do?" I asked her.

"Do whatever you want. If God's behind this, you will know," she matter-of-factly offered.

"The Lord is good unto those who wait for Him, to the soul that seeks Him." (Lamentations 3:25)

UNFORGETTABLE

The following morning, I awoke with the feeling I should go to the racetrack. However, I was reluctant. I really couldn't be sure God was behind the whole experience I had the night before. Since I barely had enough money to pay my bills, I surely didn't want to gamble any of it away.

I made my way into the kitchen and bid my girl friend good morning.

"What are you going to do? Are you going to the track?" she curiously inquired.

"I don't know. First, I have to go to get a money order and send off some bill payments. After I'm finished, I'll see what happens," I responded.

After we finished breakfast, I gathered up the bills and bid her goodbye. As I drove to the post office, I took my time. I was not in a hurry. I was in fact stalling for time. Although I felt compelled to go to the track, I really didn't want to go there. I just couldn't believe God would send me to the racetrack to make a bet. I was not sure what to make of it all.

As I think back on it, I guess I thought if I waited long enough, God would show me it wasn't His will after all. As I exited the post office, I decided to go to the nearest gas station and fill up my tank.

Once I arrived at the filling station, I proceeded to pump gas into my car’s tank. While the gas was pumping, I opened the hood and started checking the engine fluids. I was in no hurry to go anywhere. I cleaned my windshield and considered checking the air in my tires next.

All of a sudden, the thought came into my mind I should go to the racetrack immediately. However, I knew that thought was not my own. Yet, at that instant, I knew I had to go to the racetrack. I had to find out what this was all about. I didn't hesitate for one second longer.

I responded to what I had just heard by quickly closing the hood of my car, getting into my vehicle and starting the motor.

By this time, the adrenalin in my body was flowing full throttle. All of a sudden, I had absolutely no doubt God was about to give me an awesome display of His power. I put the car into drive and took off towards the city of Hallandale Beach. From past experience, I was aware the Florida racing circuit was having their Gulfstream Park meet at the time and they would be racing there..

As I was driving along, I had no idea how long it would take for me to arrive at my destination. Yet, I had no doubt I would get there at the exact moment God wanted me to arrive. Even though I was quite anxious by then, I knew there was no need to hurry.

When I arrived at the track, I considered where I should park. Since I was no longer a jockey, I didn't have a horseman's sticker. This would have allowed me to park in the horseman's parking lot. I realized my only option was to park in the grandstand parking lot and pay the fee.

As I turned off of US 1 and into the parking lot of Gulfstream Park Racetrack, a parking attendant directed me into the grandstand parking lot. As I approached the ticket booth, I paid the parking fee and was directed to a row of empty parking spots.

As the attendant waved me on, I noticed I would be parking my car in aisle 35. There it was again! When I saw the three and five on the sign in the parking lot, I could've jumped through the roof of my car. At that moment, the Lord spoke to me in my spirit again.

"Go right in and bet the three and the five," He firmly instructed me.

I couldn't get to the entrance fast enough. On my way there, I briefly considered buying the Racing Form. This was a customary practice for me all during my racing career. Although I rarely gambled, I was a pretty good handicapper and would usually be able to figure out what horses were worth a bet and what ones weren't. Since I hated wasting money, I guess I wanted to check out the three and five before I made a wager on them. I still wasn't sure God was behind my experience.

However, I was soon assured I needn't 'waste' my money on the racing form this time.

"Just go," He urged.

I paid my entrance fee and immediately did exactly as directed. After I had placed my bet, I picked up a track program and made my way to a seat in the upper grandstand. Once I sat in the seat I had selected, I looked up at the tote board. It indicated there was three minutes left until post time for the third race.

There it was. I had been subjected to the three again and again. At that moment, it dawned on me the Lord had told me the three was going to win the race. All of a sudden, He spoke to my spirit again and reminded me He had told me in the beginning the three was going to win. Suddenly, I had absolutely no doubt the three was going to win. At that point, I decided I had to exercise faith and absolutely should bet more on the three.

God had graciously just been given an additional surge of faith. I decided to go for it. I was now so sure of it, I would have bet my life on the three. I knew that I knew I had definitely heard from God and He couldn't be wrong. There was no other logical explanation.

I quickly made my way back to the betting windows. Once I arrived there, I took out my wallet and placed all I could afford to bet on the number three to win. Afterwards, I made my way back to the seat I had chosen.

Once I arrived, there, I sat down to watch the race. Seconds later, the race started and the number three horse went to the front. At that point, I don't remember what position the five horse was in but that didn't matter.

As the horses approached the stretch, the three was still leading the pack. Then, the five made his move. As the horses crossed the finish line, the three was first and the five was second. I was in awe. My knees started to shake and I recalled the account in the Bible when Isaiah the prophet had an encounter with God. At that point, I knew exactly how Isaiah must have felt.

As he stood in the physical presence of God, Isaiah stated, "Oh woe is me, for I am undone; because I am a man of unclean lips…for mine eyes have seen the King, the Lord of hosts." (Isaiah 6:5)

Although I didn't physically see God, I was awed by the fact He was definitely right there--with me! In that instant, I felt like a cockroach. There I stood in the middle of the floor and someone had just turned on the light. It was too late. I had no where to run. I was so vulnerable. I had never felt so inadequate in all my life.

Oh my God, why me? Why would the awesome Creator of the universes choose me? I am the least of the least. What did I do to deserve such an honor, I questioned Him in my spirit?

In His gentle comforting way He spoke to my heart again.

"Don't be afraid. I am for you. Truly, what you have just witnessed is unlike anything you have ever experienced, or heard of, in all of your years on the racetrack. I have given you this insight so you will never again doubt I Am is in complete control of your life. I Am is omnipotent, omnipresent, and omniscient. I will provide for you. Everything will be alright. Only trust Me". He proclaimed.

God had just beaten me at my own game so-to-speak. In the many years I had been involved in horse racing, I had never witnessed anything even remotely close to what had just taken place. He had just brought home His point in a way I never would have imagined was possible. .

Later, He reminded me what I had read earlier in the book of Jeremiah Chapter 33 verse 3. It states:"Call unto me and I will answer you, and show you great and mighty things, which you know nothing about."

Wow! He sure made that scripture a realization

to me today, I thought to myself. That afternoon, I came to the realization God was in total control of every little detail of my life. In fact, I had no doubts ever again. I know without a doubt nothing, absolutely nothing on this green earth can ever happen which is not under His control.

Most importantly, I had just learned, beyond any shadow of a doubt, He was the One I could always depend on. Even when I couldn't depend on myself, He would be there to take control of my circumstances. I was so amazed. I still am.

Before I go any further, I want to make something known to all who are reading this book. I don't believe for one moment that God condones gambling. I also want it to be known God never told me to go to the racetrack and place a bet ever again. Nor did he lead me to gamble in any other way, shape, or form.

However, concerning the incident I just described in this chapter, I don't believe God was ever coaxing me to gamble. After all, He already knew the outcome of the race before it started - didn't He? God is indeed omniscient. I do believe He made this point to me that day in a way far beyond my wildest imagination. In so doing, He proved to me He has not changed. He still knows everything from the beginning to the end. If I ever had any doubts about that, He put them to rest once and for all.

The point is that God still does what He wants to, when He wants to. Events such as the one I just described may prove to be too intense for some people's religious upbringing. God understands. However, He is still challenging us to let Him out of the box we have placed Him in.

Dare to trust Him with your whole life. Believe the scriptures. "For with God, nothing shall be impossible." (Luke 1:37) After all, every last word contained in the Bible is from the very mouth of God. Have the faith of a child and you too will see things you never imagined were possible.

If you diligently seek God, and get to know His will for your life, He will indeed show Himself to you in a variety of ways you never even imagined were possible. This verse of scripture from Matthew 5:8 promises, if your motives are pure you shall see Him. "Blessed are the pure in heart; for they shall see God."

If you seek God with all your heart, He promises you will find Him. I encourage you to read the Bible as much as you possibly can. Your faith will never grow unless you do. "So then, faith comes by hearing and hearing by the word of God." (Romans 10:17)

I believe God is just waiting for His followers to take a leap of faith. When we do, He can and will gladly reveal Himself to us in ways only He can imagine. "But without faith it is impossible to please Him; for he that comes to God must believe that He is, and that He is a rewarder of them that diligently seek Him." (Hebrews11:6)

A personal relationship with the God of all creation is an awesome thing! It should be treasured and sought after by anyone who professes to be a child of His. Why live a mundane life? There is so much more to this life than we can see. God is just waiting for us to reach out to Him so He can show us what we have been missing. "For the eyes of the Lord run to and fro throughout the whole earth, in order that He may show Himself strong in the behalf of them whose heart is perfect toward Him." (II Chronicles 16:9)

"My thoughts are not your thoughts, neither are my ways your ways says the LORD." (Isaiah 55:8)

NOT SO SWEET SURRENDER

As promised, God provided me with all of my needs. Shortly after my racetrack experience, He brought me into a better job. One afternoon, I happened to be looking in the newspaper for job opportunities. I was in my sister's apartment. While I was there, a friend of my sister's, Betty, came by to visit her.

She saw me looking in the classified ads and asked what kind of work I was looking for. I told her I was looking for a job as a server. She told me there was an ad in that day's paper for phone sales people. It stated they were looking for people to sell home improvements via the telephone. My first response was negative. However, Betty pointed out the salary they offered also included a commission. It was very good.

Since I had been working for a labor pool receiving minimum wages at the time, I gave the ad serious consideration. I had been doing back breaking work unloading boxcars in the hot, Florida sun. I figured I didn't have anything to lose, so I called the number listed. The gentleman who answered the phone, told me to come in for an interview that afternoon.

I showed up for the interview and to my surprise I was hired. I was scheduled to start the following day. I didn't know how long the job would last, but I figured I would hang on as long as I could. I had hopes something better would eventually be sent my way.

My hourly pay was about $3.00 an hour more than the pay I had been receiving for busting my hump unloading boxcars. I marveled at the fact I was getting paid such a high hourly wage to sit in an air conditioned office and make phone calls. Once again, I thanked God for His goodness to me.

However, my first day on the job left me with serious doubts as to how long I could actually survive doing that kind of work. This was due to the fact that the office manager fired the young man who was seated right next to me within my first two hours of employment. It seemed the young man wasn't producing enough to please him.

The office manager showed no mercy for the employee and made no bones about telling the young man what he thought of his sales abilities. Afterwards, he rudely told the guy to pack up his gear and hit the road. I remember thinking what a cold hearted, slave driver my new boss was.

I figured my days in that environment were undoubtedly numbered. Since I wasn't a very experienced salesman, I didn't think I would be able to please this guy for very long. If I couldn't produce, I knew what my fate would be.

But, the Lord had a plan. As I sat at my desk, I prayed and asked Him to help me to do my job in a way which would please my boss. After praying, I reviewed the sales pitch that the office manager had provided me with. As I spoke with prospective buyers, I was supposed to read the pitch which had been given to me verbatim. However, while using their pitch I didn't have much success. So, I prayed again and the Lord gave me a better one to use.

Immediately after my prayer, He gave me the thoughts and I quickly put them into words on a piece of paper. As soon as I started using the pitch he had given me, I began to make sales. Within a few days, I had become the office manager's favorite salesperson. In the meantime, he had noticed I was using my own pitch and rightly attributed that to my success. In fact, he asked me if I would give the pitch I was using to my co-workers. I readily agreed. My boss then vowed to give me a $500.00 bonus for doing so.

It seemed as though all my troubles were over. I finally had a nice, easy, well-paying job. Needless to say, I was very grateful for what the Lord had done in my life. I had been trying my best to live a life that was pleasing to Him and I appreciated the way He was rewarding my efforts.

Although things were indeed looking up, my trials weren't over yet. A few weeks later, I received a phone call from my lawyer. He informed me he had received notice from the courts that I had lost my appeal. He was told to instruct me to surrender to Judge Harper's court in West Palm Beach on the following Monday.

However, there was a bright side to it. My lawyer promised me he was sure he could get me back out on a federal appeal bond shortly after my surrender. He estimated I would be back out on the street within a couple of weeks.

As instructed, I surrendered to the Palm Beach county authorities. In my mind, Lee would swiftly arrange for me to post the federal appeals bond and I would be able to go home right from the county jail.

A few days later, those hopes were shattered. While I was still in the county jail, I was awakened from my sleep at about 3 a.m. and shipped to Lake Butler, Florida. I never imagined I was going to wind up back in 'red neck' country, but here I was.

I couldn't understand why God was allowing this to happen to me. After all, I had done all I could to live up to His expectations. I never believed I was going to have to spend any more time in prison than I already had.

Since the police had conducted an illegal search in order to obtain the evidence used in my conviction, I was sure my sentence would eventually be discarded. I was dumbfounded God allowed me to lose my appeal and now I was on my way back to prison.

I consoled myself with Lee's promise he would probably have me released on a federal appeal bond. I imagined there was a certain amount of red tape which had to be processed before my release. I just hoped this wouldn't take too long. *Maybe God just needed me to witness to someone who was being held at the Lake Butler Reception Center,* I thought to myself.

While I was being held there, I received notice my girlfriend had gone into labor and delivered a healthy, baby girl. She named her Faith. It was bittersweet news. I wasn't there to welcome my only daughter into the world. Worse yet, I couldn't even hold her in my arms. However, I was very grateful God had blessed me with my daughter. In the process, He once again proved He rewards our faith.

I was pleased, but I was also heartbroken. Another bitter disappointment soon followed my heartache. Shortly after I received the news of my newborn daughter, I was transferred back to Baker Correctional. Within a week of my arrival there, my lawyer informed me he was unable to convince the federal court to set a bond for me. I was told there was nothing else he could do.

I couldn't believe it. I had run out of options. I couldn't do a thing about my situation. From what Lee had told me, the federal court had accepted my appeal, but denied me a bond. Once again, I was at the mercy of the Department of Corrections. I was destined to serve more time.

Due to God's grace, I had no clue as to just how much time I would be forced to serve. That was a good thing. If I would have known I was going to be forced to serve another 13 years and 8 months in the Florida prison system, I probably wouldn't have been able to handle it.

Before I was recommitted, I had been out on an appeal bond for 10 months. During this time, I had been the recipient of many miracles. Therefore, I really wanted to share those experiences with other prisoners. In fact, I had prayed and asked God to put me into the prison ministry full time. I guess you could say I learned the hard way to be careful what you ask for.

At any rate, now I had a full time ministry to prisoners and I was determined to make the best of it.

Although this was not the way I had planned to begin my prison ministry, I still trusted God would work it all out for good.

By His grace, I made it through the next few months of adjusting to my life back in bondage. Meanwhile, my girlfriend tried to deal with her new life as a mom twice over. Unfortunately, she was still not mature enough to deal with her situation. In order to cope, she had resorted to drugs. The devil was quick to send men her way who were more than willing to fulfill her hunger for illegal drugs.

At the time, my girlfriend was living in the very same apartment building where my mom and my sister, Geri, lived. This created problems. She wanted to go on with her life and party hearty.

However, my mom and sister felt she was accountable to me. They tried to persuade her to consider take her responsibility as a mother and a 'wife' more seriously.

Being a hard-headed Italian, my girlfriend was bent on living her life on her own terms. I couldn't fault her for that. After all, hadn't I been exactly like her? But, my sister and my mom couldn't deal with it. Several times my sister had observed my girlfriend in some guy's apartment. Eventually, my sister was hurling accusations at her. The strife between the two of them began to escalate. One day, my sister and my girlfriend actually exchanged blows.

I was hearing stories from both ends. Worst of all, I couldn't do a thing about any of this. One day my mom informed me that my son, Justin, had just fallen off of the second story balcony at the apartment building. Thank God, he wasn't seriously injured from the fall.

At that point, I was totally at my wit's end. Fortunately for me, I did the right thing. I prayed. Actually, I cried out to God. I told Him I couldn't go on any longer. I asked Him to intervene in my situation right then and there. He did. He told me to open up my Bible. When I did, I looked down at the verse of scripture which caught my immediate attention.

"Why are you cast down o my soul, and why are you disquieted within me? Hope thou in God, for you shall yet praise Him for the help of His countenance." (Psalms 42:5) This was not what I had in mind, when I asked God for help. I was looking for physical deliverance. However, He gave me something more important than instant gratification.

The verse of scripture I read calmed my spirit down immediately. At that point, I had no doubt everything was going to be alright. In spite of my helplessness, I knew I was in God's hands and He was able. I will never forget how that one verse of scripture gave me the strength to go on. Just like God promised in His Word, I had the peace that passes all understanding.

He brought me to the realization there was absolutely nothing I could do for my girlfriend or my children. He knew exactly what it was going to take to get me to cast my burdens on Him. It was a hard thing to do. I had always been so self-sufficient. I was having the struggle of my life with this new concept of depending totally on God.

Thankfully, I had learned God's Word couldn't come back void. (This is written in the scriptures in Isaiah 55:11). Previously, He had shown me this was absolutely true again and again.

In His Word, He promised to take care of me and my family. I knew I couldn't do it. So, He made it easier for me by giving me the good sense to realize I had nothing to lose by trusting in Him -completely.

I simply did as He instructed and gave everything up to Him. It was quitting time for me once again. After I finally made up my mind to do that, I made a telephone call to my family and instructed them to leave my girlfriend alone. I explained she was doing the best she knew how and was going to do what she wanted to do anyway. I told them I was no longer concerned about what my girlfriend did or didn't do. Should she be there for me whenever I got out of prison, all would be forgiven. If not, I would survive.

After I spoke to my family, I wrote my girlfriend a long letter and explained my feelings to her. In the letter I explained what God had led me to do. I ended the letter by telling her I didn't want to hear from her or my family concerning what she was doing with her life anymore.

I also told her I was looking forward to my release some day and, if she was there when it Happened, we could start over. If not, we could just be friends. I told her I would always love and care for those children of ours. I prayed over the letter and sent it out in the mail that night. Once I did that, I felt my burden was completely lifted.

A short time later, I spoke with Lee and he told me we had run out of options. He informed me it looked like I was going to have to do the time after all. This was not what I wanted to hear, but I knew he had done all he could.

"When am I going to get out?" I pleaded.

"Well, the judge structured the sentence in order for you to be eligible for parole after three years. I don't see any reason for them to keep you any longer; as long as you keep your nose clean," he optimistically consoled me.

After hearing his explanation, I resigned myself to the fact I wasn't going to be paroled until I had served at least three years of my life sentence. Although I had no clue as to what was actually going to happen, I was determined to get my prison term over with as soon as possible.

At any rate, it wasn't easy trying to keep my nose clean as I went about my daily life in prison. It seemed like there was always someone who was looking for trouble bumping heads with me. Every time I turned around, there were other inmates who seemed to be bent on making my life miserable.

The first thing which really stood out to me in the prison environment was the lack of maturity among most inmates. I could hardly believe how they could make such problems for one another from the simplest of situations. It seemed to me they would have grown out of such behavior at much earlier stages in their lives.

From day one, I had determined in my heart I wasn't going to be taken advantage of. I would not allow anyone to have an inch when it came to exalting themselves over me. Throughout my life, I had always stood up for my rights. I wasn't about to stop doing this in a prison environment. I knew if the other inmates saw compromise, or any type of submission, it would be a sign of weakness.

If anything, I intended to show everybody I was one little Italian who was a force to be reckoned with. Unfortunately, this was not a very good Christian witness. In my mind, I felt my strength would also serve notice to the unbelievers that just because someone is a Christian, it doesn't necessarily mean he is weak.

It was with this mindset I served the first few years of my prison time. During this period, I had many altercations with other inmates. Some were unavoidable; for instance some other inmates tried to force themselves on me sexually. However, some of the other fights I was involved in could have been avoided. I realize now, if I would have just focused more on showing everybody the love of Jesus, I wouldn't have been so easily provoked.

I did try to witness about Jesus everywhere I went in the prison. Unfortunately, most of the inmates didn't want to hear what I had to say. Furthermore, most inmates just wanted to wreck my testimony and prove all Christians are phonies. As the Bible promises: " For the flesh lusts against the Spirit and the Spirit against the flesh; and these are contrary the one to the other; so that you cannot do the things that you would." (Galatians 5:17)

Knowing the Word of God as I did, I should have expected persecution from most of the other inmates. In my spirit, I understood what was happening.

But, in my flesh I couldn't accept the way some inmates would ‘try’ me for no apparent reason. This really agitated me and I would be quick to respond to the opposition in the only way they seemed to understand - with violence. Eventually, I realized this was not what God wanted from me.

He was gracious enough to give me space to grow. However, I didn’t get it. One day, He decided to put me into the position where I had to rely totally on Him and not on my martial arts black-belt skills. It all started with an altercation I had with an inmate in the staff dining room earlier that day.

I had been working in the staff dining room that morning. All of a sudden this inmate, along with a few of his buddies, gained entrance into the area where I was working. They were attempting to steal some things there. Since I was responsible for whatever we had stored in the staff dining room that day, I attempted to intervene.

I was quickly met with physical threats. Since I was not one to wait for the evil-doers to strike the first blow, I threw a side kick at the inmate closest to me. As the kick struck his ribs, it knocked him back into his buddies which were standing behind him.

Before the rest of the crew had a chance to respond to my aggressiveness, one of the officers who was working in the kitchen caught a glimpse of what was going on. He quickly intervened and called for backup. The authorities quickly put an end to the whole situation.

As was the procedure, the officers carted all us inmates off to the Lieutenant's office. Once we arrived there, he was quick to inform us we could both be thrown into the hole for our altercation. However, he offered to let us both off the hook if we were willing to let bygones be bygones. None of us wanted to go to the hole, so we agreed to make peace with one another.

The lieutenant released us all back onto the compound. I was glad it had all ended the way it did.

After all, I held no animosity for anyone involved in the whole situation. However, I soon learned my foe was not so forgiving.

It seems I had bruised his ego and he was not about to accept the fact I had made him look bad in front of his 'home' boys. He concocted a scheme to get his paybacks. Unbeknownst to me, he and his buddies were plotting to jump me.

After we left the lieutenant's office that afternoon, I set out to do my daily routine. Usually, I would do exercises to stretch out my limbs. Afterwards, I would kick and punch a hanging bag for about half an hour. Once I finished doing this, I would run for about 8 miles along the perimeter of the compound.

On this day, I stretched out as usual. After doing that, I suddenly got the thought I shouldn't work out too hard on this particular afternoon. This led me to decide I would postpone from working out by throwing kicks and punches at the hanging bag. However, I chose to just go ahead and do my run.

I enjoyed doing my laps around the perimeter of the compound that afternoon. The weather was beautiful. It was rather hot, but I liked to run in the heat. I enjoyed sweating the impurities out of my system. As I was about to start running my sixth mile, I was flagged down by another inmate. He claimed he had heard my name being called over the intercom. He told me they said I had a visitor waiting for me in the visiting park.

I immediately stopped running and started walking towards my dormitory. At that point, I was about 30 yards from the entrance. As I was proceeding, I was catching my breath and thinking about whether or not I should try to take a fast shower before going to the visiting park. Since I was only clothed with running shorts at the time, I figured I might as well just jump right into the shower. I wasn't even wearing any shoes; because I liked to run barefoot.

As I attempted to open the side door of the dormitory, whoever was behind me at the time grabbed me around the neck. As this took place, whoever it was that was standing directly in front of me unleashed a round house punch catching me on left side of my face.

All of a sudden, I heard a bunch of other inmates yelling: "kill that cracker!"

I knew I was in for the fight of my life. I quickly pushed back into the side door of the dorm. As I did so, I slammed the inmate who was on my back into it. At this point, he quickly let go of me.

Immediately, I started to throw kicks and punches to thwart off the rest of my would-be attackers. My kicks were horrible because my legs were extremely tired from the running. However, for some strange reason they were still good enough to cause my attackers to back off long enough for me to gain a little composure.

The next thing I realized was the fact I was encircled by a group of black inmates. Suddenly, I saw the inmate whom I had the confrontation with earlier that afternoon. He lunged at me. As he did so, I was quick to respond with a left jab. He hesitated momentarily.

The last thing I wanted to do was fight. First of all, I was dog tired. Secondly, I didn't want to be thrown into the hole for fighting with this inmate again. Also, I knew once I beat him the rest of the inmates would probably jump me.

Since we were in a blind spot on the side of the dorm, I wasn't expecting the authorities to intervene. At that point, I knew I didn't have any other choice. The fight was on. My attacker lunged at me again. I stepped to the side and avoided his advance. I confidently threw another jab. Once again, he backed off. Again, I heard the crowd chant: "Kill that cracker"!

As my opponent came within range of me again, I threw a punch at him and started circling to his left. He backed off again. At that point, I knew he didn't really want to fight me one on one. He was just trying to save face. Hoping to discourage him, I went on the attack again.

However, I was only able to throw one punch at my opponent at a time. Normally, I would have launched three or four punches in quick succession. For some reason I just couldn't put any combinations together. This had never happened to me in any other fight I had in my entire life.

I wondered how long I could hold off the rest of my attackers at the rate I was going. Then, I heard someone in the crowd yell out: "the Man!" I was never so glad to hear that expression. Only God knows how much longer I could have avoided an attack by the others gathered there against me.

By God's grace the authorities quickly discovered my predicament. Once I heard the inmate warning his home boys, I knew my battle would soon be over. At that point, I danced around my opponent and threw out another jab in an effort to keep him away from me. I was just stalling for time.

Seconds later, we were interrupted by a group of officers who had come to break up our fight. As they separated us, one of the officers asked me what had happened. I quickly explained the situation to him and pointed out the other inmates who were involved in the attack on me.

They protested, but the officers placed them in handcuffs and carted us all off to the lieutenant's office. Once we arrived there, I explained what had just happened. The other inmates tried to talk their way out of the situation, but the lieutenant didn't believe them. Common sense told him I wouldn't have been the one to attack them without provocation.

The lieutenant listened patiently to their side of the story and then told the officers to write out disciplinary reports on the three inmates who attacked me. Then, he ordered the inmates to be placed into confinement. Finally, he instructed one of the officers to escort me back to my dormitory.

Once I arrived there, I went to my bunk and sat

down. At the time, they were having a count. (This was a time set aside for counting the inmate population - in order to make sure we were all there).
After the officers did their count and left the dorm, a few of the blacks started making comments in reference to me. The inmates were from Miami and they didn't like the idea I had gotten away from the fighting unscathed. These guys were the 'home boys' of the man I had fought.

The instigators stirred up some of the other blacks. They threatened to jump me, once the yard was opened back up. As I sat there on my bunk listening to these trouble makers stir up strife against me, I became enraged. I never started trouble. However, I was often placed into the position of defending myself. Why should anyone else be concerned about the outcome of this last altercation? As far as I was concerned, I was sick and tired of these idiots who were constantly looking for a reason to start trouble.

At that point, I had it in my mind to seriously hurt the next person who confronted me. The Lord had a different plan and He told me so. However, I didn't believe there was any other way to deal with these guys except violence.

"What am I supposed to do? These fools don't understand anything but violence," I argued with God.

"Let me fight the battle. You have been trying to do it on your own all along and it hasn't worked," He responded

"What do I do to stop their attacks?" I argued.

"Read your Word," He calmly instructed.

At that moment, I took my Bible out from my locker. As I opened it up, I saw it was in the book of Isaiah, Chapter 59. I looked right at verse 19. It states: "When the enemy shall come in like a flood, the Spirit of the Lord shall lift up a standard against him".

Immediately, that verse of scripture penetrated my thick skull. I now knew exactly what God was trying to teach me. As soon as they cleared the count, I went over to one of my Christian brother's bunk. The evil doers had also threatened him during the count time and he seemed a bit fearful. His name was Ronnie. Simply because he was my friend, the evil doers had promised to hurt him also.

Ronnie was a small, young, black man. In fact, he was smaller than me. I don't believe he knew much in the way of self-defense. Understandably, he was visibly shaken. I showed him the verse of scripture the Lord had just shown me.

"God will deliver us if we will trust Him" I confidently promised my fellow believer.

"Pray with me, brother. The Lord just gave me a word to stand on," I encouraged Ronnie.

He quickly agreed to my request. We both got down on our knees and I prayed that verse out loud. I told God we were going to depend on Him to fight our battles.

"Since we are putting our trust in Your Word, it is up to You to manifest the promise Father," I declared.

Once our dorm was released for chow, Ronnie and I walked to the mess hall together. After we had eaten, we were exiting the chow hall. At this point, we were confronted by one of the inmates from the Miami click. We didn't know what to expect.

"We decided to let that go," he said as he approached us.

I didn't know what to say.

"We realized it wasn't your fault, you were just defending yourself. It's over," he solemnly promised.

Then, he turned and walked away. Needless to say, we were relieved. We both started praising God right there on the walkway. I could hardly believe what I had just witnessed. Ever since I had become a Christian, I had been defending myself and bringing reproach on the name of Jesus. Now, I
Finally realized my heavenly Father had to purposely put me into the position where I wasn't even able to use my self-defense skills. He alone had delivered me from

my enemies - who grossly outnumbered me.

By His grace and through His power alone, He had indeed delivered me from my foes. Through it all, I had learned a very valuable lesson that day.

"Unless Your law had been my delights, I should have perished in my affliction." (Psalms 119:92)

LESSON LEARNED

During the next few years of my incarceration, there were many more valuable lessons I learned. Some had to be taught to me time and time again. I am a little dense. However, God was very patient. He is never in a hurry and He never gives up on His children. If He did, I never would have survived the years I was destined to spend in prison.

During the first three years of my incarceration, I did manage to keep a clean record. As the time drew near for my parole hearing, I gathered up as many good character references as I could. In order to encourage the parole board to grant me parole, I felt I would need to show them how I had changed. I even managed to line up a job. I brought the paperwork for my proposed job offer with me to my parole hearing.

When I arrived at the administration building of the prison for my interview, I didn't have a doubt in my mind. I was sure I was going to be paroled as soon as possible. After all, I had done everything required of me and I had been a model inmate. Furthermore, the judge who sentenced me recommended I be paroled after serving three years of my sentence.

Unfortunately, I was in for a very rude awakening. When I walked into the office to see the parole examiner, I expected to be commended for my good behavior and to be joyfully granted what I had worked so hard for. Instead, I was greeted by a rude, cold, judgmental bureaucrat who didn't want to hear anything I had to say.

As I attempted to give him the paperwork I had amassed, he abruptly told me the parole board didn't need it. That was the slap in the face I was greeted with. Then, he proceeded to present me with my sentence according to his calculations.

"Your proposed release date is 2006," he sternly stated.

When I heard those words, I almost fell off the chair I had just sat upon. This release date was about 17 years in the future. *How could this be*? I wondered. I questioned the examiner as to why my sentence was so far off. Then, I tried to reason with him that the time he had calculated I should serve was not the original intention of the judge who had sentenced me. He sarcastically replied this was the way the parole board chose to punish me. He made it clear there was no reasoning with him and that my destiny was no longer up to the judge.

"But, the judge specifically recommended I be paroled after I served three years," I desperately pleaded.

I don't remember his exact response to that statement-although I should. Perhaps, I blocked it out because I couldn't accept what was happening to me. At any rate, the examiner made it quite clear he wasn't interested in anything I had to say. He made it quite clear I was in no position to argue with his decision.

After I left the parole examiner's presence, I probably had steam coming out of my ears. I was dumbfounded. I took a long walk around the perimeter of the prison compound. I couldn't think straight. At this point, I had no recourse but to cry out to God.

"How could you allow this to happen to me?" I demanded. "Didn't I do everything I was supposed to do? Why? Why? Why?" I desperately questioned my Maker.

But, He didn't answer. I couldn't hear His still, small voice in my hysteria. I was too busy presenting my side of the controversy. I was demanding an explanation-as though God should be accountable to me.

On the other hand, God is a perfect gentleman. He doesn't ever scream in order to get His point across to us. If we aren't ready to listen, He just waits until we are. He doesn't have to force the issue. That is exactly what He did. He simply allowed me to vent my frustrations.

Once I calmed down enough to hear Him, He

explained that He wasn't through with me yet. He had more work for me to do in that prison. He also had some more work to do on my character. Contrary to my opinion, it wasn't quitting time just yet.

Speaking of quitting time, He also reminded me I had a book to write. Years earlier, He suggested I write this book you are reading. However, I figured it would be easier to do this once I had access to a typewriter. Since I didn’t work in a clerical position yet, I wasn’t able to use a typewriter while incarcerated. Therefore, I put it off. I figured I would start this venture once I was released from prison.

At any rate, this was not what I wanted to hear. Yet, I knew it was God's will and I was in no position to argue. I needed to accept this and start working on the book. If I had to write it by hand, so be it. There was a bright side to this. I figured writing this book would help me to keep my mind off of the streets.

It was indeed a hard pill to swallow, but our gracious Father didn't leave me out there in the water all alone. He soon led me to a verse of scripture in His Word to console me and give me the strength I needed to go on.

Romans 8:28 is that word of wisdom. It states: "And we know that all things work together for good to them that love God, to them who are the called according to His purpose." After receiving this Word, I realized it didn't matter what my circumstances were. God promised to work it all out for good. I couldn't lose. Although I had lost my physical freedom and all my earthly possessions, I no longer had to fight the world system to try to overcome. God had already done that for me in the person of Jesus.

I accepted the fact He was in total control of every situation I would ever come across. The second part of this verse states I was called according to His purpose. This means I have to accept whatever mission He sends me on. This was scary to me. I must admit it wasn't at all easy to surrender my will to this concept.

Yet, in my spirit, I knew there was no better way to go through this life.

I realized I had been withholding part of me all along. I got down on my knees and asked God to take all of me. I had finally come to my final quitting time - spiritually. I didn't know it at the time, but I had just taken a giant step towards maturity in Christ.

I faced many more tests, but He always prepared me for them. Then, He always provided me with whatever I needed to be victorious. As I traveled down the long road to my physical freedom, I had the peace of knowing I was already free in Jesus. It no longer weighed heavy on my spirit that I was in physical bondage.

Due to the Holy Spirit's guidance, I had the joy of knowing I was a servant of the living God. I was doing His will. Man was no longer directing my paths. God Almighty was leading the way. I finally understood the parole board was not in control of my life. He was. I trusted He would never make me travel any of the paths He placed me on unless it was for my good. I also knew He would never make me go it alone.

Our heavenly Father constantly used His Holy Word to guide me through each trial I experienced. As I continued to dig into His Word, I received all the strength, comfort, and wisdom I ever needed. This alone is what enabled me to have the victory over my circumstances.

I don't believe I ever would have gotten out of prison had it not been for God's guidance. Surely, I would have allowed my circumstances to get the best of me. In fact, I almost lost it on more than one occasion. I experienced strife from the hard core inmates, persecution from the prison officials, and tribulation from some of the other inmates who claimed they were followers of Christ.

During the many years I was serving my sentence in prison, I felt as though I were in some kind of a pressure cooker. I expected this pressure cooker to blow at any given moment. I knew I had no control over anything happening in my daily life. Thankfully, God assured me He would take care of each situation I faced as it presented itself. He did. He is faithful…even when I'm not.

The more I studied God's Word and applied it to the situations I found myself in, the more my faith and trust in Him continued to grow. His purpose was to bring me to the point where I would believe without a doubt that nothing could happen to me unless He was allowing it. In fact, He proved this to be absolutely true time and time again.

If God allowed something to come my way, He would work it out for my good as promised. This was the confidence I had gained. In the beginning years of my life, I had always considered life to be a crap shoot. However, as far as I could tell, my dice were now loaded. All I could roll were winning numbers. My best Friend was in control of this game. No matter what the other players rolled, I couldn't lose. No matter how the dice tumbled, I was sure to roll sevens. Wow!

With this assurance, I went about my daily life in prison. As far as I was concerned, I was blessed to be living right in my mission field. Although I knew I was always under the magnifying glass of the inmates I lived with, this worked to my advantage.

Many inmates eagerly anticipated my fall. Others watched me because they saw the joy and peace I was experiencing and wondered how it could be possible. I was a living Bible. My testimony couldn't have been more impacting.

There was a downside to this, though. Because I professed to be a Christian, most of the inmates felt they couldn't trust me. They feared I would snitch on them should I see them doing something wrong. As if not being trusted weren't enough, I knew I couldn't trust others. Among this number were some of the men who professed to know Jesus. There were many wolves in sheep's clothing in prison.

Over the years, I came into contact with many of these individuals. Unfortunately, they had no clue about the love of God and they could be quite vindictive. At first, I was shocked when I saw how unloving some of these so-called Christians were. I had always assumed all Christians had a loving nature and were kind to people. I sure had a rude awakening on that one.

I learned first hand what Jesus was talking about when He said, "Not every one that says unto me, Lord, Lord, shall enter into the kingdom of heaven: but he that does the will of my Father which is in heaven. Many will say unto me in that day, Lord, Lord, have we not prophesied in thy name? And in your name have cast out devils? And in your name have done many wonderful works? And then I will profess unto them, I never knew you, depart from me, you that work iniquity," (Matthew 7:21-23)

Some of those wolves in sheep's clothing even had the audacity to give themselves elaborate titles. Unfortunately, they really did damage to the cause of Christ; because other inmates, who weren't yet born again, saw their hypocritical actions and were driven further away from God.

Yet, God was still in control and sometimes He harshly judged such individuals. At one point during my incarceration I played the piano for the weekly services and was director of the chapel choir. Unfortunately, many of the men who would attempt to join our choir were doing so for their own glory. Then, there were others who were just claiming to be Christians and were flat out living in sin.

I didn't want anyone, who wasn't a living witness for Jesus, to be a part of our choir. I really felt this would be a terrible witness. Contrary to what some may have thought, I didn't think I was any less a sinner than the next person. However, I did try my best to be the witness God had called me to be. I felt this was my duty and my calling. I took it seriously. As far as I was concerned, leading the prison choir was an important part of my ministry and an honor.

I had made a conscious decision that I didn't want to live like a sinner anymore and I expected anyone who professed the name of Jesus to do the same. Even so, I never got to the point in my spiritual walk where I stopped battling my flesh. I still do. Yet, I always did make an attempt to act the way I understood a Christian should act. My main goal was to lead as many of the inmates into a personal relationship with Jesus as I possibly could. Therefore, I felt everyone who dared to minister through our choir should also be sincere in their commitment to Jesus.

The chaplains agreed with my convictions. However, because of certain Department of Corrections regulations, they couldn't prevent anyone from joining the prison choir. The institution had their own little set of rules and the chaplains had to abide by them. If an inmate complained to the authorities he was being discriminated against; because he wasn't allowed to join the prison choir, the establishment would come down on the chaplains

I didn't have to deal with the authorities on that matter, though, because I knew God had the final say. I had no doubt He would back me on my convictions. I also depended on Him to show me which men weren't fit to minister in His name. He backed me up completely. He always answered my prayers to move out from among the choir members all those men who were unworthy to represent Jesus.

I caught a lot of flack from other inmates because of my stand on this. But, I didn't let this affect my determination. I was rewarded accordingly. I never had to fight any of the battles alone. God always took care of the 'thorns' in my flesh one way or another.

One of the so-called Christian brothers, who sang in our choir, was involved in some shady dealings on the compound. I didn't look for this information. The Lord used an unbeliever to enlighten me about it.

When I found out some disturbing news about

this particular brother, I approached him concerning the allegations. He denied any wrongdoing. I explained to him it would not be right for him to engage in any conduct that would bring shame to the cross of Jesus. I tried to convince him the lost men on the compound were watching those who claimed to be God's children very closely.

I emphasized again and again to those who claimed to be Christians that they had the responsibility of setting a good example for others to follow. Unfortunately, this particular inmate had to learn the hard way.

After our talk ended by him emphatically denying any wrongdoing, I prayed and asked the Lord to expose any shady activities this man was involved in. I also prayed He would forgive him if he were lying to me and bring him back into a right standing with Jesus.

The next time we had choir practice this man was absent. When I inquired as to his whereabouts, someone told me he was in confinement. As it turned out, he had some homemade liquor brewing in his locker. He had it stored in the dorm where he lived. The plastic bag, in which the mixture was being fermented in, blew apart from the pressure inside. Once this took place, the whole dorm started reeking of alcohol.

Moments after the incident took place the officer on duty was making his rounds in the dorm counting inmates. He discovered the mess and took the appropriate action. Shortly after I heard this report, the Lord brought to my mind His Word in Numbers Chapter 32 verse 23b: "be sure your sin will find you out."

I learned from the experience and kept moving on with Jesus. I prayed my 'brother' did likewise. At any rate, I knew it would all work out for good in the end. In some instances, I was really tempted to despise the hypocrites. It was hard not to. But, but I did not seek their hurt. I believed God meant it when He said vengeance is mine. Anyway, those men were not hurting me. They were only hurting themselves.

Actually, the Lord brought good out of those experiences too. Before I became a Christian, I was an expert in getting my revenge on those who crossed me. I had prided myself for always being able to get more than even with those certain individuals. No matter how powerful they were, and no matter how smart they were, I had always managed to get a step ahead of them and pay them back to a far greater degree than they had hurt me.

Of course, I now knew this wasn't God's way and that I shouldn't continue this practice. He soon taught me I should start out by casting aside any thoughts of revenge which would come into my mind.

Yet, every time I would see those individuals who had done me harm, I would feel resentment towards them. Since I knew I was incapable of controlling my feelings towards those who had hurt me, I prayed and asked God to give me the strength to deal with those situations.

He swiftly answered that prayer and told me I had to surrender my grudges to Him. He instructed me to pray for everyone I resented each time they crossed my path. He also told me I should ask Him to bless them as well.

Lunacy! That's what my natural man thought about this. Yet, I was now in a spiritual war and I knew I could only defeat my enemies by doing things God's way. In spite of my feelings, I did exactly what I was told to do. Eventually, I overcame the resentment I had in each and every instance. To top it off, I got blessed for my obedience.

While I was in prison, I also had to deal with the authorities. As far as most of the prison staff was concerned, I was an inmate and couldn't be trusted. No matter how long I stayed on the path of righteousness, I was always going to be considered a convict to some of the officers on the compound. According to most of them, a convict is just looking for an angle and another chance to beat the system.

I couldn't blame the officers for their attitudes towards inmates. Most convicts in prison were constantly trying to pull something shady off. More often than not, this was just for the sake of 'winning' the challenge to get away with something - anything. I guess it made them feel superior whenever they would succeed.

In some ways this was amusing. Like an old flat nosed, glass jawed, cauliflower eared, want-to-be champion boxer, some of my fellow convicts were only too willing to jump into the ring with the reigning champ - the authorities. No matter how many rounds were lost, no matter how many times they got knocked down, the fighting just couldn't end. There was always another round to go. The opportunity to launch their haymaker and bring down the authorities was always a possibility. This mindset was a product of their worst enemy - the devil. Unfortunately, most of them didn't seem to be aware of this.

All things considered, I didn't expect the authorities to accept me for who I really had become in Jesus. Although I did my best to display His character, I could tell very few of the officials I had come in contact with actually believed I was trustworthy. I always knew I would constantly have to prove myself to everyone.

Yet, I didn't have a problem with that. After all, I was the one who had really messed up their life. I was the convict. Why should anyone trust me? I knew why. However, only those who knew the life-changing power of Jesus Christ could understand and accept this.

I had good reason not to challenge the authorities that be. First of all, I knew in my heart, if I broke the law, the same God who controls everything would cause my transgression to come to light. He tells us in His Word the authorities that be, are ordained by Him. Therefore, I knew trying to beat the system would cause me to be held accountable by God. I never had any desire to deliberately disobey His commands.

The moment I surrendered my life to Jesus, my

desire to get my way by any means necessary was gone forever. Even though I wasn't yet perfected, I was in the process of being formed into the image of God's only perfect Son. The Bible says, "We are His workmanship created in Christ Jesus unto good works, which He hath before ordained that we should walk therein."

Because of the work God had done in my heart, it was now truly my sincere desire to only do what was right. All I really wanted, more than anything else, was to be pleasing to Him. I knew without a doubt there is nothing more rewarding in this life than doing His will.

Because of this change of heart, I was no longer a threat to society. Unfortunately, my greatest challenge was to convince the powers that be of this. In the process, I learned firsthand why God tells us to judge no man. Since we don’t know what is in another person’s heart, how can we understand their motives and their intents? On the other hand, God even knows our thoughts long before they enter our mind. I suppose that is why He doesn’t need us to do the judging.

In spite of my circumstances, I considered myself to be blessed. I knew I had already overcome and God promised to complete the work He had started in me. "He who has begun a good work in you will complete it until the day of Christ Jesus." (Philippians 1:6) In God's eyes, I am still a tender plant. He is the gentle Gardener and will continue to cultivate my character until I’m molded into the image of His glorious Son. Awesome!

Though I was considered the dregs of society, I was grafted into God's family. This is something the world can’t understand. I can’t blame them. I could barely comprehend it myself. What had taken place in my wretched life was beyond reason. Furthermore, I didn't deserve it - but who does?

Whatever God's reason for choosing me, I was just grateful He did. My so-called wife, my family, my friends, and the world system had all written me off. But, God chose to shed His grace on me. I will never be able to thank Him enough. However, I am willing to spend the rest of my life here on earth trying.

I was determined to take it one day at a time. I knew I still had lots to learn. This alone was the driving force causing me to grow closer to my Father and my Saviour. I had no idea what each day would bring, but I did know God was with me. He continually encouraged me of this.

When I think back on my prison experience, I'm glad I didn't have any idea I was going to serve almost 15 years. In God's wisdom, He chose to keep this information from me. He was gracious enough to give me hope all along the way.

During my first few years of incarceration, I was given the hope my case was going to get overturned in the courts. When I didn't get any relief from the courts, I started focusing on getting paroled. When that door didn't open, the Lord opened up a new door for me in the court system. When He did this, I was able to file a variety of different motions in the federal courts. I was encouraged by the fact the doors could swing wide open for me at any moment. I really had the faith to believe this was eventually going to happen.

However, I learned the hard way faith in itself is not a means to an end. This was another hard pill to swallow, but eventually brought the desired cure. Meanwhile, my days of anxious waiting turned into months and the months turned into years. I felt as though I was in the marathon of my life. There I was the runner who just couldn't muster up enough energy to finish the final segment of the race. Just when it seemed like I was going to catch up to the leaders of the pack, they always managed to come up with enough energy to draw farther away from me.

Every time I filed a new motion to one of the courts, it seemed as though I had the right argument. I was sure my motion was going to be granted. After all, I assured myself, my petition was right on the mark. I couldn't see any reason for an honest judge to deny my argument. After all, it made perfect sense.

“It is good that a man should both hope and quietly wait for the salvation of the Lord.” (Lamentations 3:26)

TIME OUT

Unfortunately, the court system doesn't revolve around making sense. Even though a person has the right argument, they won't get anywhere unless they have the right judge. Since they are only human, judges have their own opinions and interpretations of the laws of the land. Unfortunately, they also have their own prejudices too.

I just couldn't seem to find a judge who would agree that the police did indeed conduct an illegal search in my case. No matter how much evidence I presented to prove this to the court, the judge always seemed to come up with another excuse to disagree.

When I received a ruling in favor of the state, I just moved on to the next level in the judicial process. As long as there were other options in the federal court system, my hope was still alive. During this whole scenario, I continued to draw nearer to God.

By His grace, He inspired me to keep myself busy. Eventually, I completed a college course in business. I learned how to play the piano, and the guitar. I took a music course and I learned how to read as well as write music. I became involved with the prison chapel music programs and this led to my being designated to be the choir director.

Any time there was a Bible study given, or an outside group came in to minister to the inmates, I was there. I knew I would receive something from God at each of these functions. I was never disappointed. It was at one of these Bible studies where I met many great friends and brothers and sisters in Jesus. (I will go into detail about these God-given helpers later on in this book.)

I also attended most of the prayer meetings which were held in the prisons where I was being incarcerated. Some of these meetings were conducted by inmates. Others were conducted by the prison chaplains.

One Saturday morning, I was among a group of Christians who had met with the chaplain in order to have one of these prayer meetings. Shortly after our praying had begun, an inmate barged into the room where we were meeting. He announced another inmate had just been stabbed out on the rec field directly behind the building where we were located.

Immediately after the inmate finished his announcement, sirens began sounding and they announced over the PA system all inmates were to return to their housing units. At that point the chaplain dismissed us. As we exited the building, I noticed the chaos all around us. I didn't see any officers on the compound, but I did see groups of inmates running wildly throughout the compound.

As I began walking towards my dormitory, I noticed a group of black inmates running towards me. At the time, I was on a cement path which ran parallel to the building I had just exited. The inmates had just come around from the back of the building and were headed right towards me. Many of the inmates were brandishing various weapons.

Obviously, these were some of the rioters. I estimated there to be about a dozen of them. I didn't have any place to go, so I looked straight ahead and continued walking. Just then, the Holy Spirit brought to my mind, "A thousand shall fall at your side, and ten thousand at your right hand but it shall not come near you." (Psalms 91:7)

Seconds before the Holy Spirit quickened those words to my spirit, I briefly considered veering off the path I was on and making a dash for my dormitory. When that scripture was brought to mind, I knew God was with me and His Word would not come back void.

I continued walking straight down the path I was on. Seconds later, the group of men who were heading straight for me veered off to the left and ran towards the canteen. (The canteen is a store where inmates can buy just about everything one could find at a convenience store).

When they arrived there, they began beating several of the inmates who had been in line waiting for their turn to make a purchase. As I witnessed this, I gradually made my way off the path and on to the grass which was on my right. I knew I couldn't stay straight on the path because I would have had to walk right into the disturbance which was taking place.

A short time later, I arrived at my dorm safe and sound. Afterwards, the compound was on a complete lock down. This lasted for several days. After we were released back on to the compound, I found out the riot was caused by the stabbing of a black inmate by two white inmates. The black inmate who had been stabbed later died.

It turned out he was stabbed because he had been extorting money from one of the white inmates. The inmate who had been having a problem with the deceased inmate told his ‘lover’ what was going on. It seems the inmate's lover decided he wasn't going to put up with that so he stabbed him.

Actually, the white inmate approached the black man and tried to work it out. However, the black man refused to rectify the situation and this resulted in his being stabbed. In prison, many stabbings occur strictly over pride. This was a prime example of that.

Later, I learned the man who was stabbed had been staying in the same dormitory where one of my Christian brothers lived. This brother told me he had been witnessing to the man who was killed on the very day of his death. It seems the deceased was constantly trying to bully other inmates and was taking their property from them. The brother witnessed this firsthand, because he lived in the same quad as this inmate.

Apparently, he had tried to reason with the man and had told him he could not go on doing the things he had been doing without having some repercussions. He tried to explain that God was using him to try to help him to get out of the lifestyle he was living in. However, the man stated he wasn't ready to change just yet. He even told the brother who had been witnessing to him that many of his family members were devout Christians and they were praying for him.

Unfortunately, even though this man came from a Christian family who encouraged and supported him, he wouldn't submit to God's authority. Maybe he thought he would give up his lifestyle some day, only God knows. The thing is he had refused God's offer one too many times.

The Bible clearly states: "Today if you will hear His voice, harden not your hearts, as in the provocation, in the day of trial in the wilderness," (Hebrews 3:7)

I witnessed God's judgment fall on several of the inmates I was incarcerated with over the years. Thankfully, I also played a part in some awesome conversions during this time. I saw God take some of the hardest hearted inmates I encountered and change their character completely. One of these conversions took place in a red neck known as 'Gator'.

I had lived in the same dorm as Gator for about two years. His bunk was several bunks away from my bunk. He was situated right next to a small, black, Christian, brother named Ronnie. Ronnie and I were very close. Because we constantly witnessed about the love of Jesus, Gator constantly mocked my friend and me.

One night, Ronnie and I were having a Bible study together. I was sitting on the foot of Gator's bunk. This was a common practice among inmates. I had no reason to believe I was provoking anyone for doing this. All of a sudden, Gator came storming over to us and began shouting obscenities. I can't remember exactly what was said, but it was something to the effect he didn't want to hear any crap about no Jesus and didn't want us having a Bible study anywhere near his bunk.

Although Gator was quite a big dude and very threatening, I didn't fear him. Yet, for the sake of being a good witness and helping him to see Christianity in action I held my peace that night. We moved over to my bunk and we continued to hold our Bible studies there.

A few days after this incident, I was returning from work and was on my way to my bunk. Since I worked in the staff dining room. I had access to many things the other inmates were deprived of. In my hand, I held a couple of pieces of fruit which I had planned on using for my dinner.

As I was passing Gator's bunk, he asked me to give him the fruit which I held in my hand. *He has got to be kidding! Why should I give this guy my dinner?* I asked myself. I soon found the answer to my question. The Lord had different plans for that fruit.

"Give Gator the fruit," He insisted.

I knew I had just heard from my Creator, so I didn't hesitate to toss the fruit to him. As I did, I told him Jesus loved him. Afterwards, I knew I wasn't going to be hungry although I had just given up my dinner. I wasn’t. This incident reminded me of the time the disciples were offering Jesus some food and He declined their offer. They questioned among themselves if someone had given Jesus food earlier. Jesus told them “My food is to do the will of Him that sent me.” (John 4:34)

I had no doubt the gesture of giving Gator that piece of fruit was a seed-planting. I knew in my heart God was going to use that incident to break his rock-hard heart. I wasn’t disappointed. He did. A short time after this incident, Gator accepted Jesus as his Saviour. He soon became full of the Spirit and went about preaching the Gospel to the other inmates. He was really on fire for God.

Even though I believed God was working on Gator, I really didn't expect his conversion to be so dramatic. In fact, I wasn't even sure I was going to see the fruit of my labor in this life. Once again, God showed me He is indeed able to do much more than we can ask or think.

I don't know why I should have been taken by surprise. In Ephesians Chapter 3 verse 20 God promises, "Now unto Him that is able to do exceeding abundantly above all that we ask or think…" One of the main things God had been teaching me is His Word does not come back void. If He said it, it will be. Nothing can ever change that.

All throughout my journey in the Florida prison system, God proved His faithfulness to me. He continually provided my needs - even when those I depended on weren't able to do so. As I think back on it, one such time comes to mind.

In the Florida prison system, they have what is called a weekly draw. This was a designated day at which time the inmates could withdraw money from their bank accounts within the prison system. About five days before draw, the inmates would fill out a draw slip and signify the amount they wished to withdraw from their accounts. If they had the funds, they would be paid the amount requested in cash on the designated day.

On one such draw night, I was waiting patiently to get my draw. While the officers were issuing the money to the inmates, one evil-doer came over to my bunk and asked me for a cup of coffee. This same person had done much evil to another Christian brother and me. However, I know the Lord instructs us to bless our enemies. Even so, I found that hard to do in a prison setting.

In spite of this, the Lord showed me how much our obedience to Him influences the amount of blessings we receive. Since I did not like the person asking me for a cup of coffee, I had no feelings of guilt for saying no to his request because I was out of coffee anyway.

A short time later, my name was called and I went to pick up my draw. I swiftly got off my bunk and made my way to the officer's station. When I arrived there I was told I didn't have sufficient funds in my account. I was frustrated. I was out of coffee and I didn't have money to buy a new bag of coffee for the coming week. I didn't need much. All I usually spent money on was coffee, shampoo, soap, and batteries for my radio. As far as I knew, I couldn't buy my customary bag of coffee this particular week.

Once I made my way back to my bunk, I sat down on it and I started to think of ways I could get a bag of coffee to hold me over until the following week's draw. Although I still had a dime, this was all the money I had left over from the money I drew the previous week. I knew this wasn’t going to get me too far.

All of a sudden the thought came into my mind I should give my last dime to the evil-doer who had asked me for a cup of coffee earlier. I had no doubt where that thought came from. I knew it wasn't my idea.

I also knew the evil-doer who had asked me for a cup of coffee could use my last dime to buy a cup of coffee from one of the other inmates in our dorm. At the time, ten cents would buy an inmate a cup of coffee from other inmates who sold their coffee by the cup. *Why should I give my last dime to an enemy of righteousness?* I thought to myself.

It didn't take long for the Lord to convince me how dumb my question was, so I called the guy over to my bunk and told him God loves him. Then, I told him I didn't have any coffee but I did have a dime.

"God loves you and wants you to have this. Go and buy yourself a cup of coffee," I told him. Then, I gladly gave him my last dime.

Without even thanking me, he turned and walked away from my bunk to go get his cup of coffee. I didn’t care. I was glad because I had been obedient to God. If nothing else, I sure had the joy of the Lord. However, I soon found out this was not my only reward.

A short time later, the man who had the bunk across from mine came back from picking up his weekly draw. Though I had lived in the bunk across from this inmate for several months, he had hardly ever spoken a word to me up until this moment.

"Jimmy, do me a favor. I have just drawn some

money and I still have money left over from last week. Please hold $20.00 for me until tomorrow and I'll give you $5.00," he proposed.

He and I both knew there was a rule in effect which stated that inmates could not have more than twenty- five dollars in their possession at any one time. If this man had kept the money he had left over from the week before, along with the money he had just acquired, he would have been in violation.

Since I didn't have any money, I saw no reason why I couldn't hold his money for him until the following day. I agreed to his request. For doing him the favor, he kept his word and gave me $5.00 of the money I had held for him overnight. God works in mysterious ways.

One thing which took me quite a long time to accept is the fact God's timing isn't the same as ours. Many things I would have done yesterday seemed to take God forever. For instance, I had always wanted to work in the chaplain's office while I was incarcerated at Baker Correctional. I really admired the chaplain there and I got along well with the other inmates who were clerking for him at the time.

Among the most sincere brothers I met there was another inmate named Ken Copper. He had such a sweet spirit and the love of Jesus seemed to flow out of him like a river. (Actually, this is what Jesus promised us). He didn't just profess to be a Christian. He emulated our Saviour in every respect.

Consequently, God did a major miracle in his life by causing him to be released from prison against all odds. You see, the judge who sentenced him had gone far beyond the norm and given him a very long sentence. As if that weren't enough, he withheld jurisdiction for 60 years. This meant there was no way he could receive a parole without this judge's personal consent.

At any rate, God opened the doors wide and Ken was released after serving only three years on his sentence. After his release, he started a prison ministry in Jacksonville, Florida called Prisoners For Christ. Eventually, he wrote a very powerful book concerning what Jesus had done in his life. (Ken had been a serial bank robber). The book is entitled: "Held Hostage" and was published by Chosen Books.

I also met George Roberts at Baker. He was a black brother and a sweet spirited man of God. He played the bass guitar. The Lord placed him in my path in order that we could write songs together. We both loved glorifying our Saviour. George also taught me how to play the guitar and was instrumental in getting me hired as one of the chaplain's clerks.

Although the chaplain had several openings for a clerical position during the first three years I was at Baker, he didn't choose me for the position. This was in spite of the fact that George, Ken, and several of the other clerks working for him had recommended me for the various positions whenever they had become available. I couldn't understand why I had been rejected time and again. However, I knew God had a plan.

During my fourth year at Baker, the Chaplain finally hired me. I was elated. I was hired to be the chaplain's assistant. I had my own office, which was adjacent to his. In my office there was a piano. The Lord used that piano to get me into the music ministry for the remainder of my incarceration.

Had I been hired by the chaplain at an earlier time, my position with him would not have allowed me to have access to the piano or the time to practice playing it. Praise God! As He often does, He saved the best for last. I could not have been more pleased with my job in the chaplain's office at Baker.

During my time as a chaplain's assistant at Baker, my spiritual man grew immensely. My faith just blossomed. One afternoon, a man came into my office and I noticed he was visibly shaken. I asked him what was troubling him. The man told me he had just returned from the medical center at Lake Butler and had been diagnosed with terminal liver cancer.

I asked him if he was a Christian. He told me he was. At that moment I felt led to ask another believer who worked for the chaplain to join me in praying for the man's healing. I had never done anything of the sort before. Without a doubt, the Spirit of God prompted this. I felt compassion for the man and I knew God could heal him.

I told the man to wait in my office, while I went next door in order to get one of my co-workers to help me pray for him. After I explained the man's situation to my brother, Tito, he agreed with me that it was God's will for the man to be healed. Together, we went back into my office and prayed for the distressed man.

During prayer, I remember quoting God's Word which states, "If two of you shall agree on earth as touching anything that they shall ask, it shall be done for them by my Father which is in heaven." (Matthew 18:19) Afterwards, I told the man we two had come into agreement and therefore, God's Word would not come back void.

About two weeks later, the man we prayed for came bursting into my office. He was overjoyed. He explained he had just come back from the Lake Butler medical center. They had been testing him in order to see how far advanced his cancer was. To everyone's surprise, they didn't find any trace at all of the cancer that had been ravaging his body. Praise God!

"Be still, and know that I am God." (Psalms 46:10)

MORE THAN ENOUGH

I was really enjoying my job as a clerk for the chaplain. The time just seemed to be flying by. I was enjoying the opportunities I had to witness to so many more inmates. Then, without warning, God chose to move me out of my comfort zone at Baker C.I.

It was time for me to be tested again. I was about to learn much more in His school of hard knocks. To my dismay, I found out His will doesn't necessarily coincide with our plans. At the time, my will was to ride out my sentence in the surroundings I had learned to enjoy.

However, one afternoon the chaplain called me into his office and informed me the administration was planning to ship me out to another institution. This news hit me like a ton of bricks. I didn't want to go to another institution and have to start all over again. The only two places I wanted to go was home or heaven.

I asked the chaplain if there was anything he could do to prevent this transfer from taking place. He told me he would call my classification officer and see what could be done to stop this procedure. I thanked him and left his office. I immediately set out to find a place where I could be alone with God.

When I found a suitable spot, I began to plead my case to Him. I had questions. I had apprehensions. To top it off, I didn't have a clue as to why this was happening to me? I was sure He would rectify my situation by preventing my transfer. In fact, I begged Him to do so. However, I also told Him even if He said no to my request I was ready to accept His will.

Afterwards, I had peace once again. The news of my impending transfer had turned my little world upside down in an instant. Just a few moments in His presence and everything was put into the right perspective for me again. Once again, I knew I was still in His hands and nothing else mattered.

Later on that afternoon, the chaplain called me into his office and informed me he had spoken to my classification officer and nothing could be done to prevent my transfer. I was disappointed but I wasn't discouraged. I knew God had a plan. I was ready to move on if this is what He wanted me to do.

For a brief moment, I thought about the pitfalls of being transferred. First of all, I would have to establish myself in my new environment. I was sure there would be those who would 'try' me to see whether or not I was an easy mark. I dreaded this inevitable situation. Mainly, because I feared that during my trials I would revert back to my old ways of dealing with inmates who sought out the weak.

I absolutely abhorred such behavior. All of my life I had despised those who would take advantage of the weak. I used to welcome the opportunity to teach such evil-doers a lesson. I was also too proud to allow anyone to exalt themselves over me. However, I had to trust my faith in God would give me the strength to overcome my fleshly nature. Somehow, He managed to give me the peace which overwhelmed any fears I might have had.

I spent the rest of my final day at Baker CI bidding farewell to the staff members and inmates I had befriended. The following morning, I awoke with the anticipation of moving on. I was actually looking forward to it. I was now a little anxious to see what God had in store for me next.

The Comforter Jesus spoke about in John Chapter 15 was truly just that to me. Later that morning, the bus came to make the transfer and I was totally ready. I knew I was in the great big hands of my Creator and trusted His judgment completely.

As my journey wore on, the Comforter made His presence known to me in greater measure. In fact, while being transferred, I became full of the Spirit. I had such joy and peace many of the other inmates thought I was crazy.

When we arrived at Charlotte Correctional Institution, I was more confident than ever my God was greater than any threats coming my way. Although rumor had it Charlotte had a reputation for being the most dangerous prison in the system, I wasn’t the least bit fearful of my new surroundings.

Once I was settled into my dorm at Charlotte, I met an awesome brother in the Lord named Jim Cash. Jim was a short, burly, determined, strong man of God. He was one of the most sincere Christians I met during my incarceration. By God’s grace, I had the privilege of rooming with Jim for a while.

During that time, he and I studied our music and the Word of God together. I soon came to realize God had answered my prayer to help me advance in music by sending me to Charlotte. Had I stayed at Baker, I doubt I would have enhanced my musical abilities as quickly. I also don't think I would have gotten my theology down quite as good had I not met this dear brother.

If I were to make a comparison between Jim and me on a spiritual level, I would have to say he was on the collegiate level and I was still in high school when we met. Although he had already spent around 15 years in prison by that time, he had a sweet disposition and didn't hesitate to help others find the saving grace of God through Jesus Christ. He was very strong in the faith and he was well respected throughout the compound.

Unfortunately, there came a time that God chose to separate us. This happened way too quickly for my liking. One afternoon, Jim was suddenly surprised to be informed he was being transferred to another institution. He hadn't put in for a transfer. In fact, he had asked to be transferred closer to home and was sent to Charlotte. He was actually quite happy right where he was.

Since both of us knew God was in control, neither of us fretted over the matter. He left as scheduled the following morning. Our time together had ended, but our friendship was far from over. It was years before we got to hear from each other again but we were in each others thoughts constantly. Though we didn't know whether our reunion would take place here on earth or in our Father's kingdom, we had something to look forward to.

After Jim left Charlotte, I continued to develop my musical abilities. This kept my mind off of my loss and helped me to be a more profitable servant to my Lord. He continued to use me in the music ministry there. In fact, I was very involved in most of the chapel sponsored programs right from the start.

This proved to be rewarding in more ways than I had imagined. In fact, at one of these prayer gatherings He chose to show all of us He still hears the prayers of the prisoners. One morning, a group of us inmate Christians and the chaplain were gathered together for prayer. Just before we started to pray, one of the brothers mentioned we should pray for one of our choir members who had recently been placed into confinement. According to what this brother had heard, the choir member was being mistreated.

In fact, rumor had it he had been physically beaten by one of the captains who worked at Charlotte. This particular captain had a reputation for being mean and unfair in his dealings with inmates. As we prayed, I asked the Lord to protect our brother and to keep him from harm during his stay in confinement. I also prayed the Lord would reveal it to the proper authorities if the captain and his men were indeed abusing inmates.

Within a couple of days, the captain and some of his men were indicted for prisoner abuse. The Lord had indeed brought their wrongdoing to the light. It turns out the captain and some of his officers were under investigation for some time. Eventually, the investigators received the information which had confirmed their suspicions. What a God-incidence.

He used that situation to show me no one is immune to His correction. I used to wonder why some of the people who were in authority seemed to be getting away with their wrongdoing. Now I know they're not. They will all answer to Him - some sooner than others. They too will reap what they have sown.

Not all of our prayers brought negative results on others. In fact, one answered petition which came from our prayer group resulted in the building of a beautiful chapel at Charlotte. Along with this chapel, we were given a lot of new musical equipment which really enhanced our music ministry there.

I had been working for the chaplains long before the chapel was built. After the chapel was finally completed, I was in la-la land. The time seemed to pass by more swiftly than ever before. I kept quite busy between my job in the Chapel and the music ministry I was involved with.

Before I realized it, I had spent a few years at Charlotte. During this time, I had filed various motions to the federal courts concerning my release. At one point, I really thought I was on the verge of being granted my freedom. As a result of my petition to the court, I was granted a hearing in the federal court in Miami, Florida.

To top it all off, my court-appointed federal lawyer was actually able to present a witness to the court on my behalf. It was the girl I was with at the time of my arrest. To protect her identity, let's just say her name was Sherry. She had witnessed the illegal search and seizure the police had performed on me the day of my arrest. I had not seen or heard from her in years. Yet, the Lord saw fit to put her in touch with my lawyer just before my hearing and she had agreed to testify for me.

Sherry's testimony on my behalf was flawless. When one of the arresting officers testified, he made the mistake of claiming he was just following police procedure when he conducted the search of my luggage. My lawyer quickly pointed out that the police officer was not being truthful, because the procedure he supposedly used was not in accordance with the actual police procedure which was in effect at that time.

At that point, I thought the judge was sure to rule on my behalf. Even though my lawyer had told me earlier that the judge presiding over my hearing was bias against convicted felons, I really did believe she was going to grant my motion. This would have resulted in me being released from custody.

To my dismay, she decided she was not going to rule on the matter. According to her, she had to review the testimony given that day in court before doing so. This was not a good sign. Yet, I was not discouraged. I still thought the judge had heard enough of the truth to convince her to grant my motion.

After my hearing, I was sent back to Charlotte. Each day I listened very closely to every announcement coming over the P.A. system. I was expecting to hear my name called over the prison intercom at any time.

I really believed I would be called up to the administration building at any moment and told I was being released by the federal authorities. Unfortunately, this never happened. It wasn't the Lord's will to have me released through the court system.

Through it all, I learned that just because one has the faith to believe it doesn't necessarily mean what they believe is God's will for that person at that particular time. I didn't understand this at that time. Yet, in spite of the disappointments, He gave me the strength to bite the bullet and go on.

I had no idea whether or not I would ever see the streets again. However, He continued to give me hope against all hope. I chose to trust Him and He had a surprise in store for me.

Although I had no way of knowing it at the time, He planned to grant me my freedom a little at a time. I never for a moment imagined the way He had already chosen to free me. During my crusade for what seemed to be a hopeless cause, I just held onto His unchanging promises. I figured I was on His time and if I were ever going to be released it would happen when He willed.

While I awaited the outcome of the various motions I had filed, I was on an emotional roller-coaster. Whenever I had received a rejection concerning one of my motions, I would feel like there was no light at the end of my tunnel. During those times, the Lord would always open up another door for me and this would renew my hopes. I never lost hope I would one day obtain my freedom through the federal court system.

However, even though many doors continued to open along the way, each one was slammed in my face. Then the final blow came. One day, I received the judge's ruling concerning the hearing I had in the Miami federal court. I couldn't help but think this was the last nail in my coffin.

At this point, I figured I would never get out of prison. She had ruled against me. Turns out she threw my case out because of a mistake my lawyer had made when she filed some motion on my behalf. How bogus.

The judge never ruled on the evidence my lawyer presented in court. She claimed the hearing was ruled null and void because my lawyer made some sort of an error. I couldn't believe this would happen in a federal court. This is the highest form of justice an American citizen is afforded. Yet, I came to the realization I had clearly been discriminated against.

This was devastating to me. I will never forget how crushed I was. I wasn't so much concerned about what the court had done. My deepest concern was the fact God had allowed this to happen to me. I wasted no time taking my plea to the high court of heaven. I questioned God about the outcome of my hearing.

"How could you let this happen to me. You know the police officer lied on the stand at my hearing and you know the judge was biased. You witnessed the illegal search of my baggage. My lawyer proved our case. Why should a mistake by my lawyer cause me to lose my appeal? Why are you going to let them get away with this?" I demandingly pleaded.

In reply, God reminded me of something I had

recently read in the Bible. In the book of Genesis Chapter 37, He gave us a record of how Joseph was imprisoned. Although he didn't even commit any crimes, Joseph's own brothers were jealous of him and they sold him into slavery. He wound up in Egypt working for one of the Pharaoh's military leaders.

At the time, Joseph made the best of a bad situation. He worked hard and stayed faithful to God. His master favored him. Eventually, he was put in charge of all that his master had. However, his good fortune didn't last long. Eventually, his master's wife tried to coax him into having sex with her.
Joseph's reply: "How can I sin against God and my master?"

The woman's reply was to yell rape. She screamed so loud her whole household of servants came running. Joseph was falsely accused by her and for the second time he was forced to pay for a crime he didn't commit. This time, he was put into prison.

Once again, Joseph stayed faithful to God and he was blessed by becoming the warden's right hand man. Consequently, he wound up spending a total of 13 years in captivity. Considering the fact he never deserved this punishment, it is amazing to me he never questioned God.

In the long run, Joseph's faith and patience paid off. God caused him to be released from prison and placed him into the position of being the co-ruler with the Pharaoh of Egypt. Eventually, God used him to bless His people, the tribes of Israel, by bringing them into Egypt and sustaining them. This took place at the time the rest of the world was experiencing a severe famine.

Because Joseph trusted God, not only was he blessed beyond his wildest dreams, but his entire family was blessed as well. As I thought back on this historical account of God's dealings with His faithful servant, I felt ashamed.

Although it was true the police performed an illegal search and seizure in order to get evidence they used at my trial, I was still guilty of a crime. Furthermore, if I had been caught for even a small fraction of the number of crimes I had committed during my lifetime, I would have had absolutely no chance of ever seeing the streets again.

Worse yet, I deserved to go to hell for sinning against God. Anything I received short of that was pure grace. What right did I have to question God's judgment? How could I complain to a Holy, Holy, Holy, God?

At that moment, I decided it was absolutely my quitting time. I knew I had to stop trying to take my life back. I had to stop focusing on obtaining my physical freedom and start being more determined to live the rest of my life for God so I could indeed be used for His purposes.

I finally made the decision I would no longer concern myself with where I would be spending the rest of my life. I promised God I would leave that up to Him. I trusted Him with my life. Why should I be concerned whether or not I would ever get out of prison alive?

Then, it dawned on me God caused His beloved Israel to go into captivity and once they had completed the exact amount of time He had promised them in captivity, He caused the Jews to be set free. He even put it into the new ruler's heart to help the Jews to build their country back up. Afterwards, the ruling dictator actually helped to pay for the rebuilding of the Jewish temple. How great and Godly is that?

In order that my faith didn't falter, He always gave me just enough revelation of His awesome Presence in the various situations I found myself. As He continued to build my faith, I became more and more confident everything was going to work out fine in the end. Sometimes it seemed to me like the end of my imprisonment would never come, but in spite of a few lapses in my faith, I knew He was going to supply me with the strength I needed to make it through.

I knew I couldn't make it on my own, but I also

knew God promised me He would be my strength. I was willing to take Him at His Word. I found myself in many situations where all I could do was cry out to God. During those times of need, He had always come through for me.

When I needed Him most, He always led me to His Word. It was there where He showed me the solutions to my problems. He never failed me. As I think back on it now, I had the most awesome experiences with God during my lowest points. Imagine that? I think God was trying to tell me something all along.

In fact, He said it through Paul in 2 Corinthians Chapter 12 and verse 9: "and (God) said unto me, my grace is sufficient for you: for my strength is made perfect in weakness." The apostle Paul penned those words many years before my existence. At the time, he was asking God to move something out of his way.

It appears Paul was plagued by demonic oppression. Three times Paul asked God to free him from whatever seemed to be tormenting him. God refused. Can you feel it? You are putting your life on the line to sell this company's product. You are hunted down by the opposition. They want to kill you, but you are faithful to the call. You just keep plodding along trying to inform people of this awesome deal God has for them. You get run out of New York. You flee to New Jersey. The mobs in Jersey are no more merciful than their New York counterparts.

You manage to make it to Philly (Philadelphia). However, it doesn't take long for the opposition to mount up again. Many nights you go to bed hungry. You rarely even get to sleep on a real bed, but you never stop spreading the good news about your product. Progress is being made. However, after much blood, sweat, and tears, you finally run out of options. You simply ask the head of the corporation for a small favor. What does he do? He rejects your plea.

Tell me, would you send out your resume post haste? Most of us would. Not Paul. He knew the importance of sacrifice. He knew and trusted the God of Abraham, Isaac, and Jacob. He understood we can't always understand the infinite One, but he was still willing to go to his death for such a One. Eventually, he did just that.

I don't believe Paul had any regrets about giving up his very life for the cause of Christ. During his time of service to the Master, he learned an awesome truth. I am ever grateful he passed it on to the rest of us. It is that whenever we are at our weakest point, Jehovah-Jireh, our provider, is right there with us. He is able. He will supply every ounce of strength needed to get us to the next level. Meanwhile, because we are dearly beloved children of His, He will comfort us.

Jesus wasn't just blowing off steam when He told His disciples: "I will not leave you comfort less; I will come to you." (John 14:18) The Master himself, in the form of the Holy Spirit, has come. He indwells all true believers. I know this piece of information is not just historically factual. I too have had the honor of experiencing God's Presence through the very same Spirit ever since I gave my life to Jesus.

I truly surrendered my heart to the Lord of glory and He continually manifested Himself in my life- in the very same ways Jesus had promised. He never stopped delivering on the promises He gave His children over 2000 years ago.

Awesome! No wonder I could stand up to the onslaught of the enemy again and again. Surely, this was no accomplishment of mine. Just as God promised, He chose me, He called me, and He sustained me through it all.

To top it all off, I have found a Friend who sticks closer than a brother. In all my first 33 years of life on this planet, I had not found too many people I would really consider friends. I used to wonder why people were so unreliable. Although I longed to really have a close personal relationship with someone, I never found such a one who would always be there for me. It seemed as though the more I gave, the less I received back from people. I didn't think I would ever find what I was looking for in a relationship. Then, I met the Master.

"**My grace is sufficient for you, for my strength is made perfect in weakness." (2 Corinthians 12:9)**

RAY OF HOPE

Sometimes, God used others to steer me into getting His will done in my life. The following is an example of this. I had never been given any kind of hope from the parole board. It was 1995. In over six years, my original proposed release date of 2006 had not changed. I had established an excellent record as a 'model' inmate. However, this didn't seem to matter. Needless to say, I was quite discouraged. Then, one day another inmate suggested to me I get my family to go to my upcoming parole hearing. The thought had never crossed my mind before.

It seemed to me the parole board had every intention of keeping me right up until 2006. To say the least, this was very frustrating to me. As the years passed by and the parole board refused to take any time off of my proposed sentence for my good behavior, I gave up all hope of ever getting paroled.

Since I fully expected God was going to do some kind of a miracle to get me released, I never gave it a second thought. By this time, I was no longer focusing on my release. I had already made up my mind I was going to serve God and not get distracted by anything else. If it was meant to be, I was prepared to spend the rest of my life in prison.

Thankfully, this was not God's plan. Instead, He chose to send me the right information at just the right time. When I heard the parole board had been taking time off because family members stood up for their loved ones, this made me realize there was a chance I could indeed get some time deducted from my proposed sentence. If my people would stand up for me, I could finally catch a break.

Although I really didn't think I had much of a chance with the parole board, I asked my family if they would give it a try. I was surprised, as well as grateful, when my mom and my sister, Geri, volunteered to go to my parole hearing.

After my sister and my mom had attended the hearing, I called my sister. I was shocked by her report. She informed me the parole board had deducted five years from my sentence. There was light at the end of the tunnel. Finally, they had made it possible for me to obtain a parole. I was ecstatic.

Although I hadn't been focusing on my release, it was quite a relief to know my physical freedom was now within reach. As I reflected on my situation, I could understand God was moving on my behalf because I had finally let go. Before, I was focusing on getting out, more than on serving Him. Once I had truly given up my quest for freedom, He rewarded my faithfulness.

As time went on, I continued to serve God with all of my might. As far as the state was concerned, I was serving time. In reality, I was serving God. I knew who was in control. I was still in prison because God was still working on me and using me to reach others with His truth.

The realization of this put my circumstances into a totally different light. First of all, I was honored. God had chosen me in spite of me. Secondly, I enjoyed having the great Potter work on me. I was the unfinished masterpiece still in progress.

I must admit it wasn't always easy having things from my character chipped away by the Master. However, it helped to know it was for my own good. As I continued on my journey to spiritual maturity, God taught me He doesn't waste any of our tears. In fact, the Bible tells us He keeps them in a bottle. They too are precious to Him. If God takes something from us, it is not just because of a whim of His. No, He is the real and true Father of mercies and the God of all comfort.

Sometimes, He is just pulling us from the fire. Like the tot who is going straight for the hot iron in the fireplace, we are sometimes unaware of the dangers and consequences of our actions. The glow of the hot iron looks so inviting.

Sometimes, we question why He doesn't cease from interfering with our pleasure? We fail to realize, should He withdraw His restraints on us, we would get 'burned'. Should He allow us to have our way and we do get burned, we often times blame Him for our pain. Don't we have a lot of nerve?

Somewhere along the way, I learned God only took the things from me which hindered my walk with Him. In effect, such things were stunting my spiritual growth. When I was willing to give up whatever the Holy Spirit would be dealing with me about, my daily walk became a joyous experience again. This resulted in my experiencing the joy of the Lord in abundance. Being imprisoned didn't affect this blessing one bit.

However, the joy of the Lord eluded me when I wasn't focused on His will. It seems there was one major hindrance to my reaching the mountain tops and making spiritual progress - me. Just as the apostle Paul had stated in the book of Romans Chapter 7 verses 18 through 25:

"For I know that in me (that is in my flesh,) dwells no good thing; for to will is present with me; but how to perform that which is good I find not. For the good that I would, I do not; but the evil which I would not, that I do. Now if I do that I would not, it is no more I that do it, but sin that dwells in me. I find then a law, that when I would do good, evil is present with me. For I delight in the law of God after the inward man: But I see another law in my members, warring against the law of my mind, and bringing me into captivity to the law of sin which is in my members. O wretched man that I am! Who shall deliver me from the body of this death"?

He wasn't copping out when he penned these words. He was simply explaining why Christians often run aground. It seems our ship has rudder problems. We try to steer our vessel in one direction but we sometimes encounter overwhelming resistance. In our quest for independence, we strive to keep the course. We will to please God and are bound and determined to use all of our own strength to do this.

However, our fleshly desires lead us into trouble more often than not. We certainly don't want to hit the rocks of our consequences, but we just can't seem to avoid them. Once we shipwreck, the devil starts hurling accusations at us.

"You're not a Christian. God can't be pleased with your walk. You're not cut out for this Christianity stuff," he accuses.

It's no wonder many baby Christians give up. They try to please God with their flawless conduct and fail every time. The accuser of the brethren launches one fiery dart after another. How can anyone stand up against one who has been around for thousands of years and knows every deceitful trick in the book?

Thank God, I have found the answer to this dilemma. Grace is the answer. In the very next verse Paul penned out, he explains: "I thank God through Jesus Christ our Lord." (Romans7:26)

Paul accepted God's grace in Jesus and counted on His strength to help him overcome his own fleshly desires. Like Paul, I have come to realize I can't do it. Though I would love to, I can't serve God without error. My spirit man has one desire and that is to please God. On the other hand, my flesh has one desire and that is to indulge. Whatever feels good, do it.

There is only one way for us to keep this monster called self under control. Like the apostle Paul, I learned I must die daily. But, self refuses to stay in the grave. If allowed, the spirit man will keep him restrained. Yet, this will only happen when I surrender my will to Jesus every day of my life.

The first thing I had to do in order to be an over comer, was to determine to read God's Word daily. Then, I had to be a doer of what I was taught. If I allow it to mold my character into what God wants me to be, I get victory over the flesh.

The more I read, the easier it was for God to increase my faith and strengthen my spirit man. He always prepared me for the inevitable battles I would face. Whenever I would feel weak and inadequate for the task ahead, He would lead me to verses like: "I can do all things through Christ, which strengthens me." (Philippians 4:13)

Sometimes, I didn't even have enough strength of will to do what I knew God wanted me to do.
I just couldn't kick some habits I knew were not pleasing to God. I desperately prayed again and again. Finally, during one such trial, He answered my prayers by leading me to Philippians 2:13. This verse states: "It is God which works in you both to will and to do of His good pleasure."

I shall never forget how I took Him up on this promise. Thereafter, whenever I got to the point where I realized some form of sinful behavior was just overwhelming me, I got on my knees and begged God to manifest Philippians 2:13 in my life.

When I meant business, He was quick to show me He did too. I can't even begin to count the number of times He manifested His promise to work it in me to 'do' His good pleasure. As if that weren't enough, He also revealed to me He promises never to allow us to be tempted beyond what we are able. He proved true to His Word and has pulled this rock-headed child of His out of the fire on numerous occasions.

I know there is no way I could possibly please God on my own. I still have my sinful nature. Therefore, I have to trust and rely on His grace. He has promised me He will keep on rescuing me. Jesus already paid the debt for every sin I will ever commit. Since I have faith in this promise, I am pleasing to God. "Without faith it is impossible to please God." (Hebrews 11:6)

This gift of faith He has given me, continually guided me as I made my long journey through the prison system. Time and time again, my faith in our heavenly Father opened the doors I needed opened in order to be able to enjoy my physical freedom once again.

One such instance came to pass while I was still

in prison at Charlotte Correctional. At the time, I came to the realization I couldn't make any more progress in my quest for physical freedom. I came to the point where I couldn't show the parole board I was making progress because there weren't any more programs I was eligible to participate in. However, insofar as the parole board is concerned, an inmate needed to participate in these various programs in order to get time off of his sentence.

In between reviews by the parole board, it was required of an inmate to show them he was constantly preparing himself for his release back into society. Things such as earning a GED, participating in AA, (Alcoholics Anonymous) NAA, (Narcotics Anonymous) and taking college courses, or completing any other programs sanctioned by the Department of Corrections would be looked upon by the parole board favorably. Hence, the inmate would receive time off for his good behavior.

Since I had already taken part in every program I was eligible for at Charlotte, I needed to transfer from Charlotte to some institution that offered me a program I hadn't already completed. After I participated and completed the program, I would be eligible for some more time off of my proposed release date.

However, transfers were not easy to come by at Charlotte Correctional Institution. With this in mind, I turned to the only One whom I knew was capable of helping me overcome my situation. I prayed a simple prayer and explained my situation to my heavenly Father. Of course, I knew He already knew. Since His Word tells us to be specific, I felt I should explain myself. So, I did. I asked Him to arrange a transfer to whatever institution He wanted me to go to.

Shortly after I prayed that prayer, I was given a custody reduction. This meant I would be able to go outside the prison gates each day. This was a good thing, but there was one drawback. I had to give up my job working for the prison chaplain. Consequently, this meant I would no longer be able to attend and conduct the choir practices which we had twice a week. I begged classification to allow me to stay in the chaplain's office to no avail.

I was assigned to work as a clerk in the warehouse outside the prison. I no longer had a choice in the matter. I briefly considered refusing to go to my new job assignment, but I was told I would be put in solitary confinement if I didn't report for work as scheduled.

I knew a trip to the prison confinement wouldn't set well with the parole board. Therefore, I started my new job as scheduled. Once I was on the job, I enjoyed my new surroundings. The warehouse manager was a pleasant man to work for. It also felt good to get away from the atmosphere of the prison for a little while each day. I felt as though I was out of the pressure cooker during such periods of time.

Then, I was made aware that skilled clerks with medium custody weren't easy to find at Charlotte. This too would work against my ever getting transferred. With my natural mind, I figured there was no way I was leaving Charlotte. I was between a rock and a hard place. As far as the natural eye could see, I had no options.

Thankfully, I had an ace-in-the-hole. My prayer did not fall on deaf ears. God wasn't about to let me down. To top it all off, He came through in a way I never would have imagined. He never ceases to amaze me.

It happened on one otherwise ordinary afternoon. While I was going through my daily routine of speed walking around the compound, God set His plan into motion. At the time, I was in the fenced-in recreation field. The field is about a sixteenth of a mile long and half as wide. As I was ending my routine, I was at the far end of the field. Suddenly, I noticed some inmate coming from the outside toilet enclosure. He was brandishing a very large knife.

When I saw this, my first instinct was to quickly

make my way to the exit gate at the opposite end of the rec field. I had no clue as to what was happening. I only knew I wanted to be as far away as possible from the huge knife I saw the inmate wielding.

Although I didn't yet know it, by the time I had reached the exit, this inmate had stabbed someone. Before I could make my exit, I was approached by one of the officers. He commanded me to go with him back to the opposite end of the rec field.

I didn't understand why the officer was leading me back to the opposite end of the rec field. In fact, I was protesting to him because I had already done my share of walking. At that point, all I wanted to do was head back to my dorm and take a hot shower.

However, the officer thought I was involved in the stabbing which had just taken place. While we were both walking towards the other end of the field, he was questioning me about the stabbing. He explained to me that I was a suspect in the stabbing.

I was shocked. I told the officer I was a Christian and had never possessed a knife as long as I had been in prison.

"I don't need a weapon to fight my battles. Jesus is my deliverer," I protested.

As we continued our walk, I noticed another officer and a group of inmates were walking towards us. I never suspected what would happen next. Once the inmates had come closer to us, one Spanish inmate shouted to me:

"You have a big mouth!"

Immediately after this, he punched me in the mouth. Afterwards, a group of other Spanish inmates, which were then within range of me, proceeded to throw punches and kicks at me. I noticed the officer quickly jumping back out of the way of the scuffle. My first reaction was to cover up. I didn't want to be written up for fighting. Thankfully, I had already learned He would be fighting my battles anyway. With this in mind, I just rolled with the punches.

Shortly after the assault on me had started, reinforcements arrived in the form of a group of prison guards. They quickly proceeded to break up the gang of assailants. Needless to say, I was sure glad to see those guys.

The officers quickly placed my attackers in handcuffs and took them away. Then, one of the officers gave the command for me to be escorted to the infirmary. As a result of the attack on me, I had received a bloody lip. Since it is a DOC policy to have any inmates involved in any sort of a physical confrontation checked out by the medical staff, I understood what to expect next.

I was quickly given medical attention. After I had been treated, the officer escorted me to the lieutenant's office. When I arrived there, they were in the process of trying to sort out what had taken place earlier. By the time I was called on, they pretty much knew what was going on.

The lieutenant explained to me there had been a case of mistaken identity. Somehow, the officers had gotten word I was the inmate who had committed the stabbing on the recreation field.

"This was a gang-related assault. The 'Latin Kings' are responsible and they seem to think you were snitching on them. We feel you won't be safe on the compound right now, so we are placing you into protective custody," the lieutenant explained.

I in no way wanted this, so I tried to convince the lieutenant I would not be harmed.

“I have been in prison for over 10 years and the Lord has always protected me. He has gotten me this far and I don’t think the Latin Kings are bigger than Him,” I protested.

However, the lieutenant didn’t have my kind of faith. He ordered an officer to take me to my quarters and allow me to pack up all of my belongings. At the time, the entire compound was on lock down. This was a precautionary measure to help prevent the spread of violence.

While I was being escorted to my room, some of the inmates in my housing area shouted out:

"Snitch"!

I tried to just ignore the slurs. (The dorm was divided up into four wings with about sixty two-man rooms in each section). Yet, I was taken aback by the fact it was the inmates in my section who were hurling the insults at me.

This really saddened me. I thought I had been friends with the majority of those. I had always tried to be an example of a true believer to those guys. At that moment, I was mainly disappointed because I figured my entire testimony to the inmates at Charlotte Correctional was totally destroyed.

I was really discouraged by this turn of events. I didn't want to be taken off the compound under those conditions. I also knew I was going to miss working outside the fence and exercising my newly acquired custody. Worse yet, I would be missing playing the piano in the Sunday service.

There was one upside to all of this. I knew I was going to be in a solitary cell and all alone with God. Plus, I figured He was going to work the whole situation out for good eventually. Until He did so, I planned to take advantage of being in a cell by myself. Since the first day I was incarcerated, I hadn't been alone in my own room. Being able to meditate on God's Word undisturbed made going into confinement appealing to me.

After I packed up all of my belongings, the officer escorted me to the confinement area. A few minutes later, I was placed in a room by myself. Before I even finished unpacking my belongings, I heard an inmate call out to me. Surprisingly, he knew my name. As he called it out, he boasted that he was the one who punched me in the mouth earlier that day.

I responded by telling him I forgave him and that Jesus loved him. Then, I asked him what caused him to attack me. He explained it was because I snitched on one of his gang members. I told him I didn't snitch on anybody. Then, I tried to explain what it was that I had been trying to convey to the officer who had brought me over to him and his buddies.

At this point, I could sense this inmate's confusion. I prayed and asked God to touch this man's heart and bring him to Jesus. As soon as we ended our conversation, I started reading my Bible. A few hours later, the inmate who had boasted about assaulting me called out to me again. This time, it was to issue an apology to me. He explained one of his buddies had found out it was not me who snitched on his gang after all.

Evidently, I was cleared of all guilt. I was delighted to hear this. I thanked the inmate and told him I was praying for him. Then, I proceeded to enjoy some quiet time with the Lord. The next few days seemed to fly by. Then, I was told I was going to be interviewed by a review committee. I figured this would result in my being released back out onto the compound. I was delighted.

However, once I was brought before the committee they denied my request. According to their estimates, there were quite a few of the Latin Kings gang members at Charlotte. They explained they were not going to take a chance by allowing me to be released back into the general prison population.

I tried to convince the members of the committee I was no longer in any danger. I explained what I was told by one of my assailants. However, the committee wouldn't accept an inmate's testimony. Therefore, I knew there was nothing else to be said. It was inevitable the committee was going to have me transferred.

At this point, it dawned on me. This was God's answer to my prayer. Duh! It didn't come in the way that I thought it would, but God has the prerogative to do whatever He wills. Although I had enough experience with His ways to understand this, I still missed it.

Nevertheless, now I understood and was grateful. I thanked Him for it.

God had once again turned what I considered a bad situation into a blessing. Although I was sad I was leaving behind some good, Christian brothers, I looked forward to finding out what He had in store for me next.

"For I know the thoughts that I think toward you, says the Lord, thoughts of peace and not of evil, to give you an expected end." (Jeremiah 29:11)

SURPRISE, SURPRISE!

While I awaited my transfer, I really enjoyed my time alone with God. He really blessed me. He even gave me some opportunities to witness to some of the other men who were being held in protective custody.

A few days after I faced the review board, I was transferred to the South Florida Reception Center. I was excited. I knew a new chapter in the book of my life had just begun. Although I had no clue where I was heading, I was confident I was in store for a blessing.

I arrived at the South Florida Reception Center without incident. This institution is where most inmates, who have been convicted in the southern half of the state, are sent from the various county jails. While there, they are evaluated and assigned to their permanent institution. Whenever an inmate, who is already in the system, is transferred needs various types of medical attention, or is on their way to a court hearing, they usually wind up in SFRC.

Once everyone who traveled on the bus with me was processed, we were assigned to our temporary housing. I had barely settled into my new quarters when our dorm was called out for chow. After chow, I was anxious to get out into the yard. I hadn't been able to enjoy a good walk in a couple of weeks. Once our dorm was released, I wasted no time making my way around the rec field.

It was a beautiful south Florida evening. As I was just about finished with my walk, I came upon an inmate I had known years earlier. I was shocked to see this person back in prison. The last time I had seen him he was being paroled from Baker Correctional Institution. I don't remember his name right now. I do remember the last time I had seen him he seemed to be on fire for Jesus. In fact, while he was at Baker, he had been an awesome witness for Jesus.

Once he recognized me, he greeted me with a

strong Christian hug. As he did so, I cut to the chase and asked him what had happened? I was curious to know the reason why this strong man of God was on his way back to prison.

He was real enough to take the blame for his own actions. He explained he had hooked up with some woman shortly after his release from prison. He began to have sex with her even though he knew
God frowns on sexual relations outside the boundaries of marriage. In fact, it is called fornication in the Bible. This relationship was the beginning of his downfall. He was too ashamed to go into further details and I didn't press the issue.

At any rate, this brother gave in to the desires of his flesh. As a result he was on his way back to prison with a lot of fresh time to serve. If anybody would have told me this was going to happen to this dear brother, I would not have believed them. This served as a stern warning to me. The Bible makes it clear promises you shall reap what you sow. I had just witnessed proof of that.

I determined right then and there I would under no circumstances commit fornication once I was released. By experience and examples, I had no doubt God chastises His children when they are disobedient to His commandments. He still loves them and He won't renege on any of His promises to them. Yet, a child of God who willingly sins will undoubtedly be punished. In the process of sinning, they unknowingly open up the door to cursing. This allows the devil the freedom to wreak havoc in their lives and circumstances. There is no way to avoid such repercussions.

You see, God allows Satan to punish His disobedient children. This is something the devil is only too glad to do. God has clearly shown us this spiritual law in the book of Job. He also made it quite evident the devil can only go as far as He allows. Hence, this evil-doer is merely a pawn in God's overall plan. In effect, He uses the devil to mete out punishment to teach His children obedience. Then, He works even all such things out for the good of them who love Him.

I prayed with this dear brother and wished him Godspeed. Shortly thereafter, the yard was closed and we both had to report to our dormitories. I never saw this brother again. But, I am sure he is back on track and is serving God again. It is sad he had to fall, but I am sure God will use even this for His glory.

The following morning, I was transferred to Hendry Correctional. I had always heard good things about Hendry. Therefore, I was glad when I learned this institution was my next stop. Once I arrived there, I was assigned to my temporary quarters. After a long trip and the slow process of being assigned to my housing unit, I was exhausted. To my delight, I was placed into a private room. I had expected to be assigned to an open-bay dorm. That type of dorm is usually noisy and overcrowded, so I was pleasantly surprised.

Once I mingled in with the population at Hendry, I was informed I would be interviewed by a classification officer within three or four days. At that time, I would be given a job and assigned to my permanent quarters.

During my first few days there, I met quite a few Christians and I attended just about every Christian function offered. I quickly became acquainted with some of the Christian musicians. Some of the other brothers befriended me and tried to help me in various ways.

One brother introduced me to the chaplain and helped me to get the opportunity to play the keyboard in their chapel band. Another brother offered to get me a job working for the chaplain. I also had an offer to take a position as a tutor in the GED program at Hendry.

I was delighted the Lord had brought so many sincere Christians my way so swiftly. It seemed to me He had opened the doors for me to enjoy a nice 'cushy' job at Hendry. However, I wanted to exercise my custody by working outside of the fence. I figured this would be the best way to get my custody lowered even more. I hoped this would eventually lead me to a work-release program.

I prayed about it and asked the Lord to just place me where He wanted me to be. When I went for my interview with the classification officer, I received another one of those DOC slaps in the face. I don't remember the gentleman's name, but I do remember how snippy he was.

I also remember how shocked I was to hear I was being assigned to work in the kitchen at Hendry. This was the last place I wanted to work. I had my fill of kitchen work at Baker. In fact, I swore I would never again place myself in that position. This rude dude told me I had no choice. I was going to work in the kitchen.

I explained to him I wanted to exercise my custody and, therefore, wanted a position outside the fence. He still refused to change my job assignment. As a last resort, I told him I was offered a job working for the chaplain as well as a position in the school at Hendry. This didn't faze him at all.

"You're going in the kitchen!" he forcefully declared.

Needless to say, this really got my goat. I was dumbfounded this was happening to me. After all, I was the victim here. How could the DOC take away a privilege I had earned for no fault of my own? Why was I being persecuted? I had a good mind to tell this evil messenger of Satan to take his job and shove it.

Yet, I knew I would be the loser if I did. Once again, there was nothing I could do. However, I could go over this meatball's head. I did just that. I complained to God. However, He didn't seem impressed either. Once again, I was put in a position I could not comprehend.

"Why? What have I done wrong?" I questioned my Maker.

At that point, it seemed as though I was going backwards. To top it all off, I got assigned to sleep in an open-bay dorm. It looked as though I had quickly gone from being blessed to being cursed.

However, God reminded me He was still in control. He didn't mess up. All I had to do was to remain faithful to Him and I would be blessed through it all. He assured me this was just another opportunity to exercise my faith. When I grasped that, I decided I was going to work in the kitchen and do the best job I could.

I remembered I had read in God's Word, "And whatsoever you do in word or deed, do all in the name of the Lord Jesus, giving thanks to God and the Father by him." (Colossians 3:17) I also read in Colossians 3:23, "and whatsoever you do, do it heartily, as to the Lord, and not unto men."

As far as I could figure this was a no-brainer. I had to obey God's Word. I quickly settled into my new job in the kitchen and tried to make the best of my situation. Since I worked the early morning shift in the kitchen, I had much of my day free. Therefore, I exercised daily and practiced playing the guitar with another brother who had befriended me.

I don't remember how much time slipped by. At any rate, one day I was awakened and told I was being shipped to the work camp. The work camp was a few miles away from the institution at Hendry. I looked forward to going to the work camp. Mainly, because I had been told it was a much more peaceful atmosphere than the prison.

There were only about 200 men being housed at the work camp. This was a far cry from the institution's population - which ranged from 900 to 1,100 inmates. I was also told the food was much better at the work camp. According to the info I had received, the inmates were given bigger portions of food there as well.

The main reason I looked forward to going to the work camp was because I would be able to exercise my custody there. Most of the inmates who are housed at work camps are assigned jobs which are located outside the fence.

Once again, I was confident I was on the verge

of a blessing. This time I was right. It seemed like the Lord had prepared the way for me well before I arrived at the work camp. He used a Christian friend of mine from Hendry to do so. This inmate, named Joe, had become good friends with me during my short stay there. Then, one day without warning, he was shipped out to the work camp.

While Joe was at the work camp, he became friends with an inmate who worked in the motor pool outside the fence. As God would have it, Joe's friend told him his boss needed a clerk for the motor pool. When I arrived on the scene, he asked me if I wanted the job. I jumped at the opportunity.

Since I always enjoyed working on motor vehicles, and I was a good clerk, I figured this was a perfect spot for me. I imagined this was an opportunity for me to learn some more things about auto mechanics as well. I jumped at the chance for this position.

Later that day, Joe saw his friend and told him I was very interested in the clerk's position.
To my delight, I was hired the following day. When I arrived at the work camp, I was given a new classification officer. No love lost there. I was so glad I didn't have to deal with my former persecutor. My new classification officer was quite an improvement from the old one. He actually seemed willing to help me. He asked me where I would like to work. I explained I was offered a job as a clerk in the motor pool. He told me he would confirm this offer. He did so and afterwards assign me to the motor pool. I was delighted.

I reported for work the next day. My new boss picked up the inmate who got me the job, another inmate, and myself and took us to the motor pool. My new boss was a nice, easy going, young redneck. He and I hit it off right away.

Once we arrived at the motor pool, I was shown to my office. Then, he explained what would be my main duties as clerk. Afterwards, he told me to have a look around the rest of the complex which was connected to the motor pool. While I did so, he took off on some mission. I didn't see him again until it was around the time for the inmates who worked outside the fence to report back to the work camp.

It turned out this was pretty much the daily routine at my new job assignment. I was amazed and delighted at my new found freedom. Since my boss usually left me alone in the motor pool office, I enjoyed having a little privacy for a change. I was amazed I was no longer being constantly monitored by the authorities who were in charge of me.

Inside the fences, an inmate has absolutely no privacy. They are under constant surveillance. I can understand this. After all, most of the time the authorities are watching us for our own safety. Still, I got tired of living a life similar to that of a fish in a bowl.

After I had worked in the motor pool for about two months, the Lord had another pleasant surprise for me. I don’t remember who, but He used someone to make the suggestion to me that I ask my boss to put me in for a custody change.

Once again, God was on the move. I had no intentions of asking for a custody change until that idea was brought up. Actually, I didn't even think my boss would go along with the idea for fear of losing me. He had expressed he was happy to have a good clerk whom he knew he could trust for a change. It seemed that he hadn’t had too many of those in the past. Therefore, I wouldn’t have blamed him for wanting to keep me as long as possible.

Even if my boss granted my request, I wasn't sure my classification office would be willing to drop my custody at that point in time. However, I figured I had nothing to lose. I went ahead and asked my boss. To my surprise, he was quite willing to put me in for a custody change.

It was an even greater surprise to me when I was given minimum custody status a few days later.

In the interim, my good friend, Joe, had been transferred to the Fort Myers work-release center. I missed him, but I was thankful for the time we had shared Jesus with one another.

Once I had the minimum custody status, the Lord used somebody else to suggest I put in for work-release. Again, I don't remember who came up with the idea, but I figured it was worth a try. I sent in a request and asked to be transferred to the same work-release camp Joe was sent to. I really didn't think this was going to happen.

First of all, I still had over three years left before my proposed release date. Also, I remembered the way the D.O.C. had rated my conviction. It was well known they didn't give too many felons much leeway. To top it off, several other inmates, who had charges similar to mine, had recently committed more crimes while they were at a work-release facility. In light of that, I sincerely doubted there was even a faint hope of my ever being accepted for the work-release program.

In spite of all this, I figured God had sent someone across my path to bring me that suggestion for a reason. Up until then, He had been doing things like that to get me to step out in faith. Once again, I figured I had nothing to lose, so I was willing to give it a try.

I filled out a request form and sent it to my classification officer. Shortly after I submitted the request, I was granted a transfer to the Fort Myers work-release center. This really caught me by surprise - in a good way. I never imagined I was going to be blessed in so many ways in such a short amount of time. Once again, I witnessed firsthand God is faithful. He loves to reward those who diligently seek Him. Since I passed the tests, this was just His way of rewarding me for putting all of my trust in Him.

"For you will light my candle: the LORD my God will enlighten my darkness."

(Psalms 18:28)

GREATER HORIZONS

Once I arrived at the work-release center, I was reunited with my good friend Joe. It just so happened he was the laundry man there. This was the best job for a permanent party work-release inmate. (An inmate is not allowed to go out into the community and work until they have 18 months or less left on their sentence. These inmates are considered permanent party. These inmates can be assigned to a work-release center with three years or less left on their sentence. These inmates are allowed to do public works, and community service, but only while under supervision.)

It turned out Joe didn't like being inside the work-release center all of the time. He told me he had planned to get a job change. He wanted to get a job working on the logging crew. As he explained it, he just wanted to get out of the center and into the 'free' world.

Coincidentally, I found out that I was being assigned to the logging crew. I was not a happy camper. Once I found this out, I was very disappointed. I did not want to be out in the hot, Florida sun chopping down trees. I was well into my forties by this time and I had no desire to do the kind of labor required of the inmates who worked on the logging crew. Since I had been working as a clerk most of the time I had been in prison, I didn't think I was physically fit for this type of manual labor anymore.

Once again, I was being tried. In response, I chose to take my situation to the Lord in prayer. I thanked Him once again for bringing me to the work-release center in the first place. Then, I asked Him, if it were possible, would He please get me a better job. Afterwards, I explained whatever His will was concerning my job assignment I was ready to accept it.

Shortly after I prayed that prayer, Joe approached

me and offered to recommend me for the laundry man position he was vacating. He promised to speak to the classification officer and suggest to him that he would like to take my place on the logging crew.

I was so grateful. Even if it didn't work out, I appreciated his effort on my behalf. I didn't hesitate to let him know this. The following day, Joe told me the classification officer wanted to see me. I assumed I was in for a blessing. I swiftly arrived at his office. He cordially greeted me and he told me to have a seat.

"You have been highly recommended. Therefore, I am going to assign you to work as the laundry man here at the work-release center," he said. I was shocked. I had never received a note of approval from any of the DOC administration in all my years of incarceration. Needless to say, my heart jumped for joy as I heard those words.

During the next few months, my stay at the Fort Myers work-release center was like being in a different world. Time seemed to pass by much quicker. I loved my job and I was comfortable with the peaceful atmosphere there. Compared to my prison experience, I was living on easy street.

To top it off, I was given one eight-hour furlough each week. My entire family was living on the opposite coast of Florida, so I couldn't go home for my furloughs. However, the Lord had a plan. He wasn't going to allow that blessing to go unclaimed.

Two of my very dear brothers-in-Christ, Les Lemke, and Ray Gegner, opened up their homes to me. These were the brothers I had met earlier at Charlotte Correctional. They held a Bible study there every Friday evening. This fellowship was usually the highlight of my week. During that time, we had all become very close brothers in the Lord.

Once I arrived at work-release, they came to visit me and offered to take me to their homes once I was granted furloughs. As soon as I was given this liberty, one of those dear brothers would pick me up at the center and bring me to his home. On the following week, the other brother picked me up and brought me to his home.

To my delight, both of their wives were excellent cooks. Needless to say, I never ended any of my furloughs on an empty stomach. Both of these brothers owned beautiful homes in Cape Coral and they each had a swimming pool. I was so blessed. I love swimming and on each of my furloughs I was able to enjoy taking a refreshing dip. I could not have been more delighted. For many years, I yearned to go swimming but couldn‘t. I distinctly remember how I praised my heavenly Father for the opportunity to enjoy this blessing each time I swam.

After I had been at the work-release center for several months, I was called into the front office. The officer on duty handed me a telephone receiver. On the other end of the line, was my ex. When she said hello to me, I almost fell over.

I hadn't heard a word from her or my children in years. I had no idea where they were. In fact, I didn’t know whether or not they were dead or alive. What I did know was that they were in God's hands and He would take better care of them than I ever could. He didn't disappoint me.

She soon told me everyone was fine. She informed me she had moved to New Jersey. Since she had originally lived in Long Branch, N.J, she just wanted to be near her family she explained. I didn't blame her for that.

During our conversation, she led me to believe she wanted to restart our relationship. I told her I wouldn't object to that. I wanted my children to have a stable home environment. I knew I couldn't change the past, but I could be an important part of their future.

I told her we should just play it by ear. We both had been through a lot and it wasn't quite over yet. I let her know if she were there once I was released, I was willing to pick up where we had left off. I even reassured her I would not be interested in knowing what she had or hadn't done in my absence.

As far as I was concerned, the past would be better kept in the past. I didn't want to know what she had gone through. My only interest was the fact she would be there for me in the future. As we ended our conversation, she told me to call her in a couple of days and gave me a number where she could be reached.

After I had finished speaking to her, I marveled at God's faithfulness. Not only had He taken such good care of my loved ones, He had also put me back in touch with them. I was anxious to see all of my children again. I could hardly wait to hold them in my arms.

There is simply no way to explain the emotional pain I experienced knowing I couldn't be there for them. For years on end, I hoped against hope I would be able to make it up to them. This was without a doubt the worst part of spending so many years in custody. I can't put it into words so I won't even attempt that. However, Jesus gave me the faith to believe in my heart that someday I would be there for them. The phone call I had just received was confirmation my faith had not been in vain.

Everything seemed to be looking up for me. Maybe, this was because I had learned how to look up...to God. Over the years, He had been quite patient with me. I can only imagine how He had longed to bless me, but I kept getting in the way. Once I passed my final exam in the school of hard knocks, He wasted no time opening up the windows of heaven in order to pour out His grace upon me.

Being at the work-release center was a mountain top experience for me. Even though I couldn't go out of the center and work just yet, I had many other things to be thankful for. Then, I was reminded, a spiritual high is usually followed by a trek through the valley.

The very next time I spoke to my ex, I discovered she had a change of heart. She didn't want to her boyfriend prior to contacting me the first time. I assumed she was looking to use me as a replacement for him at that time. It turns out she had since made up with him.

During our second conversation she made it clear she wasn't really ready to restart our relationship. When I heard that, it was quite a let down for me. Yet, I knew God had a plan. I wasn't about to force the situation. I let her know I had no problem with her choice. I only wanted to be able to see my children once I was released. She told me she wanted me to see them. On that note, we ended our conversation.

About a week after the big let down I was given, the Colonel in charge of the Fort Myers work-release center had some more bad news for me. One afternoon, he made an announcement over the PA system. At that time, he ordered all the inmates at the center to come into the recreation room for a mandatory meeting.

Once we were all assembled, the Colonel gave us the bad news. It seemed the Department of Corrections had decided to convert the Fort Myers work-release center into a work camp. He informed us, that all inmates who were left in the center, at the time of the transformation, would be kept there until their sentence was completed.

This was really bad news for me. I was not yet eligible to leave the center to work an outside job. Therefore, I didn't think I stood a chance of transferring out to another work-release center until I had 18 months or less left on my sentence. Once they put a fence around the center, I wouldn't ever be able to go out into the surrounding community again until I was paroled.

If they converted to a work camp, this would mean no more furloughs and I wouldn't even be allowed to go to an outside church for worship services anymore. They also wouldn't give me an opportunity to go out on any shopping trips to community stores. In fact, I wouldn't be able to go to any of the outside functions, which I had become accustomed to attending on a regular basis. Worst of all, I would have to spend the rest of my time being fenced in once again. From my point of view, it was as though I was being sent back to prison. I didn't do anything wrong to warrant this. My initial reaction was to question God? How could He allow this to happen?

Before I got too carried away, the Holy Spirit quickly led me to gather up my thoughts by bringing God's Word to my remembrance. As usual, He had the solution to my problem. By this time, I had been reading the Bible on a daily basis for about 15 years. Since I had an abundance of God's Word stored up in my heart, He was able to remind me what was promised to me and to comfort me in my hour of desperation. This is exactly what Jesus promised us in the Gospel of John Chapter 14 verse 26:

"But the Comforter, who is the Holy Spirit, whom the Father will send in my name, he shall teach you all things and bring all things to your remembrance, whatever I have said to you."

The scripture He brought to my mind was: "For the Lord God is a sun and shield; the Lord will give grace and glory; no good thing will He withhold from them that walk uprightly." (Psalms 84:11) At that point, I trusted God would shield me from the attempts of the devil to place me back into a prison environment. In my heart, I knew old slew foot was trying to get me to have a lapse in my faith. I also knew he was out to rob me of any blessings God had already bestowed upon me.

I understood this fact because Jesus told us (in John 10:10) "The thief comes to steal, and to kill, and to destroy. I am come that you might have life, and that more abundantly." Jesus was referring to Satan. He is the thief. From what I understood of the scriptures, Jesus came to give me blessings. On the other hand, Satan is out to curse God's children by stealing our blessings.

Yet, the devil couldn't just snatch away my blessings. I was under the umbrella of God's protection as a child of His. Unless I was living in rebellion to

God's commands, I knew the Bible promises that I could rule in this life as an heir of God. "..they which receive abundance of grace and of the gift of righteousness shall reign in life by one, Jesus Christ.' (Romans 5:17)

Since I knew the Word of God, I was determined to stand on it and hold onto what He had already given me. I turned to Him in prayer and asked Him to make a way for me to transfer out of the Fort Myers work-release center before it was converted into a work camp. I was hoping He would make a way for me to transfer to Hollywood work-release center.

In spite of the department of corrections rule stating inmates must have no more than 18 months left, before they could go out into society and work, I prayed He would give me favor and cause me to be an exception to the rule. After praying, I felt at peace. I knew in my heart God had a plan.

As the laundry man at the work-release center, some of my duties included cleaning the staff restrooms, the Colonel's office, and the staff snack area. Therefore, during the course of my duties I had often come into contact with the Colonel. During my stay there, we had several conversations and were on pretty friendly terms. We had learned we both had something in common. Among other things, the Colonel loved to run and so did I.

Suddenly, I felt led to approach him and ask him if there was anything he could do to help me to obtain a transfer. A short time later, I was given the opportunity and I spoke with him. After I explained my situation to him, he told me he would try to help me in any way he possibly could. He promised to put me in for a transfer. After our conversation, I knew in my heart everything would work out in my favor.

About a week later, the Colonel called me into his office. He told me my transfer had been approved. I was going to the Hollywood work-release center. I was ecstatic. Yet, I really had no idea how many more awesome blessings God was preparing to pour out upon me.

When I arrived at the Hollywood work-release center, one of the first people I 'happened' across was my Christian brother, Joe. It seemed that God wanted us two to be together for a while longer. He joyfully showed me around the center and let me know what to expect from the authorities there.

During this time, he told me another good friend of mine was at the center. According to him, my friend was also a former jockey. I was surprised to find out it was my old buddy, Ricci Squartino. I hadn't seen or heard from him in about 13 years. In fact, the last time I had seen him was while I was out on an appeal bond.

Before I got saved, I knew Ricci. I first met him when he was aspiring to become a jockey. We immediately became good friends. I could identify with the struggle he was going through. Years earlier, I had already experienced those same pains.

When I first saw Ricci exercise a racehorse, I knew he was a natural. I decided to try to help him further his career along. Although he hadn't ridden in any races up to that time, I gave him his first mount.

The horse I put Ricci on was the best one I owned at the time. Unfortunately, he wasn't able to make much of a showing in his first race. As it turned out my horse, was injured. At any rate, he broke the ice that day. This was a crucial point in his career as a jockey. Most trainers won't ride an apprentice jockey until he has already shown them what he is capable of doing on a horse in an actual race.

Since I had faced this same 'catch 22' situation as an apprentice jockey, I was pleased to be able to help Ricci to overcome that obstacle. A short time later, Ricci made it into the limelight on the Florida racing circuit.

Before his career bloomed, Ricci and I were getting acquainted with one another and we did some wild things together. I am not going to go into the details concerning the specific situations we were involved in simply because I'm not willing to give the devil any glory. However, I just want the readers of this book to understand he was well acquainted with the very wild and absolutely crazy guy I used to be.

When I was a fugitive from justice, Ricci and I suddenly lost contact with one another. This was due to the fact that I had gotten myself into the situation which eventually landed me in prison. I did not have a clue our paths would ever cross again.

While I was out on an appeal bond, this came about. Two years after Ricci and me had last seen each other he came strolling into the restaurant where I had been working. On that occasion, he was driving a Mercedes Benz and I knew he had done quite well for himself. I also knew he didn't know what the real purpose of his life was.

I wasted no time sharing with him what God had taught me. I witnessed to him and explained how God had been working in my life. I did my best to steer Ricci to Jesus that day. I assured him his fame and fortune would waste away should he refuse to surrender his life to God. Unfortunately, at that time he wasn't ready to give his life to Jesus.

The next time we met (about 10 years later), he told me he had lost everything. In fact, he was on the verge of completing his second stint as an inmate in the Florida prison system. As we got reacquainted, he explained how far he had fallen.

Turns out, he had gone to New York and climbed up to the top in the jockey standings there. He lived life in the fast lane and eventually became addicted to cocaine. As though this weren't enough, he moved on to crack cocaine and the rest is history.

It was a very sad thing for me to see how his life had taken such a downward spiral. I knew he was searching for the same thing everyone else is. He was looking for peace, contentment, love, and acceptance. Like most of us, he was looking for these things in all the wrong places. I tried to convey this to him.

First, I told him how God had brought me through the many years of captivity I had experienced. Then, I explained how awesome God was and how He had changed me. I was hoping he too would be willing to give Jesus a shot at improving his life. I soon discovered he hadn't yet gotten to that point in his life. He was still desperately trying to hold onto something he had no control over.

A few days later, I got to meet his wife and his son. As I witnessed Ricci interacting with his son, on one of his visits, I knew he had a deep love for that boy. As I became acquainted with his wife, I realized she too was into drugs. Due to what I had learned about his lifestyle in that short period of time, I didn't believe he would be able to stay out of prison for very long.

Since I really cared about his well being, I told him straight up.

"If you love your son, you need to surrender your life to Jesus. From what I see, you have quite a hurdle to overcome. If you don't get your drug problem under control, there is no way you will be there for him," I emphatically insisted.

I knew in my heart, what I was saying was definitely going to come to pass. I only wish he would have believed me. Unfortunately, he refused to turn his troubled heart over to Jesus that day. A few months later, he was released from custody and I lost contact with him once again.

"Present your bodies a living sacrifice, holy, acceptable to God, which is your reasonable service. And be not conformed to this world, but be transformed by the renewing of your mind, that you may prove what is that good, and acceptable, and perfect will of God." (Romans, 12:1,2)

ONE FOOT OUT

My stay with the Department of Corrections was still a long way from over. However, I was being blessed in every way I could imagine. First of all, I got a job in a very popular restaurant in Pembroke Pines as a waiter. This in itself was a miracle. No one on record at the work-release center had ever worked as a server. They offered positions in restaurants such as dishwashers, cooks, and prep workers. There was a multitude of other unskilled labor positions available to inmates as well. But, they did not have any opportunities available for servers.

However, I wasn't about to work for minimum wage doing manual labor at my age. (I was about 48 years old at the time). I knew I could make a decent living serving tables and I enjoyed serving people. It was my plan that I do this kind of work once I was released. Therefore, I figured I would get my foot in the door while I worked my way out of the prison system.

Although none of the local restaurants had advertised for servers, I thought I would apply anyway. By God's grace, I was able to convince the officer, who was in charge of helping inmates find their employment, that I was capable of obtaining work as a server. Once this obstacle had been cleared, I had to prove myself to my potential employer.

This proved to be the greater task. The particular restaurant I chose to apply at was a corporate owned establishment. Although they had hired several inmates from the work-release center, they didn't seem to want to hire any inmate servers. I figured this was due to the fact they didn't trust ex-cons to handle money transactions.

I can't say I blamed them. Yet, I was out to change their minds. Not only did I want the job, I also wanted to prove an ex-con who has Jesus in his life is able to be trusted. (Actually, they can be trusted even more than the most outstanding citizen who doesn't acknowledge Jesus' lordship).

After several phone calls, I was able to schedule myself an interview with one of the managers of the restaurant. Then, I was taken there by van from the work-release center. I was dropped off and instructed to call the center once my interview was completed.

After I had filled out several pages of the employment application, the manager interviewed me. He and I hit it off pretty well, so I figured I would be hired the same day. We talked for about half an hour and then the manager handed me a fairly thick folder. To my surprise, the interview was only the beginning of a very long process I would have to endure.

He instructed me to study the menu inside the folder. After I learned the entire menu and the ingredients of each dish, I was to call and schedule another interview. At this point, I realized this was not going to be as easy as I had thought.

When I opened the folder and examined its contents, my suspicions were confirmed. Inside the folder, I found about 10 pages listing the entrees and the ingredients of each dish served at this restaurant. They served Italian food. Although I am an Italian-American, I had never heard of many of the ingredients listed on the menu. I wasn't about to give up, though. I was determined to give it my all. I believed God's Word which states in Philippians 4:13 "I can do all things through Christ, which strengthens me."

I took the menu back to the work-release center and studied it in its entirety for about a week. Then, I made my appointment for a second interview. Once I arrived at the restaurant, I had another surprise waiting for me. I had expected to be interviewed by the same manager. Not so, I was told that particular manager was not on duty that day.

I unexpectedly got to meet another of the restaurant's managers. Once this manager had quizzed me on the menu, he asked me if I knew about certain ingredients in the various dishes. I didn't totally convince him I knew the menu as well as he had expected I should. Yet, the manager was gracious enough that he took the time to explain each one of the ingredients to me.

Afterwards, he told me to familiarize myself with all of the ingredients a little better. Once I felt comfortable I knew them well enough, I could schedule my final interview. He also informed me my next interview would be conducted by the general manager.

I almost got discouraged. After all, I had never been through such a long process to obtain a job in my whole life. Usually whenever I sought employment, I was hired on the spot. However, I realized this was a whole new ballgame and I just had to play according to their rules.

I was grateful I was even given the opportunity to work for this corporation. Since I was a convicted felon, I could have been passed over on that basis alone. I had come too far already. I wasn't going to let this opportunity slip away.

I studied hard. Then, I studied some more. Finally, I felt I had every one of the ingredients in the restaurants dishes down to a science. Then, I made an appointment for my final interview. I was fortunate enough to schedule one immediately.

During my interview, the general manager told me how impressed he was with my knowledge of the menu. He wasted no time in hiring me. Needless to say, I was quite relieved the whole process was over. I knew, had I not prayed and trusted God, I never could have succeeded in landing this job.

I began work a few days later. I was delighted to be able to go out into society and do what most of the general public was doing. I soon received another blessing. The work- release center informed me I could take a bus to work every day, if I chose this method of transportation. It wasn't mandatory for me to ride to work on the DOC van.

To the average person, riding on a bus is not much of a blessing. However, after being under constant supervision for about 10 years, riding the public transportation was a privilege to me. Being out in public and not having someone looking over my shoulder gave me a real sense of freedom.

Once I started work at the restaurant, I quickly adjusted to the system they used there. I really enjoyed serving people and my co-workers were all very friendly. In fact, some were too friendly. I was doing my very best to please the Lord, but old slew foot kept trying his best to entrap me.

There were some real pretty, young girls serving tables with me at the restaurant. One of these young women, I'll call her Mary, was constantly hitting on me. She would hold onto me and grapple me, while I was at the computer trying to send my orders into the kitchen.

Since I had no supervision while at work, I had no doubt I could have left the restaurant on any given day and I could have taken Mary to the nearest motel. Since I was on good terms with all of my supervisors there, I would have been given the green light to take care of 'personal' business during some of my scheduled work hours.

The supervisors at the restaurant thought they were doing the men from work-release a favor by giving them the opportunity to have sexual encounters during working hours. It was a common practice for them to allow the inmates to leave work and go out on their own for periods of time. As long as this did not interfere with the inmate's work performance, everybody was happy.

I had quite a battle with this one. I didn't want to be entrapped by the hater of my soul. I prayed. I asked the Lord to deliver me from the temptation to indulge my flesh. I also prayed for Him to send me a good, Christian woman once I was paroled.

After I did my part, He did His. He literally manifested the scripture which states: "God is faithful, who will not allow you to be tempted above that you are able, but will with the temptation also make a way of escape, that you are able to bear it." (1 Cor. 10:13)

Just to be sure, He manifested this scripture in my situation as well: "Now unto Him that is able to do exceeding abundantly above all that we ask or think, according to the power that works within us, Unto Him be glory." (Ephesians 3:20)

About a week after I prayed, the Lord chose to send me the best woman I have ever met. He not only delivered me from my lusts He also gave me exceedingly abundantly more than I would have dreamed of.

He used my sister, Geri, to introduce me to my exceedingly great reward. One day, she came to Hollywood work-release center to visit me. Since she didn't want to take the ride from Miami to Hollywood by herself, she had asked her good friend, June, to accompany her on the trip.

Consequently, June lived in the same apartment building in Miami Beach as her and my mom. She had been friends with my family for some time. She readily agreed to take the ride with my sister on that fateful day.

As soon as I met June, I was attracted to her. She wasn't like the other women I had in my life before I had come to Jesus. She was as mature as she was pretty. That was an unusual quality. The majority of the women I had gone with were pretty to look at, but they lacked character. Also, most of the prettiest women I lived with were high maintenance. To put it bluntly, they were spoiled.

I soon found out June was a far cry from those women. She is a giver, a hard worker, and she is very unselfish. As far as I could tell, she lived a simple lifestyle. She had two children from a previous marriage and was a dedicated mother to them. She really caught my attention.

After I learned a little more about her, I sensed she was the one for me. I also felt vibes from her that she was attracted to me. However, she wouldn't let on. I soon learned why. She had been hurt by her first husband. Then, she was hurt again by the man whom she had lived with after her divorce. As we talked, I discovered she wasn't quite ready to open up and let herself be vulnerable again.

Yet, I knew if it were God's will, June would someday be mine. My sister, Geri, was very pessimistic about this. In fact, one time when we were discussing my relationship with June, she told me to forget it.

"June is out of your league," she insisted.

When she made that statement, my sister was referring to the fact I was an ex-con. June was a respectable member of society. Furthermore, she came from a very wealthy family. However, I didn't see this as an obstacle for me. I didn't care. I was God's child and, therefore, I was also a respectable member of society. I believed what the Bible said. I had unlimited resources and an account in the bank of heaven.

As far as I was concerned, June could even be my wife someday. I knew this could only happen if it were God's will. However, that is the only way I wanted for it to be so. At any rate, I felt peace about the whole situation and I was willing to let God work it all out on His time schedule.

June soon began coming with my sister to pick me up for my weekly furloughs. Eventually, we began to get acquainted with one another. A short while later, she told me she would like to be able to visit me on Saturday mornings. I told her I would be delighted.

She soon started visiting me - on a weekly basis. We also talked over the phone daily. Our relationship continued to grow. Among the many good things I learned about her was the fact she was a devout Christian. I soon became convinced she was the one for me.

I didn't know it at the time, but God was soon to confirm this fact to both of us. One day shortly before June's birthday, I was taking my daily walk around the rec field at the center. I was talking to the Lord. During this conversation, I asked Him to help me find the best gift I could possibly get to give to her for the occasion.

I had no clue what I could give to a woman who seemed to already have everything. Also, my ability to get to the mall was very limited-not to mention my funds. Inmates at the work-release center were only allowed to have $35.00 per week in their possession. Therefore, I didn't have a lot to work with. I knew it would be quite difficult to get her something special with such limited funds. Also, I had very little time in which to shop around for a gift.

However, the Lord quickly gave me a solution to my problem. His reply to my prayer:

"Write her a song," He told me.

Wow! How unique. I hadn't thought of that.

"Thanks Father," I gratefully replied.

I had no doubt I would indeed write June a good song for her birthday. While I was in prison, the Lord had prepared me for this mission. I was excited. I quickly took to the task. Within an hour, I had penned a song for her.

A short time later, I undertook recording the song. On several of my weekly eight-hour furloughs, I managed to get the job done. On the day we celebrated June's birthday, I was home on a furlough. We were at my mom's and we had a birthday cake for her.

After we sang 'Happy Birthday' to her, I presented her with a cassette tape of the song the Lord had given me for her. As she listened to the recording, she wept. I didn't know what to make of this. Once she regained her composure, she explained to me she had prayed and asked God to have me write her a song. She did this in order to have God confirm I was the right one for her.

How awesome. Prior to the day we were celebrating her birthday, she never mentioned this prayer to me or anyone else. I knew all along God brought us together. His confirmation and approval of our relationship just added icing to the cake. It certainly helped June to accept our union for what it was. At that point, I was sure she fully understood our meeting one another had indeed been ordained by God.

As great as being in love with her was, there was a major drawback. Being incarcerated kept me from being the kind of friend, companion, and mate I wanted to be to her. Also, I knew she wasn't really sure I was the man of God I claimed to be. For that matter, my own family didn't know what I was going to be like after having served all those years in prison. Once I finally did get released, I knew I was going to have to prove myself to everybody.

I had no doubts as to what kind of a lifestyle I was going to lead. This made me all the more anxious to prove it to the world. Jesus really did make a difference in my life. There I was. Like a racehorse trapped inside the starting gate prior to a race, I anxiously awaited for the moment when the prison gates would swing open.

I had waited long enough for my race to begin. God had trained me well. I knew there was no way I could lose. I was not going to be numbered among those who become a statistic and are added to the recidivism rate shortly after their release from prison.

I had a mission and a purpose to fulfill. God had already planned out the works I was going to do to further His kingdom. In fact, He did this long ago-before I was even born. The Bible states: "We are His workmanship, created in Christ Jesus unto good works, which God has before ordained that we should walk in them."(Eph. 2:10)

I knew God hadn't taken me on my journey through the fire for nothing. I was sure He would somehow make every lesson I had learned count for something. I wasn't the least bit concerned about ever going back to my old ways. I could never turn away from God. Besides, where would I go? What could possibly be more fulfilling in this life than serving the awesome God of all creation? To me, leaving God was a sure way to fail.

Since I never was a good loser, I had no desire to desert God and join the losing team.
Considering how much I had to be grateful for, I was looking forward to giving Him my faithful service. Once I was released, I planned on being a great asset to His kingdom.

In spite of all my good intentions, this didn't come easy. I was released from the Florida Prison system in November of 1998. I had served a total of 14 years and 10 months. Through it all, I had witnessed a multitude of miracles and I had learned God is faithful above all else. His Word never comes back void. He had put me through the test. And, I had put His Word through many a test. In fact,
His Word was all I had to depend on and it got me through. It proved to be more than enough.

However, really underestimated the warfare I was about to enter into. Upon my release, Satan launched an all out attack. I guess I should have been expecting it. Yet, after over 13 straight years of fighting against the wiles of the devil in a prison environment, I expected life on the streets would be
a lot easier than the life I had been living in a prison setting. It wasn't. In fact, it seems like the war just got more intense. Life in the 'free' world was no picnic.

At the time I penned this, I have been out on parole for over 10 years. I have been blessed to be extremely happily married to June for more than six of those years. Even though I have fallen flat on my face on numerous occasions, the Lord has been all the more gracious. "My grace is sufficient for thee, for my strength is made perfect in weakness." (2 Corinthians 12:9)

I now realize it has been by His grace all along. In fact, it is only by His grace that I will continue on in my journey with Him to reach full maturity in His Son.

"For the Lord God is a sun and shield; he will give grace and glory; no good

thing will He withhold from them that walk uprightly". (Psalms 84:11)

TALK ABOUT TIMING

Since my last entry in my attempt to finish writing this book, about two years have passed. During this time, I tried and tried to put aside some time in order that I might complete the work. It seemed as though the harder I tried the tougher it became. I was getting very discouraged. I had begun to feel as though I had let God down. Yet, He gave me the peace deep down inside of knowing some day He would give me just the right words at just the right time. When He was ready, I would complete this mission which He had ordained me to do.

In the interim, I moved from Miami to North Lauderdale, Florida. Consequently, we changed churches. A mutual friend of ours who had attended a church located about 10 minutes from our home suggested we attend their worship service. Since we had been praying about it, and our friend spoke very highly of this church, we decided to try it.

We liked the way the Pastor delivered the Word there. Also, we were glad to be in a church located closer to our home. We planned to invite other people to attend the services with us. We even got involved in an evangelism course which they taught there.

A short time after we had been attending our new home church, the Pastor was scheduled to finish preaching an ongoing message on the Sabbath. However, the Lord started leading him in another direction. Therefore, he prayed and asked the Lord to confirm it if it were indeed His will for him to preach on something other than what he had been planning.

Once he arrived at the church this particular Sunday morning, he found out the electricity had been short-circuited. It seems an iguana had gotten in between one of the circuits and had been electrocuted. This power outage meant he wouldn't be able to tape the sermon. This thwarted his plan on preaching in the main sanctuary and getting it all on tape.

The Pastor realized this was God's way of answering his prayer. Therefore, he prayed again and asked the Lord to lead him to preach whatever He willed. The Father answered by leading the Pastor to preach about how God's children should focus on giving Him the glory in all things.

This message really hit home with me. As I listened intently to the message, I realized God was giving me the final chapter in this book. Still, this was easier said than done. Once again, I was met with one obstacle after another.

As I sat down at my computer to write, it seemed as though I was attempting to do the impossible. After much effort, I was able to accomplish very little. This only served to dishearten me.

I resorted to the only thing I knew I could do. I prayed - again and again. Nothing worked. I didn't get the inspiration I was praying for. I was confused. What did I do wrong? Was this whole idea of writing Quitting Time just going to fall by the wayside?

In my spirit, I knew God was still in control and He had a plan. If this book was indeed His plan, I believed He would eventually finish what I couldn't. *Hmmm. Isn't this sort of what He had been doing with my life all along?* I thought to myself.

Shortly after I had prayed, my phone rang. I answered it. It turned out it was my younger sister, Joanne, calling me. This was very unusual. I hadn't heard from my sister in quite some time. It was probably more than fifteen years. The last I had heard about her was that she had been hopelessly addicted to heroine. In fact, this vice was used by the devil to split her family completely apart. Only God knew where she had been or what her life had been like afterwards.

During our years of separation, I had been praying for Joanne, as well as the rest of my family, to be converted. I found out during our conversation, my

27 years of praying was not in vain. She excitedly explained she had given her life to Jesus. I was elated to hear this good news. I was also in shock. Although I had prayed and prayed for her, I never really expected I would get to see this happen.

In that respect, I guess I am just like so many of God's other children down here. We pray. We think we really believe God is going to do what we have asked Him to do. Yet, in our heart of hearts, we don't have the mountain moving faith we think we have.

Anyway, during our conversation Joanne went on to explain to me she was involved in a Christ centered ministry located in upstate New York. She told me she had been there for almost a year. Our phone conversation didn't last long. However, I did get to hear the greatest news I could have hoped for. She explained to me she was wholly committed to Christ. She informed me she planned to enter the ministry. Praise God! She gave me the phone number where she could be reached and we ended our conversation.

Afterwards, I rushed into our family room to share the good news with my wife and my mom. They could hardly believe it. I told them they weren't alone. This was indeed miraculous news.

Eventually, June and me invited Joanne to come to our home for the Thanksgiving holiday. Little did we know what an awesome experience God had planned for all of us. Once she accepted our invitation, anticipation set in.

A few days later, she was talking with one of her sons, Shawn, and he told her he would love to come here to Florida and meet up with her. When we found out about this, we also invited Shawn to stay with us for the holiday. About a week later, Shawn called me up and asked if it was alright for him to bring his younger brother, Mario, along. We gladly consented.

During our conversation, Shawn had told me Mario's arrival was to be a surprise for their Mom. At this point, I knew God was up to something. He didn't disappoint. Once Joanne, Shawn, and Mario were all at our home, the Lord started using Joanne and me to witness to her two sons. Neither of them had been born again.

We had a most memorable family Thanksgiving. On the following Saturday evening, Joanne invited her boys to attend church with us the next morning. I must admit, I really didn't expect them to take her up on her offer. But, they readily agreed. At this point, I was sure God was doing a mighty work among our family members.

While we were in church, I remember Shawn saying to his mom: "I never expected to see you in a church, mom, except inside of a coffin".

This statement brought tears to Joanne's eyes. It was breathtaking to witness God's work in her life. Although Shawn and Mario weren't at all religious, they realized what the Lord had done in their mom's life. This had such a great impact on them they both asked Jesus to take control of their lives as well. We all had the most fantastic family reunion for the remainder of their stay in Florida. None of us had any idea as to how memorable our Thanksgiving was going to be.

Joanne has since graduated from ministerial college. She is now working for Teen Challenge - the awesome ministry the Lord used David Wilkerson (author of The Cross and The Switchblade) to start many years ago. She is stationed in Brooklyn, New York at present. She works there as their Intake Director. God is so good.

One Sunday shortly after Thanksgiving, the Pastor was preaching about Jesus answering one of His disciples questions concerning what was the greatest commandment. "You shall love the Lord your God with all your heart, with all your soul, with all your mind, and with all of your strength", Jesus replied.

As I sat in the pew absorbing those words, the spirit of conviction came upon me. *I know I am not doing all of these things. I just can't. You know how hard*

I have tried. I confessed to God. At that point, He suddenly reminded me He promised to supply us with all of our needs. Obviously, I needed His help in the matter.

At that moment, I prayed for a Divine intervention. A short time later, I received the answer. He brought to my remembrance this scripture verse: "It is God which works in you both to will and to do all of His good pleasure." (Philippians 2:13)

Immediately, I knew this was the answer to my problem. I realized I had the will. I didn't have the do. Once again, I took God up on His Word. I asked Him to do it through me. Wow! I had no idea what an awesome journey I was about to embark upon.

Step by step, He led me into full obedience. He used a message the Pastor had preached a few weeks prior to this occasion: "Partial Obedience Is No Obedience" to give me the determination to fully commit. He prepped my heart for the work He was now actually doing in me. Apparently, this word had fallen on some fertile ground.

As I yielded more of me, I became more conformed to the image of Jesus. He filled me with more of His Holy Spirit. While this was happening, He began to lead me on a fast. I had no idea how much I was about to gain for my willingness to sacrifice a few meals.

A few days into this fast, I was at work. During my lunch break, I was feeding the birds. This was my usual custom. I would bring whatever bread happened to be left over or ready to spoil from our home and I would feed a flock of birds. They usually gathered on the branches of a tree located right across from my tool shed.

The shed was surrounded by a wooden fence. The birds would station themselves on the fence as well as on the tree. I would cast the bread out to them. Usually, I would have just enough bread on hand to feed all my fine-feathered friends.

On this particular day, there were so many birds

gathered I had seriously doubted I had enough bread on hand to feed them all. However, I just kept feeding and once I was finished feeding the entire flock of birds, I turned around to close the hanging door at the entrance to my shed.

While I was pulling the door closed, I noticed two large bags of bread sitting alongside my microwave oven inside the shed. At that moment, the Lord spoke to me and brought to my attention the fact I had just fed the entire flock of birds and yet I still had enough bread left over to feed them at least two more times. Then, He brought it to my mind Jesus had promised our Father feeds every sparrow. He pointed out to me that what I had just witnessed was more than enough proof God is still faithful to His Word today. Wow.

The very same evening, I was at home working on my computer. I heard my mom and my wife squabbling about some store-bought items my wife had brought home for my mom. It seemed my mom wanted to pay for them and my wife had told her it wasn't necessary.

This conversation was taking place in our kitchen. In order to quell this storm which was brewing, I left my computer and rushed out there. As I arrived at the scene, I saw there were three boxes of feminine pads on the left of where my mom was standing. They were sitting on the ledge of our breakfast nook.

On the right of her, there was a counter. On this counter there was a plastic bag with three rolls of bread in it. This bread had been placed there for me. I had planned to take this bread to work for the birds the following day.

At that moment, it clicked. I had been explaining to my mom time and time again over the course of the last couple of days concerning God's signature in biblical numerology. It is the number three. I had been assuring her that God does things in numerical order.

At this point, I explained to my mom the boxes of feminine pads were not from my wife. They were from God. Then, I brought it to her attention it was no coincidence there happened to be three boxes of them.

“Remember how I have been explaining to you about God's signature being the number three?” I questioned.

Then, I showed her there were also three rolls placed there on the counter for me to feed the sparrows at work.

“God's signature again,” I explained.

At that point, I told my mom and my wife what had taken place at my work earlier that day. I don't know about them, but I was astonished. It is so amazing how God uses simple everyday situations to speak to us. Yet, most of the time we are so overwhelmed with our circumstances we don't see what is right in front of us.

While I continued my fast, the Lord drew me nearer to Him. As He did so, the final chapter of this book neared its completion. The powers of darkness did not take all of this lying down. In fact, the evil one started to stir up my entire family against me. As the days drew on and the work progressed, the attacks became more blatant.

Eventually, my wife began to believe I was going off the deep end. Consequently, I was so mesmerized by the awesomeness of the Holy Spirit my behavior changed radically. She feared I had a brain tumor or something. This was due to the fact my older brother, Joe, had died recently of this affliction. Somehow or another, she rationalized this was happening to me and must have been what was causing my ‘strange’ behavior. In her mind, there was no other logical explanation.

Since she couldn’t convince me to go to the hospital and have some tests done, she decided she would ‘bring the mountain to me.’ One night, she called in the paramedics. She was convinced this was the only way she could help me to get the treatment she thought I needed.

Once the paramedics arrived and checked out my

vital signs, they found I was physically in great shape. I thought this was great. However, they thought this only meant my problem must have been mental. What happened next is hilarious.

They conferred with my wife and decided to Baker Act me. Praise God. It is amazing what lengths people will go through to try to explain away the supernatural work of God's Spirit.

However, the Lord worked even this out for good. During my incarceration, in the loony bin, I was able to witness to many people who were emotionally disturbed. I also witnessed to the doctors and the caretakers there.

While I was being detained, the Lord gave me a string of ideas. I used many of them to help further the cause of the Gospel. In fact, He used this time to plant the seeds which led me to later formulate Off The Chain 4 Jesus Ministries. Then, He inspired me to complete this book. While all this was taking place, I was being filled with His Spirit more and more.

Suddenly, everything started falling into place. As a result, the words you are now reading flowed out of my spirit like a river. I had no doubt in my heart I was doing exactly what our Father wanted me to do at exactly the right time.

However, the attack wasn't over. A short time later, I was fired from my job. I had been the maintenance man for a large homeowners association for about three years. I maintained about 144 units on the property at Lago West in Plantation. I worked for a management company which serviced this particular property.

My boss loved me. This was because, at the time he first assigned me to this property, the association there was on the verge of terminating their contract with my company. Shortly after I arrived on the scene, the association decided they loved my work ethic and made a deal with my boss to renew their contract. They stipulated this was only applicable as long as I continued working on their property. They also wanted the two other workers who had been there working with me moved to another property. The requested me as their solitary maintenance man.

While I was there performing my duties, everything seemed to be going along well and the homeowners association was kept happy. During my tour of duty there, I began to witness about the Gospel more and more. This was due to the fact I was becoming more and more filled with the Spirit.

Eventually, it got to the point I couldn't contain myself any longer. I had always shared Jesus with some of the residents on the property before. However, I had been shying away from some of the other residents. This was no longer the case.

While I was becoming very bold in my witnessing, I began to notice one of the members of the board, Mary, was getting perturbed. This was due to the fact, I had witnessed to her and the Holy Spirit had been convicting her. One day, as I warned her God has told us in the Bible He will not tolerate His children refusing to forgive another person for their wrong doing she was actually brought to tears. During our conversation, I noticed her eyes welling up as she tried to conceal her conviction.

Earlier, she had told me she hated another Christian woman who lived on the property. I shared what God's Word says about such behavior. Although I tried to explain to her she needed to ask Jesus into her heart and ask God for forgiveness, she didn't respond favorably. Apparently, she wasn't ready to relinquish control over to Him.

I felt very sad she chose to stay in her spiritual condition and keep God out of her life. I prayed for her. Although I had the love of Jesus in my heart for her, she had no qualms about causing me to be terminated a short time later.

The day following our conversation, she told me to repair a broken fence on the property. Since she was on the board for the association there, I had no problem taking orders from her. In fact, we had been working together for the duration of my employment there. In order to keep the property maintained, the board allowed her to more or less direct what work projects should be completed.

It turned out the fence she directed me to repair on that day had been smashed by a drunken driver. I started the repair work that afternoon. Since I usually ended my work day at 3:30 p.m., I tried my best to finish the repairs before my usual quitting time.

However, there was quite a bit of damage to this fence. Consequently, I had to go to the nearest Home Depot in order to get some more wood and other hardware to complete the repairs. Before leaving the job site, I had planned on bringing the golf cart I had been using back inside the compound. This is where I normally stored it.

Once I arrived at the compound, I found there was a large pile of debris and two trucks blocking my path to the entrance. I realized this was due to the fact that someone was repairing the pool which was located next to my compound. I figured they would move the debris eventually and someone could pull the cart into the fenced-in area afterwards and it would be safe and secure. I took the key out of the golf cart, locked it up, and proceeded to the Home Depot.

By the time I had gotten all of the supplies I needed, it was past 3:30 pm. When I got back to the compound, I unloaded the materials from my truck. At that time, I noticed the debris was still blocking the compound entrance. I couldn't pull the golf cart inside the compound, so I just left it in front and went home.

I was not at all concerned about the golf cart not being locked up inside the compound. This was because I knew at least one person from the association had a key for it. Since the compound was only two houses away from the president of the association, I figured either he or someone else would have noticed the golf cart sitting in front of the compound and would have placed it inside. I left and went home.

It turns out that later that day Mary noticed the golf cart wasn't locked inside the compound. Immediately, she called my boss and complained about my having left the golf cart out. When I was confronted about this situation, I explained why I had left the golf cart outside of the compound.

When my boss relayed my explanation to Mary, she insisted there was no pile of debris blocking the entrance way to the compound. She was convinced I had been negligent and insisted I was no longer responsible enough to be working on the property.

Maybe the men who were working on the pool had moved the debris before Mary arrived on the scene. Perhaps she never did see what I saw. At any rate, she gave her evil report to the president of the association and he evidently took her word over mine. My mission at Lago West was completed. What the devil meant for evil God turned into blessing.

"And we know that all things work together for good to them that love God, to them who are the called according to His purpose." (Romans 8:28)

NEW BEGINNINGS

My boss called me the following day and instructed me I had to meet with him at his office in Deerfield Beach. I suspected this wasn't going to turn out good. Once I arrived there, he explained the association did not want me to come back on to their property anymore. I must admit this turn of events really caught me by surprise.

Yet at the time my boss told me he had to terminate my employment, I felt an unexplainable peace. In my spirit, I suddenly realized this whole situation was God's way of confirming it was time for me to get into the ministry on a full time basis. Since I had already been praying concerning this, I told my boss I had no problem with the association's request.

My boss apologized and told me he didn't have any other properties he could assign me to at that time. He promised he would let me know if something should come up. I explained to him I didn't need another job because God was moving me into the ministry. At that point, he wished me well and we departed friends.

A short time later, God gave me confirmation concerning the concept for Off The Chain 4 Jesus Ministries and clarified it's goal. Since there are numerous wolves in sheep's clothing who are taking advantage of people seeking repairs for their homes, He instructed me to use the skills He gave me to help these potential victims.

He encouraged me that I could help others by providing honest, skilled workers on a volunteer basis. People in need of help could pay for the materials needed to do the job they require. OTC4J would then provide them with laborers. Once the job is complete, the homeowners could pay whatever they feel the job was worth. What an awesome concept.

Although I wasn't a skilled carpenter, I knew just enough to get this ministry going. I wasn't really sure what He wanted me to do, but I was willing to report for duty. This is all God requires of any of us. I prayed and committed myself and Off The Chain 4 Jesus to him. He did the rest.

The world's point of view on this would be quite negative. However, God has shown me and our ministry again and again He is in complete control and rewards those who willingly serve Him. Whenever we do a job and focus on ministering and not on earning wages, we get blessed beyond our greatest expectations.

I cannot begin to count the many times He has shown Himself faithful in our ministry. On numerous occasions, we have been blessed financially beyond our wildest imaginations. I can recall one time, after we had finished doing some painting and patchwork in one home, the customer asked me how much she should make out a check for in payment of our services.

I hate to give anyone a set amount that I think they should pay. In doing so, I feel like I am acting out of faith and not trusting God to bless us as He sees fit. Therefore, I told the woman to pray and ask God what He thinks she should pay. However, she insisted I give her a figure. (In my mind, I was thinking the finished work was worth about $100. $150 tops).

However, I really felt led to leave this up to God. I just couldn't bring myself to give her a set amount. Once again, I explained this is a faith-based ministry. I suggested she trust God to help her come up with the right number to place on the check.

Finally, she wrote out a check to us. Later, I pulled the check out of my pocket in order to deposit it. I saw the amount on the check. It was $300. Unbelievable! That is how our God is. I can give countless other examples of how He has blessed us far beyond anything we deserve.

The cross is not the only time He chose to give us much more than we could earn or dream of. To this day, He just loves to show His children how awesome and gracious He is. Give Him an excuse. He will give you a blessing.

Many times, on the job He has used me to encourage other believers in the faith. This in itself is such a blessing. He has also given me the privilege of leading others into the knowledge of the saving grace of Jesus. It is so thrilling to be used by the Master to help others. To me, this is worth far more than any monies I could possibly earn.

On the other hand, if I allow myself or those working with me to focus on getting paid for our labor, things never seem to work out. Whenever necessary, He reminds me I should not allow myself to fall into the trap of focusing on profits instead of ministry. Our service is to the Master.

After He taught me those valuable lessons, He gave me our motto: "Whatever you do in word or deed, do it all in the name of the Lord Jesus, giving thanks to God and the Father by Him." (Colossians 3:17) To me this means we work on each home as though it were our Lord's home. Obviously, we give it our best. ☺

We are not only committed to the homeowners. We are also committed to helping provide other believers with work. It is also our goal to help our volunteers to become more skilled in their work performance. However, this is just a small part of our mission.

Since we are in the field, we are on the front lines. The battle rages on. Therefore, we strive to help our fellow believers to become more adept in spiritual warfare. Our Father faithfully provides us with all of our needs in this area as well.

Whenever we have the funds, we have been helping to supply various food banks in the area. We also would like to assist newly released prisoners and the homeless. Hopefully, we will get enough proceeds from this book to purchase some homes and some day we will be able to place ex-cons and the homeless in them.

Not everyone who has worked with OTC4J has gotten the 'vision.' Unfortunately, some of our former volunteers were also wolves in sheep's clothing. The devil has used some of these individuals to cause numerous problems. However, our faithful Father has always revealed to us what we needed to know in order to avoid a crisis.

Local handymen are 'Off the Chain for Jesus'

By Lisa Lustig-Bennett
The Good News

HANDYMEN: James McDonald (left) started Off the Chain 4 Jesus Ministries to help men get back on their feet. [redacted] (right) is James' right hand man.

As a servant of Christ, former horse jockey and maintenance worker James McDonald was fired for witnessing to others on the job. But he saw that there was a great need for handyman services in South Florida, and the Lord gave him the idea to combine his physical and spiritual tools to reach people for Jesus.

So, McDonald, his mentor Lester Lemke, who has been a prison minister for 25 years, and Minister Buddy Malcolm founded Off the Chain 4 Jesus Ministries (OTC4J), a unique mix of mission and repair work.

OTC4J offers handyman services to the public on a "donation only" basis, unheard of in this day and age. From fixing fans and faucets to screens and sprinklers, they do almost anything and without a minimum donation price.

Some of his workers are recruited from Faith Farm, a rehabilitative center and shelter which houses about 165 men, many of whom join the program to deal with substance abuse. The men go through a nine-month orientation that teaches them the Word of God, gives them daily tasks and trains them how to survive without alcohol or drugs.

McDonald says he came up with the name "Off the Chain 4 Jesus" because he used to feel "bound to the chain of sin but now is free in Christ."

When OTC4J first began, McDonald did not know how they were going to fund the business, but they've learned to rely on the Lord to provide.

OTC4J Ministries stands upon the hope found in Philippians 4:19, *"Our God shall supply all your needs according to His riches in glory by Christ Jesus"* and Romans 8:28, *"We know that all things work together for the good to them who love God, and who are called according to His purpose."*

After a little advertising and word of mouth, James and his crew volunteered to go to homes or churches. Their clients usually pay for the materials themselves and then only pay what they can afford or are willing to give for the work. Looking to expand into Dade and Palm Beach counties, McDonald's main goal is to mobilize fellow Christian workers to help others and glorify God.

When he's doing handyman work, God will usually give McDonald an opportunity to share the Gospel. Then he will ask his clients if they know about Jesus and what would happen if they were to die today. If the clients are interested in learning more, he has been known to invite them to his house for dinner. Having a wife who loves to cook comes in mighty handy for this handyman, enabling him to get to know his guests better and minister to them.

After the donations from OTC4J are used to pay McDonald and his workers, the funds go to different ministries and McDonald hopes to one day use the funds to build or renovate a home for men trying to get back on their feet.

This article was written in the 'Good News of South Florida' newspaper shortly after the Lord led me to start this ministry. He quickly confirmed He was with me in this ministry. Come to think of it, He does promise: "It is God that works in us both to will and to do His good pleasure." (Philippians 2:13) Also, in Psalms 84:11 He promises: "No good thing will He withhold from them that walk uprightly."

Ever since I got saved about 27 years ago, I looked forward to the time I could serve God in the ministry full time. I never dreamed He would give me the skills to do home construction repairs much less give me the vision to start a volunteer handyman service as a ministry. However, I am so grateful He chose me in spite of me.

As if that wasn't enough, He chose to put me

back into the music ministry as well. Shortly after OTC4J got off the ground, I was reading the Good News. (I had become acquainted with this awesome Christian published newspaper at the outset of our ministry. The Lord had led me to this publication and then used it to create a steady flow of jobs for our volunteers. We have been running an ad in The Good News ever since). I don't normally read the classified section, but on this occasion I felt led to check it out.

Guess what? As I read on, I just 'happened' to see an ad for a Spirit-filled piano player to help lead the worship at the Faith Farm Tabernacle. Immediately, I applied and was blessed to meet Pastor Garry Steffe. From day one, I knew I was going to enjoy working with this dear brother. My wife also joined up with us and sang in the choir; along with Pastor Garry's wife and the founder of Faith Farms daughter, Dolores.

Pastor Garry is a Pentecostal preacher from Indiana who really loves the Lord. He also loved the men whom our Father chose to bring into the drug and alcohol recovery program at Faith Farm Ministries. During the past few years, we have been absolutely blessed to be used of our Father to work together and lead the worship at the Sunday morning services at the Faith Tabernacle.

For about three years, we have enjoyed our weekly practices, our fellowship together, and our ministry on Sunday mornings. What more could we ask for?

How about great preaching? Pastor Garry and Pastor Dick provided this as well. These brothers are 'real' ministers of the unabashed Word of God. When they bring forth the Word, they don't pull any punches. Not only that, they practice what they preach. I'm sure the men who went through the intense nine month recovery program at Faith Farm appreciated this.

Faith Farm was founded by Rev. Garland Eastham. He was nicknamed, 'Pappy.' He was used by the Lord to start helping the helpless about 60 years ago.

Since then, our Father has chosen to expand this ministry. They now have separate self-supporting facilities in Fort Lauderdale, Boynton, and Okeechobee, Florida. They sell new and used furniture donated by others to raise the necessary funds to cover the expenses of the ministry.

The men in the program at Faith Farm are taught the Word of God and given the proper tools to live a victorious life in Jesus. While this is taking place, they go through many crises. It really helps for them to know they are special to God. It is quite evident - to those who are open to the Gospel - that they are loved by some true believers who are also real doers of the Word. I have been so blessed to be a part of all this. I can truly relate to the men in this program.

Although our Father chose to move Pastor Garry and me from Faith Farms, we both still support the men who make the choice to give the reins of their lives over to Jesus and enter this program. They are always in our prayers and hearts. Faith Farms is also one of our top prayer priorities on a daily basis. As you can imagine, this ministry takes an enormous amount of financial support. However, as long as the center focus of this program continues to be the Lord, Jesus Christ, our Father will continue to provide everything needed to get the job done. Needless to say, this is exactly what we have always been praying for. This will continue to be the main focal point of our daily petitions on behalf of this ministry.

A short time after I got involved in the ministry at Faith Farm, my dear friend, Lester Lemke, sent me a book written by a friend of his. The title of the book is: "Can't Wait to Go Back to Prison." It was written by Dr. John Michael Domino. John was also a dear friend of Lester's. (Unfortunately, Lester went to meet Jesus before this book was completed.)

John's book is a work of God used to encourage other believers to reach out to prisoners. He gave Lester the vision for this book and used the two of them to complete the work. This is a classic example of how God coordinates the willing vessels in the body of Christ to work together for His glory.

To my surprise, He even used me to put my two cents into the mix. By His grace, He chose to help me get my feet wet in publishing by stirring Lester to encourage his co-author, John, to do an interview with me. In order to get a prisoners' insight on prison ministry, John used the information I gave him to create a chapter for their book entitled: "Brother James."

While God was preparing me for the mission work He chose to make me a part of, I was becoming more sensitive to His Spirit. Eventually, I came to the realization He was preparing me for the completion of 'Quitting Time' by causing me to cross paths with some very dear children of His who already had published works.

The wealth of information I received from John is priceless. Since he works at the Florida Gold Coast University providing instruction and guidance to interns and professional educators there, and has published mentoring books for use by Christian colleges, churches, and other Christ-centered institutions, you could say our Father gave me quite an education - for free.

As if that weren't enough, He gave me another dear brother in the Lord who is a friend I know I can depend on. John truly loves the Lord and the unfortunate lost who are incarcerated. In fact, he is a part of Love and Compassion Ministries. They reach out to incarcerated teenagers in the southwest Florida Department of Corrections.

God also used John to help another Christian and ex-prisoner write and publish a very compelling testimony of God's grace via a book entitled: "Attica: A Survivors Story." What a work God has done in that brother's life.

Speaking of authors and brothers in Christ, the Lord also saw fit to use Lester to provide me with a copy of "Shake off the Snake." The author, one A.J.

Rubano, happens to be from New Jersey. A.J. and Lester were friends. One day, Lester told A.J. I also originated from the same area of New Jersey as he had. Then, A.J. requested we meet one another.

A.J. and I soon became friends. As I delved into the book he had authored, I got so very blessed. His book is an instructional on how a Christian could overcome the wiles of the devil. I barely finished reading the third chapter of this book when God blessed me with an awesome revelation.

He let me in on a little secret. Self, stress, and strife are three things the evil one uses to distract Christians. Once they are distracted, it is an easy task for the trickster to cause them to lose the fullness of the Spirit. If you were to take the first letter of each of those three words, you would have sss. Isn't this exactly what a snake does before it strikes? How interesting.

Abba wasn't through introducing me to loving, believing doers of His Word yet. Shortly after meeting A.J., He caused me to cross paths with Rich and Dottie Kane. They are the directors of Healing Room Ministries of South Florida. One day, they called OTC4J in order to have some handyman work done at their home in Coral Springs, Florida.

Come to find out, in 1991 Dottie was miraculously healed of kidney cancer. Although Rich was a partying alcoholic musician, God chose to deliver him from this. Then, He called the Kanes into the ministry. Dottie told me they are more enthusiastic about serving Jesus than they ever were about the wild partying they did for so many years. Although, they are both over 70 years old, they assured me they will not even consider ceasing working for the Lord until He calls them home. Praise God.

At the time we first met the Kanes, none of us had any idea as to how our gracious Father was about to bless us all. During the course of the many days we spent at their home completing the work they had summoned us to do, we shared testimonies, the love of

Jesus, and prayers for each other. When all was said and done, our faith in the healing power of Jesus today was increased in more ways than one.

It never ceases to amaze me how many lives God touches. Sometimes, in the most unlikely places I could think of He chooses to introduce faithful children of His to me. For instance, I never dreamed I would someday meet a true man of God in a garage. Unfortunately, most of us already know there are many dishonest auto mechanics in this world. However, our Father has chosen to introduce me to one of his children who happens to own and operate Giant Tire in Margate, Florida. He is the epitome of honesty. His name is Bob Digiannurio.

The Bible says give everyone their due and it is my good pleasure to share the things I have learned about this dear brother in Christ. I first found out about Giant Tire through an advertisement in the Good News Newspaper. At the time, one of the vehicles our ministry was using needed some repairs. I prayed and asked our Father to lead me to a trustworthy mechanic. The thought came into my mind I should check out the Good News Newspaper for a repair shop.

As I scanned the paper, I came upon an ad. The scripture verse Bob has based his business upon was included in it. It caught my attention. “A false balance is abomination to the Lord, but a just weight is His delight.” (Proverbs 11:1). Immediately, I knew this was where I should bring our vehicle.

Although I am sometimes skeptical; because I have met many who name the name of Jesus and walk the walk of Satan, it didn’t take long for me to find out this brother is for real. While I was sitting in the waiting area at Giant Tire, I overheard some woman explaining she had brought her car there thinking she needed a brake job. After Bob checked the vehicle out, he informed her she only needed a minor adjustment and fixed the problem free of charge.

Needless to say, I was delighted to hear that. I

knew I was in good hands. On that particular day, Bob repaired our vehicle and did it completely free of charge. I was in awe. Thus began our friendship. It is so refreshing to know God has worked His way into our capitalist system. ☺

As I was putting the finishing touches on this book, our Father awakened me at 4:30 a.m. one morning and led me to tell of the good work this brother is doing. Truly, he exemplifies the honesty our Lord, Jesus has commanded His followers to display. "Let your light so shine before men, that they may see your good works, and glorify your Father, which is in heaven."

As soon as I finished writing the story concerning Bob, I realized God had caused me to do so in order to fulfill His Word to that brother. This was a prime example of how our Father uses whatever He wills to get the job done. In fact, I believe our Father gave me the awesome testimony described in this book because He wants everyone to know He always performs His Word. He has told us if we humble ourselves before Him, He will exalt us.

In my walk with the Lord, I have learned we just need to stop trying to impress the world and focus on pleasing the One who created it. Then, everything else will truly fall into place. In fact, Jesus promised just that to us in Matthew 6:33. "Seek first the kingdom of God and His righteousness and all things shall be added unto you".

I cannot finish telling the story of how God led me to write this book without explaining my relationship to my dear brother in Christ G. Booth Lusteg. While I was doing some repairs at his daughter's home in Davie, Florida, the Lord chose to introduce me to him.

Eventually, I came to find out G. Booth was an author and former NFL kicker. He received Jesus as his saviour and the Lord inspired him to many years of faithful service. He has been volunteering much of his time in order to help spread the Gospel.

In spite of his busy schedule, he has published

quite a bit of material. I was blessed to read a book he has written, "Kick Rejection…And Win." In it he gives testimony of the grueling road he traveled in order to make his mark as a kicker in the NFL. What a book. It held my attention from the moment I read the first page.

Speaking of books, once G. Booth learned I was in the process of writing this book, he volunteered to help me edit Quitting Time - free of charge. Our Father never ceases to amaze me. He used that dear brother to dedicate countless hours helping me to get the grammar corrected on this work. I shall forever be grateful. What a dear brother.

Besides all the aforementioned blessings, our Father chose to give me a very important revelation. A Christian can only progress in their spiritual walk by being filled with His awesome love. The kind of love we need is the same sacrificial love which was displayed at Calvary. God explains this to us in the Bible in 1 Corinthians Chapter 13. Yet, as most people will agree, we don't have the natural capacity to love this way on our own.

"There is no fear in love, but perfect love casts out fear…" (1 John 4:18)

TRUTH OR CONSEQUENCES

Unfortunately, many of us Christians are missing it. We strive for obedience. Of course this too is important. Religion focuses on this. However, without a personal relationship resulting in love we can't grow in Him. We may have boatloads of knowledge, but this alone won't help us to receive the power needed to change the world around us.

How then, can we get the love spoken of and displayed by Jesus? First, we must be willing vessels who yield to His Spirit completely. Then, we must ask Him to love through us. As we do, He fills us more and more. When this happens, we can't help but love everyone He brings us into contact with.

Didn't Jesus say: "If you ask anything in my name, I will do it"? (John 14:14) Once I learned this, I prayed He would fill me with His Spirit and love others through me. He answered that prayer. Jesus fulfilled His promise and is at this time enabling me to love others who aren't necessarily lovable. As a result, I have been blessed beyond measure. I have the love of our Lord and the joy which comes with it. This is awesome.

I couldn't do this for the first 27 years of my walk with Jesus. I wasn't doing the first part of the greatest commandment: "Love the Lord your God with all your heart, mind, soul and strength." How then could I love my neighbor as myself? Without His help, it was impossible.

Then, I discovered the awesome truth that, if I allow Him to do what I can't, He will use me to tear down some of the devil's strongholds. It's time for me to go on the attack. Who let the dogs out? The Holy Spirit-that's who!

I am in attack mode right now and this book is the weapon God has given me. Our Father never meant for us to be on the defense. We are supposed to be attacking and tearing down the devil's strongholds in the hearts and minds of others.

How? Using the love of God is how. This is the only way. Get it? Please get it. If you don't, slew foot will continually keep you from God's perfect will. Brothers and sisters, isn't this what you have been struggling to get all of your life?

He has given you only so much time to do His will here on this earth. Don't waste one more moment of His life. (I emphasize His). Seek His will. He is with you. He wants you to recognize Him. Wake up! Emmanuel. God is with us. And, God is love.

If we do anything, outside the spirit of love, God will not be with us on that. The more we allow old slew foot to trick us into striving with our fellow man, is the more we help him to thwart God's purposes.

As long as we stay in our Father's perfect will for us at the moment, Satan cannot steal our joy and thereby sap us of our strength. Beware Christian. The Bible clearly states the joy of the Lord is our strength. (Nehemiah 8:10) No joy - no strength.

Even as I am attempting to finish this book, I am being bombarded by the enemy. He is fighting for his life and he knows it. Our Father is indeed pouring out His Spirit in these last days. He is using ordinary people like you and me to do the extraordinary.

My question to you is would you rather continue fighting this battle on your own? Or, are you going to get on this train and ride to glory shouting and praising God all the way?

He has given us the honor of being able to experience Immanuel. Allow Him to enable you to walk in His love. If not, you are going to get hammered by the enemy. No matter how hard you try, you will not be able to fly with the eagles.

As I said earlier, self, strife, and stress is what the devil uses to clip our wings. You may still be an eagle, but you won't get off the ground. Do you know how the baby eagle flounders around while it tries to learn how to fly? He has the power to soar, but he is lacking the knowledge to do so. “My people perish for lack of knowledge.” (Hosea 4:6)

Our gracious Father has taught me that, if I want to continually walk in victory, I must allow the rivers of living water to flow out of me. Jesus said: “Rivers of living water will flow from your belly.” I submit to you this river is God's love. Get it? “God is love.” (I John 4:8)

Jesus also said: “If you continue in my Word, then are you my disciples (followers) indeed; and you shall know the truth and the truth shall make you free.” (John 8:32)

Our Father also blessed me by teaching me a Christian is not necessarily His child because they choose to follow a certain denomination. What really matters is that we choose to follow Jesus and to pursue a personal relationship with Him.

“If you continue in my Word,” He said. This means following what He has instructed you to do. In that way, you will know truth from error and you will be free from the bondage of religion.

I have a very dear aunt, Sister Josephine Riccio, who has been a Filippini nun for over 65 years. Needless to say, she is a committed servant of God. She was instrumental in my religious upbringing. I went to parochial school, received communion, etc. I will forever be grateful to my aunt who faithfully prayed for me for years on end. She has been praying for me since the day her sister, me dear mom, gave birth to me.

During the first 33 years of my life, I’m sure she must have gotten quite discouraged about my spiritual condition and my immoral behavior. Yet, I am sure she was always aware of the fact that God doesn’t always answer our prayers exactly the way we expect Him too. She kept her faith and continued to pray for me.

When He did finally remove the veil from my eyes, He did not choose to reveal Himself to me through Catholicism. Yet, as we all know, there are many born-again Catholics. So, why didn't He reach me through one of them? I don't know the answer to that one. He knew what the best way was to penetrate my hardened heart and in His time He did. All I can say is I am glad He chose to reach out to me in spite of me. I will never be able to thank Him enough.

The fact is God uses many religions to reach those who are serious about knowing Him. There is a select group of Jewish believers to whom God has chosen to reveal the truth about Jesus the Messiah. Yet, this is nothing new. The first followers of Jesus were Jewish believers. In the Gospel of John, there is an account which reveals God's requirement for entering the kingdom of heaven.

"There was a man of the Pharisees, named Nicodemus, a ruler of the Jews; the same came to Jesus by night, and said to Him, Rabbi, we know that You are a teacher come from God; for no man can do these miracles that You do, except God be with Him.

Jesus answered, and said unto him: Truly, truly, I say unto you, Except a man be born again, he cannot see the kingdom of God. Nicodemus said to Him, How can a man be born when he is old? Can he enter the second time into his mother's womb, and be born?

Jesus answered: Truly, truly, I say unto you, except a man be born of water and of the Spirit, he cannot enter into the kingdom of God. That which is born of the flesh is flesh; and that which is born of the Spirit is spirit. Marvel not that I said unto you, you must be born again." (John 3:1-7)

Peter, whom the Catholic church believes to have been the first pope, proclaims in The First Epistle of Peter: "Seeing that you have purified your souls in obeying the truth through the Spirit unto unfeigned love of the brethren, see that you love one another with a pure heart fervently, being born again, not of corruptible seed, but of incorruptible, by the Word of God, which lives and abides forever." (Verses 22 and 23)

Some might question what it means to be born again. I'm glad you asked. ☺ The key is by the Word of God. We all come into this world as sinners born of the corruptible seed which came from Adam. The Bible says we are dead in our trespasses and sins. Jesus said: "That which is born of the flesh is flesh". Therefore, we are dead spiritually. We must be born again by the incorruptible seed, "by the Word of God".

Just as Mary said yes to God when the angel, Gabriel informed her that the Messiah, Jesus, was to manifest in her womb, we must say yes to God. (See Luke 1:34-38) When we yes to God, Jesus manifests Himself in us. His Spirit takes up residence and we are sealed by the Spirit of promise Jesus told us about in the Gospel of John.

Jesus said: "And I will pray to the Father, and He shall give you another Comforter, that He may abide with you forever, Even the Spirit of truth, whom the world cannot receive, because it sees Him not, neither knows Him; but you know Him; for He dwells with you, and shall be in you. I will not leave you comfortless; I will come to you".

Unfortunately, not everybody who goes to church wants to know God or the truth of the Gospel of Jesus Christ. But if you do, be assured God will find a way to help you receive it. Once you receive the Spirit of truth, you will be His forever.

For reasons known only to Him, our Father chose to make me one of His children. I am just one more unworthy vessel through which He is pouring out His love. This is nothing new. Throughout history, He has used the base things of the world to reveal Himself to others.

He alone planned out my life and decided to give me the testimony you have just read. Now, He is using this book to lead others into His loving arms. He is also encouraging other believers to walk by faith and not by sight. Slew foot doesn't want God's children to ever read these words. More importantly, he doesn't want them to be doers of His Word. I know that I know that I know God is building His mighty army right here and now.

Because of what our Father, the one true Almighty God, has done in my life, I am a mighty warrior in His army. I can say this with all confidence. God is all and I am mighty in Him. It's not because of anything I have done. Rather, it is because of what He has done for me and in me.

The mighty Lion of the tribe of Judah defeated the enemy of our souls at the cross. Therefore, I cannot be defeated on the spiritual battlefield. "Greater is He who is in me than he who is in the world." (1 John 4:4)

"Who is this uncircumcised Philistine?" This is what David the mighty warrior in God's army shouted out as he heard Goliath taunting the army of Israel on the battlefield. Although David was small in physical stature, he was a mighty warrior in God's army.

I think you probably know the rest of the story. However, in case you didn't read the account God has given us in 1 Samuel 17:26, do yourself a big, big favor. If you want the faith of a mustard seed, which in the physical realm is the tiniest of seeds, please read the Bible. The faith which will cause you to be an over comer in this world can be found there.

Just in case you don't know this, there is absolutely no other way to obtain Satan-conquering faith. The Bible says: "Faith comes by hearing, and hearing by the Word of God." (Romans 10:17)

Do you want the faith Jesus said would enable you to say to the mountains you have before you: "be removed and be cast into the sea"? (Luke 17:6) Then, read the Word. Don't get distracted. Focus. Spend time with God every day. Feed your spiritual man and you will become victorious over all your enemies. If this is not the right way to increase your faith, why then do you think the enemy does everything he can to keep you from reading the Bible?

<u>The Bible is totally the Word of God</u>. Just take a look in John Chapter one. It states: "In the beginning

was the Word, and the Word was with God, and the Word was God." Jesus is and was the Word.

Guess what? God is in His Word. The Word is God. (Where My Word, is I AM.)

Doesn't it make sense God gave us His Word to empower us? No Word. No God. No power. Keep denying the Word of God and you will go through life complaining God hasn't done this or that for you. The devil loves a big cry baby.

The only tears God's children should be shedding are tears for the lost. Those poor souls, who are on their way to hell, deserve our tears. If you get hold of this truth, you will win this race. As you feed on the Word, you will be energized and never get tired of running the race.

"But they that wait upon the Lord shall not faint, they shall mount up with wings as eagles, they shall run and not be weary, they shall walk and not faint." (Isaiah 40:31)

Just so you know, the Bible also says: "Without FAITH you cannot please God." (Hebrews 11:6) It doesn't matter what faith you follow at this moment in time. If you are reading this book, God has ordained it. Guess what? Your spiritual ship has arrived. The answers to all the questions you have been waiting to hear are in the Word of God - the Bible.

God has given you all, and I emphasize all, you need to receive what He has planned for his children. Those who give Him their lives, to do with as He wills, are destined to be over comers. You may not see it now, but if you will just take a baby step towards Him your loving Father will run towards you.

Just as the loving father in the parable Jesus has given us in Luke 15:11-32, He will scoop you up in His bosom and lead you home one baby step at a time. Think of it. Wouldn't you do everything in your power to your own children to the highest ground they are able to stand upon.

If you are an unbeliever, God has used this book

to deliver His Word to you. Now, it's your call. If you just so happen to be in the position where you are frustrated, confused, or broken hearted, remember God is there for you.

Don't believe it? Try Him. First give up something you have no control over anyway. Give Him your life. You cannot hold onto it anyway. Just surrender it to Him and He will gladly lead you on the most awesome journey you can imagine. When it's all over, you will joyfully stand right in front of the mighty God who created you.

If you are a believer already, God has given you your sword, warrior. Take it and join His army. Do what He has called you to do. Remember Jesus said, "To whom much is given, much is expected".

God has planted the seed. It's up to you to allow Him to water it - with the water of the Word. The ball is in your court.

Whether you have come to this point in your life thinking there is no God, or you are a Christian who doubts the God you serve is the same One spoken of in the Bible, it's time to think again. Have you ever heard the expression "get a life?" God is saying this to you right now. Get a real life!

Follow the real God of the Bible and you will see miracles every day. I do. How? If you really want the answer to this question and to every other question about your life and the situations you find yourself in, read the Bible diligently. God will reveal Himself to you through His Word. As I explained earlier, there is no better way. It takes work but the rewards are truly out of this world.

In His time, the Lord opened the door for me to get into the ministry full time. Before, I was always too busy trying to make a living to put all of my focus on God's will. He solved that problem. Now, I get to minister to the people He sends me to, as I repair their homes. Awesome!

This certainly is not the way I would have

planned on getting into the ministry. However, God has ordained it. If there is one thing I learned about God over the years, it is that He does what He wants to do, how He wants to do it, and when He wants to do it. I am in no position to question Him, nor do I want to. I choose to just go with the flow.

The fact is He creates the flow. He used the book 'Held Hostage', written by my dear friend and one time fellow prisoner, Ken Cooper, to stir up the stagnated waters of my inspiration. Ken's testimony and that book reminded me if it's His will He will make a way. As He states in His Word, "With God all things are possible." (Matthew 19:26b)

Since it was God's idea for me to write this book, I assumed it would get published immediately after it was completed. Furthermore, I expected this would have taken place about five years ago. However, I somehow forgot to factor in the lesson I learned concerning God's timing years ago. His timing is not like ours. "A day with the Lord is as a thousand years". (2 Peter 3:8)

Sure, He gave me the vision and inspired me to go for it. He also gave David the vision of being king of Israel. I'm sure David was quick to latch onto that promise. However, as it is revealed in the Bible, this didn't happen overnight. Shortly after David was anointed by God's prophet to be the king of Israel, the current king turned against him.

Consequently, King Saul hunted David down for years on end. The future king spent the better part of his adult life running for his life. Surely the main question in his mind must have been: "What happened, Lord?" If anybody ever had good reason to doubt the promise of God, he surely did.

He could have started murmuring and complaining against God. Instead, David chose to just trust Him. He knew God had to have an alternate plan. So, he sat down and wrote a bunch of Psalms during those trying times of being a fugitive. Then, as was His plan from the start, God used those very words to bless untold generations of His people.

Eventually, He moved King Saul out of the way and David finally realized his dream - the dream God had given him at the outset of it all. I said all that, to say this. At this time, I don't know when or how the Lord will get this book published. I only know He will. I have done my part and completely trust Him to do the rest. Since you are now reading this, the proof is in the pudding.

If you find yourself in a position where you feel God is leading you to do something to further His kingdom here on this earth and will help to bring others into the saving knowledge of the Gospel of Jesus Christ, go for it.

Be aware. In any particular situation you find yourself, God created it. We serve the God who is omnipotent, omniscient, and omnipresent. Nothing happens by chance. Step out in faith and He will do the rest.

Sometimes, we just have to pray for what we think is the impossible. Here is a good example. My mom has smoked cigarettes for about 65 years. Her doctor and loving family members have told her she needed to quit this awful health-endangering habit on numerous occasions. She never even considered doing so.

Recently, she had an operation which kept her in the hospital for about one month. Since she hadn't been able to smoke during that period, I figured this would be a great time for her to quit. I approached her on the subject and she flat out rejected the idea. I resolved in my mind she would never quit smoking.

Once she was released from the hospital and we had brought her home, God changed all that. Shortly after she arrived back home, she was maneuvering her walker through the doorway heading to her favorite smoking lounge outside. While I observed this, I suddenly got the thought I should pray for her to quit smoking. Although I didn't really think she ever would, I obeyed that thought. I prayed to God that He would make cigarette smoking so distasteful to her she would never want to smoke a cigarette again.

Most of the time, by God's grace, I have great faith. This is undoubtedly because I have been blessed to have read the Bible more times than I can remember. ("Faith comes by hearing and hearing by the Word of God"). Yet, as I prayed that prayer I didn't really believe I would see instantaneous results. In fact, I'm not sure I believed I would ever see the results I was hoping for.

However, God had a greater purpose for leading me to pray that prayer than I could ever have imagined. Moments after my mom stepped outside, she called out to me. I rushed outside thinking she had fallen or something bad had happened. I was quite surprised when my mom informed me she had called me to tell me she just decided she was going to quit smoking for good. She explained she had taken a drag from her cigarette and it tasted awful. All glory to God!

God's purpose - besides the obvious benefits my mom and I received in all of this - was to remind us all there is still really nothing that is impossible with Him. He knew I would be sharing this experience right now with you via this book. Of course, I will also share it with everyone He leads me to in the future.

I also shared this with my nephew Shawn and he made a remark something to the effect he had no doubt God listens to my prayers. Seconds later, the Spirit told me I should share something else He pointed out to me with others. The fact is, He listens to the prayers of all His children who listen to Him. Wow.

He doesn't always say yes. He sometimes says wait. Sometimes he says no. But, if we are listening to what He has taught us in His Word, and are committed to Him, He hears every single prayer we pray. How awesome is that? Nobody has a monopoly on this. We are all the same - sinners saved by grace. This too is awesome.

Here is one last thought before I go. Jesus gave this parable: "And when he sowed, some seeds fell by the wayside. And the fouls came and devoured them up. And some fell upon stony places where they had not much earth: forthwith they sprung up. Because they had not much earth: and forthwith they sprung up because they had no deepness of earth. And when the sun was up they were scorched. And because they had no root they withered away. And some fell among thorns and the thorns sprung up and choked them. But others fell into good ground and bore fruit. Some a hundredfold, some sixty fold, and some thirty fold." (Matthew 13:3-11) Who has ears to hear, let him hear.

"And the disciples came to Jesus and said to him; why do you speak to them in parables? He answered and said to them, Because it is given unto you to know the mysteries of the kingdom of heaven, but to them it is not given.....Hear, therefore, the parable of the sower. When anyone hears the word of the kingdom, and does not understand it, then comes the wicked one, and catches away that which was sown in his heart. This is he which received seed by the wayside. But, he that received the seed into stony places, the same is he that hears the word and with joy receives it; Yet he has no root in himself, but endures for awhile: for when tribulation or persecution arises because of the word, by and by he is offended. He also that receives seed among the thorns is he that hears the word; and the care of this world, and the deceitfulness of riches, choke the word, and he becomes unfruitful. But he that received seed into the good ground is he that hears the word, and understands it." (Matthew 13:18-23)

In order to bear fruit for the Master, we must come to our quitting time. We must cease living life as if we are the sole owners of the vessels we are living in and yield to His Spirit's call. We need to focus our energies on growing in Christ daily by reading His Word and applying it to our lives as He has instructed.

On the other hand, if we choose to do our own

thing, whatever we do manage to accomplish will be worthless in the light of eternity. This is exactly why our gracious Father has inspired me to write this book. He instructed me to "Tell my people that when they quit living for themselves and start living for me, then they shall find out what real living is all about."

I pray this will be yours and my lifestyle from this moment forward. I can assure you, God has a much better plan for your life than you could ever come up with. If you will just make the effort and put in the time to reach out to Him, He will surely show you what it is. It is my sincere prayer that everyone who reads this book will take God up on His offer and become a greater fruit bearer than I.

I will leave you with the words king Solomon, by the inspiration of God's Holy Spirit, said long after he had acquired riches, wisdom and power which has yet to be exceeded by any other man: "Let us hear the conclusion of the whole matter: Fear God and keep His commandments for this is the whole duty of man. For God shall bring every work into judgment, with every secret thing, whether it is good or whether it is evil." (Ecclesiastes 12:13, 14)

The end........not really.

"To every thing there is a season and a time to every purpose under the heavens." (ECCLESIASTES. 3:1)

QUITTING TIME

Copyright page

All scripture is quoted from the two listed references below

Made in the USA
Charleston, SC
23 February 2014